COMMUNICATION UNDER LAW

Volume I:
Free Speech

JOSEPH J. HEMMER, JR.

The Scarecrow Press, Inc.
Metuchen, N.J., & London 1979

Library of Congress Cataloging in Publication Data

Hemmer, Joseph J
    Free speech.

    (His Communication under law ; v. 1)
    Bibliography: p.
    Includes indexes.
    1. Liberty of speech--United States.
2. Liberty of the press--United States.
I. Title.
KF2750.A73H46   vol. 1 [KF4772]   343'.73'0998s
ISBN 0-8108-1248-7   [342'.73'085]   79-19166

Dedicated to

MOM & DAD

Thanks for making
my education possible

PREFACE

This past half-century has witnessed growth in the complexity of communication media and systems. With a vast array of communication situations open to all citizens-- whether at the intrapersonal, interpersonal, public, mass, intercultural, or international levels--the potential for legal cases stemming from communication-related issues has increased. The rights of free expression often conflict with other treasured freedoms. Indeed, in this age, an understanding of communication law is important.

The purpose of this work is to analyze the primary issues related to communication law. The study is divided into two volumes. The first book focuses on free speech topics: dissent, assembly, academic freedom, obscenity, silence, and intrusion. The second volume considers questions related to journalistic freedom: privacy, libel, copyright, fair trial, access to information, broadcast regulation, regulation of advertising. It is hoped that the volumes provide, at a basic level, a thorough examination of communication case law.

My methodology is primarily a case-by-case treatment of the various communication-related issues. I describe actions that led up to the specific court case, place the events within a historical setting, identify the issue(s) at law to be decided in the case, reveal the majority opinion of the court, explain the reasoning behind the decision, and, where appropriate, present a sense of the controversy among court justices. When possible, I indicate the impact of the decision on society. I identify communication acts (protest, advertisement, news report, obscenity, etc.) that were performed by agents (speakers, journalists, artists, etc.) using a particular medium (speech, print, film, symbolic action, etc.) with a specific purpose (stop war, sell magazines, etc.) within a particular setting (World War II, Civil Rights Movement, etc.). Ideally, my method enables me to consider all of the elements in terms of their dynamic relationship with each other.

I am indebted to Bob Beitz. His assistance in researching, writing, editing, and proofreading contributed immeasurably to the completion of this project. Thanks also to my colleagues Paul Starr, Joe Dailey, and Pete Settle; they were willing listeners and capable advisors when I reached a standstill. Finally, I wish to express deepest appreciation to my wife, Joy, and sons, Joey and Andy. Without their assurance and understanding, this project would have been impossible.

J. J. H., Jr.

Carroll College
Waukesha, Wisconsin
September 10, 1978

TABLE OF CONTENTS

CHAPTER I

INTRODUCTION

Throughout America's brief history, its leading phi-
losophers and jurists have grappled with the issue of freedom
of expression. Inspired by Enlightenment scholars of the
seventeenth and eighteenth centuries, America early turned
to faith in man's reason as the safest basis of government.
In 1644, John Milton argued in Areopagitica that free speech
was essential to the social good. Though religious in context, his argument eventually persuaded the English Parlia-
ment to prohibit pre-publication censorship and licensing.
Almost 50 years later, John Locke expressed his belief that
every individual had certain "natural rights"--among them
being life, liberty, and property. From this philosophical
foundation, men such as James Madison and Thomas Jefferson went on to establish the freedoms of speech, press, assembly, and petition as constitutional principles.

Purposes of Free Expression

What, then, are the purposes of free speech, press,
assembly, and petition in a democratic society? By analyz-
ing the writings of the founding fathers, and subsequent opinions of the courts, four objectives are revealed: 1) self-
government, 2) search for truth, 3) social change, and 4) human dignity.

Without free and unimpaired dissemination and discussion of ideas, self-government is but a hollow fantasy. Democracy requires that all relevant views be heard and analyzed in the "marketplace of ideas." As Justice William
Douglas has said: "One main function of the First Amendment is to ensure ample opportunity for the people to determine and resolve public issues." The link between the people and their government is maintained through debate. Free
speech, then, is the tool by which democracy itself is maintained and improved.

1

Free speech is essential to the search for truth. Only through the clash of the widest diversity of ideas and information via legitimate forums of communication, can the "truth" be discerned. Arguing against English licensing and censorship, Milton noted:

> And though all the winds of doctrine were let loose to play upon the earth, so Truth be in the field, we do injuriously, by licensing and prohibiting, to misdoubt her strength. Let her and Falsehood grapple; Who ever knew Truth put to the worse in a free and open encounter?

It can be said that one man's truth is another's falsehood. Suppression of ideas, so prevalent in earlier times, is no longer accepted. Justice Felix Frankfurter wrote:

> The history of civilization is in considerable measure the displacement of error which once held sway as official truth by beliefs which in turn have yielded to other truths. Therefore the liberty of man to search for truth ought not to be fettered, no matter what orthodoxies he may challenge. Liberty of thought soon shrivels without freedom of expression.

Free speech, moreover, ensures beneficial change by allowing those not in power to criticize weaknesses within the system. Such criticism prevents the established authority from becoming isolated from the people. Free speech, by its very nature, produces an atmosphere where new ideas constantly challenge older ones. Consequently, the potential for abuse of power and the subsequent stultification of society is reduced. Free speech, in short, combats the inherent tendency of those in power to maintain the status quo. It provides a check on power and prevents the development of tyranny.

Finally, the freedom of expression grants to each citizen the dignity of his or her individual thoughts. People can speak their innermost thoughts without fear or shame. Each individual is thus able to develop his or her potential to the fullest, and to take his or her place in society as a productive citizen--a unique human being secure in his or her "natural rights."

Professor Thomas Emerson has written,

Most men have a strong inclination to suppress opposition even where differences in viewpoint are comparatively slight. But a system of free expression must be framed to withstand far greater stress. The test of any such system is not whether it tolerates minor deviations, but whether it permits criticism of the fundamental beliefs and practices of the society.

Indeed, the extent of free speech and press existing in a society provides a rough measure of freedom itself. An individual may feel free in any society, no matter how autocratic, if he or she accepts the rules of that society, but he or she can only be free in a society that is willing to allow those rules to be questioned.

Constitutional Sources of Free Expression

Some of the framers of the American Constitution questioned whether a formal Bill of Rights was actually required. Supporters of the states' rights position argued that the individual states would adequately safeguard the essential freedoms. At the Constitutional Convention in 1789, however, the delegates opted for a strong national government. The Bill of Rights was established, containing ten amendments to the Constitution. Since 1791, the First Amendment has been the basic safeguard of freedom of expression:

> Congress shall make no law respecting an establishment of religion, or prohibiting the free exercise thereof; or abridging the freedom of speech, or the press; or the right of the people peaceably to assemble and to petition the government for a redress of grievances.

Though the terms "freedom of speech" and "freedom of press" were not explicitly defined, it is generally agreed that the intent of the framers, particularly Thomas Jefferson, was to prohibit prior restraints upon publication and speech. William Blackstone, an English lawyer who had considerable effect on American law, wrote:

> The liberty of the press is indeed essential to the nature of a free state: but this consists in laying no previous restraints upon publications, and not in freedom from censure for criminal matter when

> published. Every freeman has an undoubted right to
> lay what sentiments he pleases before the public; to
> forbid this is to destroy the freedom of the press:
> but if he publishes what is improper, mischievous, or
> illegal, he must take the consequences of his own te -
> merity.

Though the freedoms of speech and press are not absolutes, the
courts have gone far in expanding their scope. Though this movement toward increased freedom has been erratic at times, the
trend is unmistakable. As the need for participation by citizens
in government has increased, the courts have responded by allowing ever-increasing protection for these freedoms.

As the states formulated their own constitutions, each
included a guarantee of freedom of expression. Yet considerable
disparity existed among state provisions. A few states developed
only a brief provision. For example, Massachusetts stipulated:
"The liberty of the press is essential to the security of freedom
in a State: it ought not, therefore, to be restrained in this Commonwealth. The right to free speech shall not be abridged. "
Other states provided specific guidelines, some of which were
designed to overcome abhorrent practices which were used in
England to deal with government critics. Accordingly, truth became an acceptable defense, and juries, rather than judges, were
given power to decide whether a particular statement was libelous.
In 1868, Congress passed the Fourteenth Amendment, which declared that no state shall "deprive any person of life, liberty, or
property, without due process of law.... " However, the states
continued to exercise broad authority in determining what constituted an abuse of free expression. Not until 1925 did the Supreme
Court declare that freedom of expression was protected from invasion by the states. In Gitlow v. New York, the Court decided
that state court rulings concerning freedom of expression were
subject to judicial review:

> ... we may and do assume that freedom of speech and
> the press--which are protected by the First Amend -
> ment from abridgement by Congress--are among the
> fundamental personal rights and liberties protected by
> the due process clause of the Fourteenth Amendment
> from impairment by the States.

The Fifth Amendment of the Bill of Rights is also relevant
to freedom of expression. It provides that "No person ... shall
be compelled in any criminal case to be a witness against himself,
nor be deprived of life, liberty, or property, without due process

of law. " While the first part establishes the right of silence, the second guarantees freedom of expression. It must be noted, however, that citizens can be deprived of liberty through "due process of law. " Freedom is not absolute.

Another provision of the Bill of Rights guards against illegal searches and seizures. The Fourth Amendment states that

> The right of the people to be secure in their persons, houses, papers, and effects, against unreasonable searches and seizures, shall not be violated, and no warrants shall issue, but upon probable cause, supported by oath or affirmation, and particularly describing the place to be searched and the persons or things to be seized.

The Fourth Amendment, in addition, has given rise to the relatively recent concept of the right of privacy--the right to be left alone.

Whereas the Fourth Amendment provides procedural safeguards against unwarranted usurpations of liberty, the First, Fifth, and Fourteenth Amendments provide the substantive and philosophical bases for the personal and group freedoms associated with communication.

Court Interpretations of Free Expression

During the presidency of John Adams, freedom of expression was vigorously restricted. Through the use of the Sedition Act of 1798 many citizens were punished who would "write, print, utter, or publish any false, scandalous, and malicious writing or writings against the government of the United States. . . . " Many political opponents of the administration were jailed for violating this law. Upon taking office, Thomas Jefferson repealed it. From that time, the U. S. Supreme Court has moved to expand the scope of expression that is constitutionally protected.

The view that the First Amendment operates not only to bar prior restraints of expression, but subsequent punishment as well, was not acknowledged until quite recently. At the outset, when the concept of free expression was novel, rigid criteria were used to regulate speech: the law of seditious libel; the test of social utility; prohibition of abusive, vituperative, false, or misleading communication; and various limitations based on

intent or motive. It was easiest simply to exclude certain groups
altogether from exercising their constitutional rights. Even today it is felt, in some quarters, that "anti-democratic" groups
should not be allowed to voice their harmful ideas. Throughout
American history, the courts have had to reconcile the conflict
between freedom of expression and other values and objectives
sought by a democratic society. Public order, equality, justice,
and moral progress are also societal aims--and occasionally
conflict with personal liberties.

Clear and Present Danger

In the 1919 case of Schenck v. United States, Justice
Oliver Wendell Holmes, while upholding convictions for violation
of the Espionage Act, suggested that the First Amendment operates to ban subsequent punishment as well as prior restraints on
expression.

> The most stringent protection of free speech would not
> protect a man in falsely shouting fire in a theatre and
> causing a panic.... The question in every case is
> whether the words used are in such a nature as to cre-
> ate a clear and present danger that they will bring
> about the substantive evils that Congress has the right
> to prevent.

The Court readily accepted the "clear and present danger" test.
Eight years later, in Whitney v. California, Justice Louis Brandeis elaborated the doctrine:

> ... even advocacy of violation [of the law] ... is not a
> justification for denying free speech where the advoca-
> cy would be immediately acted on.... In order to sup-
> port a finding of clear and present danger it must be
> shown either that immediate serious violence was to
> be expected or was advocated, or that the past conduct
> furnished reason to believe that such advocacy was
> then contemplated.

Justices Holmes and Brandeis dissented in several subsequent
cases because they felt the Court's majority was misapplying
the original test. In order to find a "clear and present danger,"
four elements had to exist: 1) the circumstances must be potentially dangerous, 2) the feared result must be "extremely serious," 3) there must be "reasonable ground to fear that the serious evil will result if free speech is practiced," and 4) the "degree of imminence" of the danger must be "extremely high."

Bad Tendency

In 1925, in Gitlow v. New York, the Court developed a
new test. Apparently having reservations about the pre-eminence
of the freedom of expression, the Court retrenched. A legislature, the majority argued, was entitled to "extinguish the spark
without waiting until it has enkindled the flame or blazed into a
conflagration." According to the "bad tendency" test, any expression which had a tendency, or which the legislature could reasonably believe had a tendency, to lead to substantial evil could be
banned. In the opinion of Justice Edward Sanford, "That a State
in the exercise of its police power may punish those utterances
inimical to the public welfare, tending to corrupt public morals,
incite to crime, or disturb the public peace, is not open to question." In short, the Court conferred a low priority to free expression. Questionable speech or advocacy was effectively "nipped in
the bud."

In 1937, in Herndon v. Lowry, the Court once again considered the doctrine of "bad tendency." Narrowly rejecting the
test, the majority argued that state power to abridge expression
was limited and to be used only where there was a reasonable
fear of danger to the state.

> The power of a State to abridge freedom of expression
> and of assembly is the exception rather than the rule,
> and the penalizing even of utterances of a defined char-
> acter must find its justification in a reasonable appre-
> hension of danger to organized government.

In overturning the Georgia Supreme Court's ruling, the Court
argued that the statute in question did not furnish a "sufficiently
ascertainable standard of guilt."

> By force of it as construed, the judge and jury trying
> an alleged offender cannot appraise the circumstances
> and character of the defendant's utterances or activi-
> ties as begetting a clear and present danger of forcible
> obstruction of a particular state function.

In Herndon, the Court returned to the 1919 concept of "clear and
present danger," and set aside the concept that speech could be
banned if it engendered a "bad tendency."

Clear and Present Danger Revisited

The Court, still not settled in its approach to the problem of regulating expression, once again turned to the clear and present danger doctrine as its main test. Though the progress of the Court in expanding the scope of protected speech was not smooth and steady, it was nonetheless apparent. Through the years, the Court increasingly drew the line of allowable expression closer to the point of action. As the Court gained confidence in its approach, it refined and reformulated the original Holmes test. Convinced of the increasing importance of free speech in a modern society, the Court continued to extend its domain--aware always of its role in public debate and social change. In 1949, Justice William Douglas wrote in Terminiello v. Chicago:

> A function of free speech under our system of government is to invite dispute. It may indeed best serve its high purpose when it induces a condition of unrest, creates dissatisfaction with conditions as they are, or even stirs people to anger. Speech is often provocative and challenging. It may strike at prejudices and preconceptions and have profound unsettling effects as it presses for acceptance of an idea. That is why freedom of speech, though not absolute ... is nevertheless protected against censorship or punishment, unless shown likely to produce a clear and present danger of a serious substantive evil that arises far above public inconvenience, annoyance, or unrest.

In 1951, in Dennis v. United States, the Court significantly altered the meaning of clear and present danger. The Court upheld the constitutionality of the Smith Act, which proscribed advocacy of the overthrow by force and violence of the United States government. Responding to the heightened apprehension of the Communist movement, the Court allowed the government more authority in banning expression.

> Overthrow of the Government by force and violence is certainly a substantial enough interest for the Government to limit speech. ... If Government is aware that a group aiming at its overthrow is attempting to indoctrinate its members and to commit them to a course whereby they will strike when the leaders feel the circumstances permit, action by the Government is required.

Chief Justice Fred Vinson accepted, word-for-word, the thinking of lower court Judge Learned Hand: "In each case [courts] must ask whether the gravity of the evil discounted by its improbability, justifies such invasion of free speech as is necessary to avoid the danger." The "gravity of the evil" became an additional element enabling the Court to justify more easily a finding of clear and present danger. In Dennis, "the gravity of the evil" facilitated the Court's upholding the convictions. While the thinking of the Court in Dennis was certainly more libertarian than the "bad tendency" test, it accorded rather limited weight to freedom of expression. Indeed, the Dennis opinion rendered the clear and present danger test, as originally devised by Justice Holmes, nearly unrecognizable.

After Terminiello, the Court stopped applying the clear and present danger test to cases involving government suppression and punishment of expression. The test's durability has been much greater in the realm of contempt-of-court cases. Up until the first part of the twentieth century, the courts generally took the position that a publication tending to obstruct the administration of justice was punishable, regardless of its truth. Beginning with Bridges v. California in 1941, however, the Court began to apply the clear and present danger test. Judges were effectively prohibited from levying contempt charges on critics unless the danger to the administration of justice was imminent and of an extremely serious nature. As recently as 1962, in Wood v. Georgia, the Court struck down a contempt citation because there was no evidence of a "substantive evil actually designed to impede the course of justice."

Balancing

In 1950, the Court began to fashion yet another test. Chief Justice Vinson, writing in American Communications Association, CIO v. Douds, rejected the clear and present danger test.

> Government's interest here is not in preventing the dissemination of Communist doctrine or the holding of particular beliefs because it is feared that unlawful action will result therefrom if free speech is practiced.... When particular conduct is regulated in the interest of public order, and the regulation results in an indirect, conditional, partial abridgement of speech, the duty of the Courts is to determine which of these two conflicting interests demands the greater protection under the particular circumstances presented.

This "balancing" test appeared again in Justice Felix Frankfurter's dissent in Dennis: "The demands of free speech in a
democratic society, as well as the interest in national security are better served by candid and informed weighing of the
competing interests, within the confines of the judicial process, than by announcing dogmas too inflexible for the non-
Euclidean problems to be solved."

The test was used throughout the 1950s and early
1960s in such cases as Konigsberg v. State Bar of California,
United States v. Robel, and Barenblatt v. United States.
Throughout its use, however, the balancing doctrine was
plagued by several flaws, chief among which were its vagueness and difficulty in application. Accordingly, the test provides no real meaning to the First Amendment, and, in fact,
is so broad that it can hardly be described as a legal test.

Absolutism

During the decade of the 1950s, opposition to balancing
was led by Justices William Douglas and Hugo Black. They
argued that the First Amendment denied the government any
power to abridge speech. Any law that abridged free expression was unconstitutional on its face. This "absolutist" doctrine was apparent in Douglas's dissenting opinions, and many
of Black's as well. By espousing such a position, the justices were not arguing that every communication deserved unqualified immunity from regulation. Rather, the test was intended to broaden the area of expression within the protection
of the Constitution. "Freedom of speech" and "abridgement"
were liberally construed. The position was perhaps best described in Justice Black's dissenting opinion in Konigsberg v.
State Bar of California. That a law abridged or deterred
speech was "sufficient to render the action of the State unconstitutional." He did not believe that constitutionally protected
rights could ever be balanced away, even if the majority of
the Court felt that the state had a legitimate interest in
abridging those rights.

> I believe that the First Amendment's unequivocal
> command that there shall be no abridgement of the
> rights of free speech and assembly, shows that the
> men who drafted our Bill of Rights did all the bal-
> ancing that was to be done in this field.

While the absolutist test unquestionably strengthened
the freedom of expression, its proponents continue to distin-

guish carefully between pure expression and subsidiary conduct. In large part, the absolutist test entails definition of the operative terms of each case. Rather than a subjective analysis of conflicting claims, as in the balancing test, the absolutist doctrine is based on liberally defined terms and their similarly liberal application to the facts of each case.

Preferred Position

Somewhere between the absolutist and balancing doctrines lies the "preferred position" test. In 1943, in Murdock v. Commonwealth of Pennsylvania, Justice Douglas noted that "Freedom of press, freedom of speech, freedom of religion are in a preferred position." The Court gave added impetus to the emerging test two years later in Thomas v. Collins. Justice Wiley Rutledge, writing for the majority, indicated that the determination of the constitutionality of restrictive or regulative legislation is "delicate ... [especially] when the usual presumption supporting legislation is balanced by the preferred place given in our scheme to the great, the indispensable democratic freedoms secured in the First Amendment." He continued: "That priority gives these liberties a sanctity and a sanction not permitting dubious intrusions." This thinking was sharply attacked by Justice Felix Frankfurter in Kovacs v. Cooper. He referred to the preferred position doctrine as "a mischievous phrase, if it carries the thought, which it may subtly imply, that any law touching communication is infected with presumptive invalidity." Justice Stanley Reed, however, stressed that "the preferred position of freedom of speech in a society that cherishes liberty for all does not require legislators to be insensible to claims by citizens to comfort and convenience." Thus, even though expression enjoys a preferred position, it is not immune from control when such action is warranted. Indeed, preferred position may be the only workable test that gives reasonable weight to the First Amendment.

Current Status of Free Expression

Regarding recent Court decisions, it is difficult to pinpoint any one particular doctrine that is consistently used by the majority. Indeed, the complexities of communication technology preclude a static approach. In the 1965 case of Cox v. Louisiana, the Court utilized the clear and present danger test, but indicated that the test was only applicable in certain

cases. Then, in 1969, in Brandenburg v. Ohio, the Court
consolidated earlier rulings to fashion the principle that "the
Constitutional guarantees of Free Speech and Free Press do
not permit a State to forbid or proscribe advocacy of the use
of force or of law violation except where such advocacy is directed to inciting or producing imminent lawless action, and is
likely to incite or produce such action." In this case, the
Court indicated its support for some reformulation of the
clear and present danger test. In recent years, the Court
has utilized two variations of the balancing test. In Roth v.
United States, New York Times Co. v. Sullivan, and Garrison
v. Louisiana, the Court used definitional balancing to prescribe certain speech that is within constitutional boundaries,
and other expression that is only provisionally protected. Situational balancing, judging each case on its particular merits,
has been applied recently when legislative limitation on expression has been challenged as unduly vague, overbroad, or otherwise improper. For example, in 1974, in Spence v. Washington, the Court considered the unique, mitigating factors behind Spence's behavior. In Lehman v. City of Shaker Heights,
the Court held that a city transit system could refuse to sell
advertising space on its buses for political advertising because
under the circumstances, the buses were not a "public forum."
When the Court uses situational balancing, the decision usually offers little guidance for future cases because it applies
only to the specifics of the particular case.

It appears that the Burger Court at this time is reeval-
uating the aggressive, often criticized innovation and liberal-
ism of the Warren Court. For more than a decade, the Warren Court ventured into uncharted constitutional waters. Many
felt that the Court had not exhibited proper judicial restraint
during that period. Freedom of expression was rapidly and
significantly strengthened.

The liberal remnants of the Warren years continue to
influence the Court. Recent appointees to the Court, however,
have been reluctant to expand the scope of allowable expression. The Court is decidedly more cautious and reserved.
Throughout the history of the Court, a period of libertarian
activism is followed by careful reevaluation and questioning.
In a sense, the Burger Court is refining and "fine-tuning" the
First Amendment advances of its predecessor. The relative
shift in the philosophical bent of the Court can be attributed
in large part to the social, political, and economic environment
in which the Court functions. During the 1960s the country was
immersed in deep internal questioning--of both foreign and

domestic policies, private and public matters. The Court responded in the only way it could--by increasing the freedom of expression. The Court was at the "cutting edge" of important events; indeed, its decisions were often the important events. Today, during a period of relative calm, the Court has responded to citizens' demands for law and order, and has had time to deal with other issues of local and individual concern. The momentum of the Warren years has been braked. If history is a guide, however, these "reflective years" represent an incubation period of newer, more tolerant, and libertarian doctrines.

Bibliography

(Sources that were helpful in the preparation of Chapter I)

Books

Bosmajian, Haig A. , ed. The Principles and Practice of Freedom of Speech. Boston: Houghton Mifflin, 1971.

DeVol, Kenneth S. , ed. Mass Media and the Supreme Court: The Legacy of the Warren Years. 2nd ed. New York: Hastings House Publishers, 1976.

Emerson, Thomas I. The System of Freedom of Expression. New York: Random House, 1970.

_____. Toward A General Theory of the First Amendment. New York: Random House, 1966.

Gilmor, Donald M. and Jerome A. Barron. Mass Communication Law. 2nd ed. St. Paul: West Publishing, 1974.

Jayson, Lester S. , ed. The Constitution of the United States of America: Analysis and Interpretation. Washington, D. C. : U. S. Government Printing Office, 1973.

Nelson, Harold L. and Dwight L. Teeter. Law of Mass Communications. Mineola, New York: Foundation Press, 1969.

Cases

American Communications Association, C. I. O v. Douds 339 U. S. 382 (1950)

Barenblatt v. United States 360 U. S. 109 (1959)

Brandenburg v. Ohio 395 U. S. 444 (1969)

Bridges v. California 314 U. S. 252 (1941)

Cox v. Louisiana 379 U. S. 536, 559 (1965)

Dennis v. United States 341 U. S. 494 (1951)

Garrison v. Louisiana 379 U. S. 64 (1964)

Gitlow v. New York 268 U. S. 652 (1925)

Herndon v. Lowry 301 U. S. 242 (1937)

Konigsberg v. State Bar of California 366 U. S. 36 (1961)

Kovacs v. Cooper 336 U. S. 77 (1949)

Lehman v. City of Shaker Heights 418 U. S. 298 (1974)

Murdock v. Commonwealth of Pennsylvania 319 U. S. 105 (1943)

New York Times Co. v. Sullivan 376 U. S. 254 (1964)

Roth v. United States 354 U. S. 476 (1957)

Schenck v. United States 249 U. S. 47 (1919)

Spence v. Washington 418 U. S. 405 (1974)

Terminiello v. Chicago 337 U. S. 1 (1949)

Thomas v. Collins 323 U. S. 516 (1945)

United States v. Robel 389 U. S. 258 (1967)

Whitney v. California 274 U. S. 357 (1927)

Wood v. Georgia 370 U. S. 375 (1962)

CHAPTER II

DISSENT

Two opposing positions characterize the history of dissent in the United States. On one hand, a zest for dissent permeates the behavior of American citizens. At the country's inception, colonial patriots expressed dissatisfaction with an oppressive English monarchy. Prior to the Civil War, abolitionists voiced opposition to the slavery institution. In the twentieth century, student activists rebelled against the power of the President to make war in Vietnam. Today, women bitterly resent a system which treats them as less than equal under the law. At the same time that citizens have lodged dissenting views on most issues, government has limited freedom of expression and punished extremism in dissent. Especially during time of war and national crisis, the government has placed restrictions on those types of dissent which might lead to a disturbance of the public order or which might endanger the national safety and security. Throughout American history, the zeal for dissent has been balanced by activities of the government designed to maintain security and preserve order. The clash of these conflicting standards presents a major focus of attention for students interested in freedom of communication.

ADVOCACY

During the twentieth century several pieces of legislation on the federal and state levels have been directed toward those "dissenters" who obstruct the military operations of the country or who advocate the overthrow of the United States government by force or violence. The constitutionality of these laws necessarily became an issue for the United States Supreme Court, and, depending upon the specifics of the case and the personnel on the Court, the decisions tended to be, at times, contradictory.

Espionage Act of 1917

In 1917, shortly after Congress declared war against Germany, it enacted the Selective Service Act as a means of raising an army. In an attempt to ward off any extreme dissent against the conscription policy, Congress included in the Espionage Act of 1917 a section which forbade using false statements to willfully interfere with the military success of the United States, promoting the success of America's enemies, attempting to cause insubordination in or resistance to military duty, or obstructing the recruiting effort of the armed services. Violators were subject to a fine of not more than ten thousand dollars and imprisonment for not more than twenty years, or both. A 1918 amendment, the Sedition Act, extended criminal prosecution to any person saying anything detrimental about the sale of government bonds, or expressing anything which subjected the American form of government, Constitution, flag, or military uniform to disrepute.

Shortly after the passage of these laws, the courts were asked to determine the extent to which political dissent in America could be regulated by the war-making powers granted to the federal government. The problem was to find a way of maintaining freedom of communication while at the same time upholding the government's power to preserve order and security during a period of national conflict and crisis.

Schenck v. United States 249 U. S. 47 (1919)

In 1917, Charles E. Schenck, general secretary of the Socialist Party, directed the printing of 15,000 leaflets which intensely criticized the conscription of men for military service. The document considered the draft as despotism in its worst form, designed to benefit the interests of Wall Street's select few. It urged draftees to "assert your rights." Anyone who refused to recognize "your right to assert your opposition to the draft" violated the Constitution. The leaflet denied the government power to send American citizens abroad to war upon people in other lands, and urged, "you must do your share to maintain, support, and uphold the rights of the people in this country." Schenck distributed the leaflets to military draftees. He was convicted of conspiracy to violate the Espionage Act of 1917.

The U. S. Supreme Court affirmed (9-0) the conviction. In his opinion, Justice Oliver Wendell Holmes introduced the "clear and present danger" test. Holmes acknowledged that in ordinary times Schenck would have been within his constitutional rights in expressing the ideas contained in the leaflet. But the circumstances in this case rendered the communication outside the boundaries of protected expression. Holmes described the test in this manner: "The question in every case is whether the words used are used in such circum- stances and are of such a nature as to create a clear and present danger that they will bring about the substantive evils that Congress has a right to prevent." The Court felt that expression designed to obstruct recruiting during a time when the country was at war constituted a "clear and present dan- ger." Schenck thus established that constitutionally protected dissent was not absolutely guaranteed but rather depended upon the specific nature of the current situation.

Debs v. United States 249 U.S. 211 (1919)

About the same time that Schenck was distributing pamphlets, Eugene V. Debs was expressing his personal oppo- sition to American entry into the war. In an address to a convention of Socialists, Debs approved the conduct of certain individuals who had been convicted of obstructing recruitment. He did not direct his speech toward soldiers nor did he urge his audience to resist the draft. Yet Debs was convicted of attempt- ing to obstruct the draft and was sentenced to ten years in prison.

The Supreme Court affirmed the conviction. The unani- mous opinion, prepared by Justice Holmes, claimed that the evi- dence was sufficient to warrant the jury's finding that one purpose and probable effect of the speech, although perhaps incidental, was to obstruct recruiting. Debs had frequently expressed his opposition to the war and the draft. He admitted it again at his trial, saying, "I have been accused of obstructing the war. I ad- mit it." According to the court, the jury had properly concluded that obstruction of recruitment probably resulted, since Debs supposedly meant that his words should have that effect. In Debs, the court provided an extremely broad construction to the Espio- nage Act of 1917. It can be argued that the Court's thinking in Debs departed from that in Schenck because the facts did not sup- port a finding of a "clear and present danger."

Abrams v. United States 250 U.S. 616 (1919)

In the same year the Court heard Abrams. Jacob Ab- rams and five associates published and distributed about 5,000 circulars in New York City. The circulars contained two articles. The first opposed the American expedition into

Russia to defeat the Bolsheviks. The leaflet opposed President Woodrow Wilson's policy of sending troups to Vladivostok
and Murmansk in the summer of 1918. It referred to the hy-
pocrisy of the "plutocratic gang in Washington," and suggested
that German militarism and allied Capitalism would combine,
though not openly, to squash the Russian revolution. The only
enemy of the workers of the world was capitalism; it was
criminal for American workers to fight the workers of Russia.
The leaflet urged "Awake! Awake, you workers of the world!
Revolutionists." The second article called for a general
strike of munitions workers: "Workers in the ammunition
factories, you are producing bullets, bayonets, cannons to murder not only the Germans, but also your dearest, best, who
are in Russia fighting for freedom." The leaflet urged,
"Workers, our reply to this barbaric intervention has to be
a general strike!", and concluded "Woe unto those who will be
in the way of progress. Let solidarity live! The Rebels."

Abrams and his colleagues were charged with violating
the Espionage Act of 1917. Even though at their trial there
was no evidence that a single person actually stopped any kind
of war work or that the leaflets actually reached a single munitions worker, the defendants were convicted and sentenced
to twenty years in prison. Abrams appealed.

The majority of the U.S. Supreme Court held (7-2) that
distribution of the circulars during the war was not protected
expression within the meaning of the First Amendment. In
Abrams, the Court failed to apply the clear and present danger
test. Instead, the majority opinion written by Justice John
Clarke stressed that even though Abrams' primary intent was
to curtail production of arms in order to aid the cause of the
Russian Revolution, an inevitable consequence of the plan was
to interfere with the war against Germany. The justices assumed that Abrams must have been aware of the effects of the
plan and therefore could be held accountable. The Court was
thus able to affirm the conviction of Abrams and his associates
for intending to hinder the prosecution of the war.

In a dissenting opinion, Holmes applied the clear and
present danger test. Brandeis agreed. Holmes claimed that
"Congress certainly cannot forbid all effort to change the
mind of the country. Now nobody can suppose that the surrep-
titious publishing of a silly leaflet by an unknown man, without
more, would present any immediate danger that its opinions
would hinder the success of the government arms or have any
appreciable tendency to do so." Holmes and Brandeis clearly

departed from the rest of the Court by holding to a liberal interpretation of "clear and present danger." However, the majority believed that the government could punish communication that had the intent to produce dangerous incidental consequences for the nation. And that power was unquestionably greater in time of war than in time of peace. Communication that would be considered innocuous in peacetime became potentially dangerous during a war.

State Criminal Anarchy and Syndicalism Acts

Beginning with the enactment of the New York Anarchy Act of 1902, which was passed shortly after the assassination of President William McKinley, several states passed similar statutes. These laws generally punished behavior which advocated the overthrow of the government by unlawful methods. The issue of the constitutionality of state criminal anarchy and syndicalism statutes came before the U. S. Supreme Court and the resolution of the issue varied with different provisions in the respective laws.

Gitlow v. New York 268 U. S. 652 (1925)

Benjamin Gitlow and three other members of the left-wing of the Socialist Party were indicted for publishing a radical "manifesto" in a pamphlet entitled The Revolutionary Age. The "manifesto" was a dull, 34-page document which predicted that "the mass struggle of the proletariat is coming into being," urged "mass strikes" and "mass action" by the proletariat, and repudiated the policy of the moderate Socialists by suggesting they were "introducing Socialism by means of legislative measures on the basis of the Bourgeois state." Sixteen-thousand copies of the document were printed; some were sold and others were mailed. The New York Criminal Anarchy statute forbade the publication or distribution of material advocating, advising, or "teaching the duty, necessity or propriety of overthrowing or overturning organized government by force or violence." The trial court convicted Gitlow and his colleagues under the statute and sentenced them to from five to ten years of hard labor.

The United States Supreme Court affirmed (7-2) the convictions, and Gitlow went to prison to serve almost three years of his sentence. The Court, through the opinion of Justice Edward Sanford, adopted the "bad tendency" test and

rejected the "clear and present danger" test.   The Court thus
concluded that words may be punished because of their undesirable nature regardless of whether there is any imminent
danger.   Holmes and Brandeis dissented, saying, "If the publication of this document had been laid as an attempt to induce
an uprising against the government at once and not at some
indefinite time in the future, it would have presented a different
question. . . .   But the indictment alleges the publication and
nothing more. "   The dissenting justices applied the clear and
present danger test and concluded that Gitlow was entitled to
disseminate the "manifesto" because it advocated uprising only
at some vague future time.

        Gitlow offered some hope for advocates of a liberal
interpretation of the First Amendment.   The Court implied the
possibility of federal protection against suppression of speech
and press by state legislatures.   Sanford claimed that freedom
of speech and press are among the fundamental personal liberties protected by the due process clause of the Fourteenth
Amendment from impairment by the states.   However, the New
York Criminal Anarchy Act did not infringe upon those freedoms, so the Court sustained the constitutionality of the statute.

Whitney v. California 274 U. S. 357 (1927)

        In 1919, California enacted the Criminal Syndicalism
Act, which defined criminal syndicalism as "any doctrine or
precept advocating, teaching, or aiding and abetting the commission of crime, sabotage . . . or unlawful methods of terrorism as a means of accomplishing a change in industrial ownership or control, or effecting any political change. "   The statute specified imprisonment from one to fourteen years for any
individual who taught, advocated, or aided criminal syndicalism;
who attempted to justify it; who disseminated written material
advocating it; who organized or became a member of a group
formed to advocate it; or who committed an act designed to
produce a change in industrial ownership or political condition.
This unique statute was not directed at the practice of criminal
syndicalism but, rather, at the preaching of it, and especially
at association with persons who proposed to advocate it.   In
the five years following the enactment of the law, 504 persons
were arrested and 264 were actually brought to trial.

        Anita Whitney, a woman nearing sixty years of age, who
was well known for philanthropic work, participated in a

convention which established the Communist Labor Party of
California. Three weeks later, she was arrested under the
Criminal Syndicalism Act on the ground that the Party was set
up to teach criminal syndicalism and that by becoming a member, she had participated in a crime. She was convicted.

Before the Supreme Court, Whitney claimed that she had
not intended to have the Communist Labor Party of California
function as a tool of terrorism or violence. She contended
that as the convention progressed it became clear that a majority of the delegates entertained views about violence which
she did not share. She should not be required to have fore-
seen that development and her mere presence at the convention should not be considered as a crime under the statute.
The Court, per Justice Sanford, held that what Whitney was
really doing was asking the Supreme Court to review questions of fact which had already been determined against her in
the lower courts. Such questions were not open to review in
the Supreme Court. The Court upheld Whitney's conviction
on the ground that concerted action involved a more significant
threat to the public order than isolated utterances and acts of
individuals. Assembling a political party designed to advocate
proletarian revolution by mass action at some future date was
outside the protection of the Fourteenth Amendment. Within
a few months of the Court's decision, Governor C. C. Young
pardoned Anita Whitney, acknowledging that "clear and present
danger" should be the vital concern, and that the Communist
Labor Party no longer posed any threat of criminal syndicalism.

DeJonge v. Oregon 299 U. S. 353 (1937)

The question of advocacy was again raised several
years later. On July 27, 1934 the Communist Party of Portland, Oregon sponsored a meeting which attracted an audience
of two to three hundred, about ten to fifteen per cent of whom
were members of the Party. The announced purpose of the
meeting was to protest illegal raids on workers' halls and
homes, and against the shooting of striking longshoremen by
Portland police. Dirk DeJonge, a member of the Communist
Party, delivered a speech in which he objected to conditions
in the county jail. He criticized the action of city police concerning the maritime strike which was then in progress. He
claimed that raids on the Communist headquarters and workers'
halls and offices were the result of efforts on the part of
steamship and stevedoring companies to break the maritime

longshoremen's and seamen's strike. He indicated that they hoped to break the strike by pitting the longshoremen and seamen against the communist movement. DeJonge also urged those in attendance to recruit members for the Communist Party and to purchase Communist literature which was sold at the meeting. The gathering was quiet and peaceful throughout.

The meeting was raided by police officers and they arrested DeJonge and charged him with violating the Criminal Syndicalism law of Oregon, which resembled the California Criminal Syndicalism Act. The indictment charged that DeJonge assisted in conducting a meeting which was called by the Communist Party, an organization which advocated criminal syndicalism. At trial, DeJonge argued that the meeting was orderly and neither criminal syndicalism nor any other unlawful behavior was taught or advocated. The prosecution stipulated several statements from Communist Party literature which advocated criminal syndicalism. DeJonge was found guilty and was sentenced to jail for seven years.

The U.S. Supreme Court unanimously found the Oregon statute in violation of the due process clause of the Fourteenth Amendment. The lower court had not established advocacy of criminal syndicalism by DeJonge. The Attorney General of Oregon admitted that the literature distributed at the meeting was not the same as that produced at DeJonge's trial. DeJonge was not found guilty of any offense other than that he assisted in conducting a meeting which was held under the sponsorship of the Communist Party. Peaceable assembly for lawful discussion could not be made a crime. If DeJonge had committed a crime elsewhere, he was subject to prosecution for that crime under another law. Oregon could not seize upon mere participation in a peaceable assembly as a basis for a criminal charge. Whatever the objectives of the Communist Party, DeJonge was still "entitled to discuss the public issues of the day, and in a lawful manner without incitement to violence or crime, to seek redress of alleged grievances. That was the essence of his guaranteed personal liberty."

Brandenburg v. Ohio 395 U.S. 444 (1969)

One of the more recent Supreme Court cases dealing with state criminal anarchy and syndicalism acts involved a leader of the Ohio Ku Klux Klan. Clarence Brandenburg telephoned a Cincinnati television station and invited a news

announcer to attend a rally. The meeting was filmed and portions were later broadcast on the local station and on a national network. One film showed twelve hooded figures, some
of whom carried firearms, gathered around a large wooden
cross. Most of the statements expressed were incomprchen-
sible, but scattered phrases which were derogatory toward
blacks and Jews could be understood. Among them were:
"How far is the nigger going to--yeah"; "this is what we are
going to do to the niggers"; "A dirty nigger"; "Send the Jews
back to Israel"; "Let's give them back to the dark garden";
"Save America"; "Let's go back to constitutional betterment";
"Bury the niggers"; "We intend to do our part"; "Give us our
state rights"; "Freedom for the whites"; "Nigger will have to
fight for every inch he gets from now on. " Another scene on
the film showed Brandenburg, in Klan regalia, delivering the
following speech:

> This is an organizers' meeting. We have had quite
> a few members here today which are--We have hun-
> dreds, hundreds of members throughout the State of
> Ohio. I can quote from a newspaper clipping from
> the Columbus, Ohio, Dispatch, five weeks ago Sun-
> day morning. The Klan has more members in the
> State of Ohio than does any other organization, but
> if our President, our Congress, our Supreme Court,
> continues to suppress the white, Caucasian race,
> it's possible that there might have to be some re-
> venge taken. We are marching on Congress, July
> the Fourth, four hundred thousand strong. From
> there we are dividing into two groups, one group to
> march on St. Augustine, Florida, the other group to
> march into Mississippi. Thank you.

A second film showed six hooded figures, one of whom was
Brandenburg. He repeated the speech except that the reference to the possibility of revenge was omitted, and a sentence
was added: "Personally, I believe the nigger should be returned to Africa, the Jew returned to Israel. " Though some
of the figures in the two films carried weapons, Brandenburg
did not.

Brandenburg was convicted, under the Ohio Criminal
Syndicalism Statute, of "advocating ... the duty, necessity, or
propriety of crime, sabotage, violence, or unlawful methods
of terrorism as a means of accomplishing industrial or political reform" and of "voluntarily assembling with any society,
group or assemblage of persons formed to teach or advocate

the doctrines of criminal syndicalism. " He was fined $1, 000 and sentenced to from one to ten years' imprisonment. He appealed.

The Supreme Court, in the Brandenburg case, rejected (9-0) the Gitlow and Whitney principle which held that "advocating" violent means to effect political and economic change involved such danger to the security of the state that the state could outlaw it. Basing its decision on a principle established in Yates v. U. S., the Court noted that the guarantee of free speech and press does not allow a state to forbid advocacy of the use of force or of law violation, except where such advocacy is directed at producing imminent lawless action. Measured by this test, Ohio's statute could not be sustained because it punished mere advocacy and assembly with others who merely advocated action. The Ohio statute was unconstitutional because it punished mere advocacy.

Smith Act

In 1940, Congress passed the Alien Registration Act, which made it a crime to advocate the violent overthrow of the government or to knowingly organize or belong to a group advocating it. This act, known as the Smith Act, was aimed at controlling subversive groups, particularly Nazis and Communists. During the 1950s the Dennis and Yates cases tested the conspiracy provisions of the Smith Act. In 1961, Scales and Noto involved convictions under the membership clause of the act.

Dennis v. United States 341 U. S. 494 (1951)

Eugene Dennis, Secretary of the Communist Party, and ten fellow communists were indicted for violating the conspiracy provisions of the Smith Act during the period from April, 1945 to July, 1948. The indictment charged Dennis with knowingly conspiring (1) to organize the Communist Party as a group that advocated the overthrow of the government by violence, and (2) willfully advocating the duty and necessity of overthrowing and destroying the government. The trial extended over nine months. The prosecution argued that Communist leaders, including Dennis, were unwilling to operate within the framework of democracy, but instead intended to initiate a violent revolution whenever the proper occasion arose. Communists were adept at infiltrating strategic positions, used aliases effectively, and tolerated no dissension from the policy laid down by Party leaders, and Communist literature advocated the general aim of achieving a successful overthrow of the government by force and violence. In response, Dennis claimed that he advocated that force and violence were necessary to achieve a communist form of government in an existing democracy only because the ruling classes would never permit the transformation to be accomplished peacefully, but would use force to defeat any peaceful political and economic gains the Communists might achieve. The jury returned a verdict of guilty. Dennis appealed.

The majority of the Supreme Court determined (6-2) that the Smith Act required proof that the intent of those who were charged was to overthrow the government by force and violence. The majority justices also agreed that a violation of the law could be sustained only when the speech or publication created a "clear and present danger" of attempting or accomplishing the prohibited crime. The overthrow of the government was a substantial enough interest for the government to restrict communication. When the government was aware that a group dedicated to its overthrow was attempting to indoctrinate its members, and to commit them to a course whereby they would strike when the leaders felt the circumstances permitted, action by the government was required. The majority opinion, written by Chief Justice Fred Vinson, concluded:

> Petitioners intended to overthrow the government of the United States as speedily as the circumstances would permit. Their conspiracy to organize the Communist Party and to teach and advocate the overthrow of the Government of the United States by force and violence created a clear and present danger of an attempt to overthrow the government by force and violence. They were properly and constitutionally convicted for violation of the Smith Act. The judgments of conviction are affirmed.

In Dennis, conspiracy to overthrow the government, rather than overthrow itself, was considered adequate to justify suppression of communication tending toward that effect. The Court found a clear and present danger of a conspiracy, and that was sufficient to offset Dennis' First Amendment claims. Holmes and Brandeis dissented. In all, twenty-nine persons served prison terms for conviction under the conspiracy provisions of the Smith Act.

Yates v. United States 354 U. S. 298 (1957)

In the Yates case, the Supreme Court provided a different interpretation of the conspiracy section of the Smith
Act. Fourteen Communist Party leaders, including Oleta
Yates, were convicted for conspiring (1) to advocate the overthrow of the government, and (2) to organize the Communist
Party as a society of persons who so advocate, with the intent
of causing the overthrow by force and violence as soon as circumstances could permit. The conspiracy allegedly originated
in 1940 and continued until the time of the indictment in 1951.
The defendants were sentenced to five years in prison and
fined $10,000 each.

The U. S. Supreme Court reversed (5-2) the decision of
the lower court on two counts. First, the term "organize"
meant to "establish," "found," or "bring into existence." It
referred to the creation of a new organization. The Communist Party was organized by 1945 at the latest. So the indictment of the fourteen, which was returned in 1951, was barred
because the three-year statute of limitations had expired.
Second, the trial judge refused to instruct the jury that in
order to convict, they had to find that the advocacy which the
defendants conspired to promote was calculated to incite persons to action. Advocacy of forcible overthrow as mere
abstract doctrine was within the free speech protection of the
First Amendment. The trial court, by allowing conviction
for mere advocacy, unrelated to the potential for producing
forcible action, resulted in an unconstitutional application of
the Smith Act. In Yates, the Court distinguished between
"advocacy of abstract doctrine," which was permissible, and
"advocacy of action," which was not. The Court reversed the
convictions, suggesting that the evidence against five defendants
was so clearly insufficient as to warrant acquittal but that re-
trial appeared justified regarding the other nine petitioners.

Scales v. United States 367 U. S. 203 (1961)

The Court further developed the distinction between
advocacy of ideas and advocacy of action in the Scales case.
Janius Irving Scales was the chairman of the North and South
Carolina Districts of the Communist Party. He recruited members for the Party and promoted the education of young Party
members. At a secret Communist school, in Scales' presence,
students were shown how to kill a person with a pencil, a
technique which was thought to be useful in a picket line.

Scales criticized American aggression in Korea and claimed
that revolution would come within a generation. He made these
statements to an FBI agent who posed as a person interested
in the Party. Scales was convicted under the membership
clause of the Smith Act which made it a felony to knowingly
hold membership in any organization which advocated the overthrow of the government by force or violence. Scales was
sentenced to six years in prison.

The U. S. Supreme Court confirmed (5-4) the conviction
of Scales for "active knowing membership" in the Communist
Party. Evidence supported a finding of advocacy of revolutionary action rather than advocacy of mere abstract revolutionary doctrine. The Court said:

> Since the evidence amply showed the Party leaders
> were continuously preaching during the indictment
> period the inevitability of eventual forcible overthrow,
> the first and basic question is a narrow one:
> whether the jury could permissibly infer that such
> preaching, in whole or in part, was aimed at build-
> ing up a seditious group and maintaining it in readi-
> ness for action at a propitious time ... the kind of
> indoctrination preparatory to action which was con-
> demned in Dennis.... On this score, we think that
> the jury, under instructions which fully satisfied the
> requirements of Yates, was entitled to infer ... that
> advocacy of action was engaged in.

In Scales, a majority of justices upheld the constitutionality
of the membership provision of the Smith Act, which they
interpreted as requiring proof of active rather than merely
nominal or passive membership in the Communist Party.

Noto v. United States 367 U. S. 290 (1961)

A companion case, Noto, also tested the validity of a
prosecution under the membership clause. The key point in
John Noto's case that the U. S. Supreme Court needed to consider was the sufficiency of evidence. The Court noted that
Smith Act violation required rigorous standards of proof. At
Noto's trial, much of the evidence came from excerpts from
the "communist classics. " This material showed the Party's
teaching of abstract doctrine that revolution was inevitable to
achieve communism in a capitalist society, but testimony
which suggested advocacy of action to accomplish that goal

during the period of indictment, 1946 to 1954, was sparse.
In Noto, the evidence of illegal Party advocacy lacked the compelling quality which, in Scales, was supplied by the defendant's own statements and behavior as a leading Party official.
In Noto, the evidence was insufficient to show that the Communist Party engaged in advocacy of the forcible overthrow of
the government. Noto's conviction was reversed (5-4).

Following this reversal, the government moved to dis-
continue pending prosecutions under the membership clause.
As a result, Janius Scales was the only person to serve a
prison sentence under the membership provision of the Smith
Act.

Censure by State Representatives

During the 1960s, as United States military involvement
in Vietnam steadily increased, groups expressed dissatisfaction
over the war policy of Lyndon Johnson's Administration. One
such group, the Student Nonviolent Coordinating Committee
(SNCC), issued a statement opposing United States involvement
in Vietnam. It said in part:

> We are in sympathy with, and support, the men in
> this country who are unwilling to respond to a mili-
> tary draft which would compel them to contribute
> their lives to United States aggression in Viet Nam
> in the name of the freedom we find so false in this
> country.... We take note of the fact that 16 per cent
> of the draftees from this country are Negroes called
> on to stifle the liberation of Viet Nam, to preserve
> a democracy which does not exist for them at home.

> ... We believe that work in the civil rights movement
> and with other human relations organizations is a
> valid alternative to the draft. We urge all Ameri-
> cans to seek this alternative, knowing full well that
> it may cost them lives--as painfully as in Viet Nam.

Bond v. Floyd 385 U.S. 116 (1966)

Julian Bond, an elected member of the Georgia House
of Representatives, publicly endorsed the SNCC statement,
"First because I like to think of myself as a pacifist ... and
secondly, I agree with this statement ... because I think it is

sorta hypocritical for us to maintain that we are fighting for
liberty in other places and we are not guaranteeing liberty to
citizens inside the continental United States.... I don't think
that I as a second-class citizen of the United States have a
requirement to support war. I think my responsibility is to
oppose things that I think are wrong, if they are in Viet Nam,
or New York, or Chicago, or Atlanta, or whatever.... I'm
against all war. I'm against that war in particular, and I
don't think people ought to participate in it. Because I'm against
war, I'm against the draft. "

Members of the Georgia House filed a petition challenging Bond's right to be seated in the legislature. Bond indicated
his willingness to take an oath to support the federal and state
constitutions. At a hearing, Bond claimed that he "admired the
courage" of people "who felt strongly enough about their convictions" to burn their draft cards, "knowing the consequences
that they will face," but pointed out that he had his own draft
card in his pocket and had "never suggested or counseled or
advocated" that anyone burn his draft card. A House committee
concluded that Bond's endorsement of the SNCC statement and
his remarks indicated that he "does not and will not" support
the federal and state constitutions, that he aided and comforted
America's enemies, that his statement violated the Selective
Service Act, and that his remarks "are reprehensible and tend
to bring discredit to the House. " Accordingly, the Georgia
House voted not to allow Bond to take the oath of office or be
seated.

A unanimous U. S. Supreme Court held that the Georgia
legislature had violated Bond's right of free expression. The
Court acknowledged that "there can be no question but that the
First Amendment protects expression in opposition to national
foreign policy in Vietnam and to the Selective Service System. "
The State of Georgia argued that it was constitutionally justified in demanding a higher standard of loyalty from public
officials than from its citizens. But the Court decided that
even though a state may require an oath to support the Constitution from its legislators which it does not require of its private
citizens, the state does not have the power to limit its legislators' capacity to express their views of local, state, and national policies.

When one compares the statement upheld by the Supreme
Court in Bond with those remarks denied protection in Schenck,
Debs, and Gitlow, it seems quite apparent that the range of pro-
tected advocacy has widened during the twentieth century.

Throughout the period, the Court clearly extended the wide
scope of First Amendment guarantees to statements and actions involving peacetime dissent, but tended to limit protection in times of military crisis. However, in Bond, the
Court applied the broader meaning of the First Amendment
to the wartime situation.

PROVOCATION

A rather small number of speakers actually advocate
the overthrow of the government by either violent or peaceful
means. Many more speakers attempt to persuade and arouse
audiences to support or oppose local, state, and national issues. Sometimes, in the course of such utterances, favorable
as well as hostile audiences may be provoked into a breach
of peace or some other form of public disturbance. In such
situations, authorities have laws at their disposal for dealing
with such instances of provocative words.

Fighting Words

An utterance which provokes another to anger but has
little if any social utility may be considered "fighting words."
This doctrine was first specified by the United States Supreme
Court in 1942.

Chaplinsky v. New Hampshire 315 U. S. 568 (1942)

Walter Chaplinsky, a Jehovah's Witness, was distributing literature on the streets of Rochester, New Hampshire
one Saturday afternoon. Local citizens complained to the
Police Chief that Chaplinsky was denouncing all religion as a
"racket." The Chief told them that Chaplinsky was legally
entitled to make such remarks, and then warned Chaplinsky
that the crowd was getting unruly. According to the complaint, Chaplinsky then remarked to the Chief: "You are a
God-damned racketeer" and "a damned Fascist and the whole
government of Rochester are Fascists or agents of Fascists."
Chaplinsky claimed that he asked the Police Chief to arrest
those citizens who were making the disturbance, but the Chief
cursed Chaplinsky and told him to come along with him to the
station. Chaplinsky was convicted for violating a New Hampshire law which forbade "addressing any offensive, derisive
or annoying word to any other person who is lawfully in any

street or other public place. " The statute also prohibited
calling such a person "by any offensive or derisive name. "

The New Hampshire Supreme Court actually created the
"fighting words" doctrine. In their opinion, "the test is what
men of common intelligence would understand to be words
likely to cause an average addressee to fight.... The English
language has a number of words and expressions which by general consent are fighting words when said without a disarming
smile.... Such words, as ordinary men know, are likely to
cause a fight. " According to the New Hampshire court, Chaplinsky's remarks constituted "fighting words. " The United
States Supreme Court said (9-0) that the New Hampshire law
did not violate the right of free expression. The words used
by Chaplinsky "are epithets likely to provoke the average person to retaliation and thereby cause a breach of the peace. "
Furthermore, the words possess low social usefulness; "such
utterances are no essential part of any exposition of ideas,
and are of such slight social value as a step to truth that any
benefit that may be derived from them is clearly outweighed
by the social interest in order and morality. " The words in
this case did not warrant First Amendment protection.

Gooding v. Wilson 405 U. S. 518 (1972)

One of the few cases to come before the United States
Supreme Court which involved the doctrine of "fighting words"
concerned a Georgia law which provided that "Any person who
shall, without provocation, use to or of another, and in his
presence ... opprobrious words or abusive language, tending
to cause a breach of peace ... shall be guilty of a misdemeanor. Johnney C. Wilson was picketing a U. S. Army
headquarters building on August 18, 1966, in protest against
the Vietnam War. He blocked the entrance so that arriving
inductees were unable to enter. When two policemen attempted
to remove him, he called policeman M. G. Redding a "White
son-of-a-bitch, I'll kill you, " and said, "You son-of-a-bitch,
I'll choke you to death. " Wilson also said to T. L. Raborn,
"You son-of-a-bitch, if you ever put your hands on me again,
I'll cut you all to pieces. " Wilson was charged with using
opprobrious words and abusive language to and of the two police officers, tending to cause a breach of the peace. Wilson
was convicted and he appealed.

The U. S. Supreme Court ruled (5-2) that the Georgia
statute was vague and too broad. In comparison with <u>Chaplinsky,</u>

in which the Court had defined "fighting words" with narrow specificity, the statute lacked such exactness. The New Hampshire statute had defined "fighting words" as language that was "offensive, derisive, or annoying." In the Georgia case, the statute was too narrowly drawn to apply only to a constitutionally unprotected class of words, "fighting words." No meaningful attempt was made to limit or properly define the terms. The dictionary definitions of "opprobrious" and "abusive" give them greater reach than "fighting words." Webster's Third New International Dictionary of 1961 defined "opprobrious" as "conveying or intended to convey disgrace," and "abusive" as "harsh insulting language." Such definitions cover incidents where words convey disgrace or insult, but fall short of "fighting words," that is, words uttered face-to-face that are derisive and annoying and that plainly tend to excite a person to a breach of peace.

Lewis v. New Orleans 415 U. S. 130 (1974)

In 1974 the U. S. Supreme Court found a Louisiana statute overly broad and facially invalid in another test of "fighting words." Mrs. Mallie Lewis, while her son was being arrested, allegedly called the police officers "goddamn motherfucking police." Mrs. Lewis was convicted for violating a city ordinance making it unlawful "to curse or revile or to use obscene or opprobrious language toward or with reference to" a police officer in the performance of his duties.

The Court reversed (6-3). Justice William Brennan, writing for the Court, declared the ordinance to be equally "susceptible of application to speech, although vulgar or offensive, that is protected" by the Constitution as it is susceptible of application to speech that is not protected. Justice Lewis Powell, in a concurring opinion, noted:

> Quite apart from the ambiguity inherent in the term 'opprobrious,' words may or may not be 'fighting words' depending upon the circumstances of their utterance. It is unlikely, for example, that the words said to have been used here would have precipitated a physical confrontation between the middle-aged woman who spoke them and the police officer in whose presence they were uttered. The words may well have conveyed anger and frustration without provoking a violent reaction from the officer.

In his view, Powell demanded a clear and present danger of violent reaction from the police officer to whom the words were addressed in order to uphold conviction.   In his opinion, such
a danger did not exist.   Also, the fears noted in Gooding
were applicable in this case because the Louisiana statute,
like the Georgia law in Gooding, was subject to virtually
open-ended interpretation by a jury.   Therefore, "persons
whose expression is constitutionally protected may well refrain
from exercising their rights for fear of criminal sanctions
provided by a statute susceptible of application to protected
expression." The Louisiana statute was declared unconstitutional.

Restless Crowds

A different type of public speaking situation which poses
a problem for police authorities occurs when a speaker communicates ideas to an audience that becomes unruly and un-
manageable.   Should the speaker be instructed to cease
speaking because the unruly crowd represents a threat to public order?   Should the speaker's right to express his or her
opinions be protected in the face of possible public chaos
while police efforts are directed at management of the unruly
crowd?   In 1949, the Court considered these questions.

Terminiello v. Chicago 337 U. S. 1 (1949)

Father Arthur W. Terminiello, a Catholic priest under
suspension by his bishop, delivered an address in an auditorium
in Chicago under the auspices of the Christian Veterans of
America.   The auditorium was filled to capacity with more
than 8, 000 persons; others were turned away.   The meeting
was called to deal with the issue: "Christian Nationalism or
World Communism--Which?" Outside, a crowd of 1, 000 protested the meeting.   Several policemen were present to maintain order, but they were unable to prevent disturbances because the crowd outside was angry and turbulent.   The crowd
interfered with access to the front door.   Members of the
crowd called Terminiello and his followers "Goddamned Fascists, " "Hitlers, " "Nazis, " and claimed they "ought to hang
the so and so's. " Bottles, stink bombs, and bricks were
tossed inside, breaking about thirty windows.   The crowd
broke the front door partially open.   Police arrested seventeen members of the crowd outside.

At the outset of his speech, Terminiello, assuming that some of his opponents had got inside, claimed, "And nothing I could say tonight could begin to express the contempt I have for the slimy scum that got in by mistake." In the main body of the speech, Terminiello viciously attacked various political and racial groups he thought were detrimental to the nation's welfare. He referred to some of the elements that were "going to destroy America by revolution." He stated that there were about "fifty-seven varieties that we have in America and we have fifty-seven varieties of pinks and reds and pastel shades in this country; and all of it can be traced back to the twelve years we spent under the New Deal, because that was the build-up for what is going on in the world today...." He also specifically attacked the "communistic Zionistic Jew, and those are not American Jews. We don't want them here; we want them to go back where they came from...." The speech provoked vehement responses from some members of the audience inside the auditorium. One person claimed, "Yes, the Jews are all killers, murderers. If we don't kill them first, they will kill us." Others said, "Yes, send the Jews back to Russia," "Kill the Jews," and "Dirty Kikes." Terminiello was arrested and charged with "breach of peace," which consisted of any "misbehavior which violates the public peace and decorum." The court held that "misbehavior may constitute a breach of peace if it stirs the public to anger, invites dispute, brings about a condition of unrest, or creates a disturbance, or if it molests the inhabitants in the enjoyment of peace and quiet by arousing alarm." Terminiello was convicted and fined $100. He appealed.

The U. S. Supreme Court ruled (5-4) that, in this case, there was no likelihood that the speech would "produce a clear and present danger of a serious substantive evil that arises far above public inconvenience, annoyance, or unrest...." Terminiello was not convicted for creating a clear danger to public disorder, but rather for causing a breach of peace by delivering a speech which stirred the public to anger, invited dispute, or brought about a condition of unrest. The Court noted that a function of free speech, perhaps its highest purpose, was to invite dispute, induce a situation of unrest, create dissatisfaction with undesirable conditions, or even stir people to anger. For this kind of public speech, Terminiello could not be punished.

Feiner v. New York 340 U. S. 315 (1951)

Two years after Terminiello, the Court examined the

remarks of a college student. On the evening of March 8, 1949, Irving Feiner addressed a crowd of about eighty persons on a street corner in Syracuse, New York. Feiner stood on a large wooden box on the sidewalk and spoke to the crowd through a loudspeaker system attached to an automobile. The primary purpose of his speech was to urge listeners to attend a meeting, sponsored by the Young Progressives, to be held that evening in the Syracuse Hotel. But Feiner also made derogatory remarks about President Truman, the American Legion, the Mayor of Syracuse, and other local political officials. Feiner said, "Mayor Costello is a champagne-sipping bum; he does not speak for the Negro people. " "The 15th Ward is run by corrupt politicians, and there are horse rooms operating there. " "President Truman is a bum. " "Mayor O'Dwyer is a bum. " "The American Legion is a Nazi Gestapo. " And "The Negroes don't have equal rights; they should rise up in arms and fight for their rights. " The Young Progressives had been given a permit for the meeting in a public school auditorium but the permit had been cancelled, so the meeting was shifted to the Hotel Syracuse. This probably sparked Feiner's remarks against city officials.

Somebody complained to the authorities and two police officers were dispatched to the scene. The officers noticed that the crowd, which spilled over into the street, was restless and that traffic was affected. At this point, Feiner gave the impression that he was attempting to arouse the black members in the audience against the whites. He urged that blacks in the audience "should rise up in arms and fight for their rights. " A white person in the audience told the policemen that if they didn't get that "son of a bitch" off the soap box, he would. The police officers feared that a fight would begin, so they approached Feiner in an attempt to coax him to break up the crowd. Three times the officers requested that Feiner stop speaking, but he continued. The crowd became more restless. Feiner was arrested for disorderly conduct, convicted, and sentenced to thirty days in the county jail.

The U. S. Supreme Court ruled (6-3) that in this case the police were not acting to stifle the opinions of Feiner, but were motivated by an interest in preserving order and the general welfare of the citizens. Feiner had not been arrested and convicted because of the content of the communication but, rather, for the reaction to it that Feiner's own behavior had produced. The majority of the Court found a clear and present danger created by Feiner's speech. In his dissenting opinion, William O. Douglas argued,

> When unpopular causes are sponsored from the pub-
> lic platform there will commonly be mutterings and
> unrest and heckling from the crowd. When a speaker
> mounts a platform it is not unusual to find him re-
> sorting to exaggeration, to vilification of ideas and
> men, to the making of false charges. But those
> extravagances ... do not justify penalizing the
> speaker by depriving him of his platform or by pun-
> ishing him for his conduct.

Certain elements clearly differentiate the situations in
Feiner and Terminiello. Terminiello addressed an audience
in a hired hall, thereby having no "captive audience" as did
Feiner, whose speech was conveyed through an amplifying system to persons walking down the street who unavoidably heard
the remarks. Terminiello was not convicted of creating any
clear and present danger to public disorder; Feiner was. The
key distinction appears to be that in Feiner, the speaker contributed substantially to the public disorder while in Terminiello, the audience, rather than the speaker, contributed significantly to the chaos. When the speaker created disorder the
communication was not protected; but when the audience was
primarily responsible, the speech fell within First Amendment
guarantees.

Threatening Words

In addition to "fighting words," any speech that can be
construed as "threatening" is illegal. A 1917 law makes it a
crime to knowingly and willfully threaten to take the life of the
President of the United States. Any violator can be fined up to
$1,000 or imprisoned not more than five years or both. A
violation of this law can be classified as "threatening speech."

Watts v. United States 394 U.S. 705 (1969)

On August 27, 1966, a public rally took place on the
Washington Monument grounds. Members of the crowd broke
up into small groups to discuss various subjects. Robert
Watts, an eighteen-year-old, joined a group discussing police
brutality. When a member of the group suggested that the
young people present should get more education, Watts replied, "They always holler at us to get an education. And now
I have already received my draft classification as I-A and I
have got to report for my physical this Monday coming. I am

not going.   If they ever make me carry a rifle the first man I
want to get in my sights is L. B. J.   They are not going to
make me kill my black brothers. " On the basis of his remark,
Watts was convicted of the felony of knowingly and willfully
threatening the President.   Watts was given a suspended sentence.   He appealed.

The U. S. Supreme Court reversed (5-4) on the grounds
that Watts made the statement in the heat of a political debate;
that what he said was uttered under pressure of a specific
event--induction into the Armed Forces; that the remark would
never actually become reality, and that the crowd actually
laughed along with Watts after the statement.   The Court did
"not believe that the kind of political hyperbole indulged in"
by Watts fits within the statutory term "willfulness. "   They also
noted that "the language of the political arena ... is often vituperative, abusive, and inexact. " Watts' statement had to be
examined in context and in this case, the remark was "a
kind of very crude offensive method of stating a political opposition to the President. "   Watts' "threatening words" were
entitled to First Amendment protection because, taken in context, the words were "political hyperbole" rather than a true
threat upon President Lyndon Johnson's life.

Offensive Words

Another form of provocation concerns words that might
be viewed as offensive to certain listeners.   In the early 1970s
the U. S. Supreme Court heard three cases that involved potentially "offensive words. " All involved protests against the
Vietnam War.

Bachellar v. Maryland 397 U. S. 564 (1970)

On March 28, 1966, Donald Bachellar was among fifteen demonstrators who protested against the Vietnam War in
front of a United States Army recruiting station located on a
downtown Baltimore street.   The marchers carried or wore
signs bearing such slogans as: "Peasant Emancipation, Not
Escalation, " "Make Love, Not War, " "Stop in the Name of
Love, " and "Why Are We in Viet Nam?"   The number of
marchers increased to around forty before the demonstration
ended.   From time to time the protestors passed out leaflets
and debated with members of the crowd that gathered nearby
and across the street.   Some members of the crowd showed

obvious displeasure with the leaflets, as well as with the demonstration. Shortly before five o'clock, Bachellar and five
other protestors entered the recruiting station and tried to
persuade a sergeant in charge to allow them to display their
antiwar posters in the windows of the station. The sergeant
informed the protestors that Army regulations forbade such a
display. According to police who were present, the protestors
then sat and lay down, thereby blocking free passage of the
sidewalk. Bachellar and his colleagues were arrested and
charged under a Maryland statute which prohibits "acting in a
disorderly manner to the disturbance of the public peace, upon
any public street...."

At the trial, the judge told the jury that a guilty verdict
could be returned if they found that the protestors had engaged
in doing or saying anything that "offends, disturbs, incites, or
tends to incite a number of people gathered in the same area. "
The judge told the jury that "refusal to obey a policeman's
command to move on when not to do so may endanger the public peace" could also constitute grounds for conviction. The
jury returned a verdict of guilty and the defendants were sentenced to sixty days in jail and fined $50. They appealed.

The U. S. Supreme Court found that, because of the
instructions given by the trial judge, the jury could have rested
its verdict on a number of grounds. The jurors could have
found the protestors refused to obey a police officer's command
to move on. They may have found that the demonstrators deliberately obstructed the sidewalk, thus disturbing and inciting
bystanders. Or, the jurors may have found that the anti-
Vietnam protest amounted to doing or saying something which
offends, disturbs, or incites people gathered in the area. According to the unanimous Supreme Court, the defendants might
have been found guilty simply because they advocated unpopular
ideas. Because conviction for expressing, publicly, opinions
that might be offensive to some of the hearers would violate
the Constitution, the Court set aside the convictions.

Cohen v. California 403 U. S. 15 (1971)

On April 26, 1968, Paul Robert Cohen stood in the corridor of the Los Angeles County Courthouse wearing a jacket
bearing the clearly visible words, "Fuck the Draft. " Women
and children were present. Cohen did not commit any violent
action, nor did he make any unusual or loud noise. In fact,
he may not have said a word until police officers arrested

him.   Cohen stated that he wore the jacket as a means of informing the public of his feelings against the Vietnam War and the draft.   Cohen was tried for violating a California statute, under which a person commits a misdemeanor when he "maliciously and willfully disturbs the peace and quiet of any neighborhood or person, by loud or unusual noise, or by tumultuous or offensive conduct. "   The court decided that Cohen's behavior had a tendency to provoke others to acts of violence.   Observers might rise up and commit a violent act against Cohen or attempt to forcibly remove his jacket.   Cohen was sentenced to thirty days' imprisonment.

The U. S. Supreme Court reversed (5-4).   The Court considered the argument that an offensive mode of expression was thrust upon unsuspecting observers and that the state had acted to protect the sensitive women and children from unavoidable exposure to the crude message.   According to the majority opinion written by Justice John Harlan, offended persons could avoid contact with the communication simply by turning their eyes away from the jacket.   The Court also noted that words are complicated because they have both cognitive and emotional meanings.   A word that is vulgar to one person may have an entirely acceptable meaning or use for another.   If the government was allowed to prohibit particular words, such a possibility might result in the suppression of ideas.   Government officials might decide to censor a particular word as a convenient system of banning the expression of unpopular views.   Making such a result possible outweighs any social benefits that might accrue from banning a single four-letter word.   Therefore, a single offensive word could not be forbidden without running a substantial risk of suppressing ideas.

Hess v. Indiana 414 U. S. 105 (1973)

At an antiwar demonstration on the campus of Indiana University, approximately 100 to 150 demonstrators moved into a public street and blocked the passage of vehicles. When the demonstrators did not respond to verbal directions from police to clear the streets, the sheriff began walking up the street.   He heard Gregory Hess utter the word "fuck" in a loud voice and immediately arrested him on a disorderly conduct charge.   Hess's specific remark was, "We'll take the fucking street later. "   Two witnesses claimed that Hess was not exhorting the crowd to go back into the street, that he was facing the crowd and not the street when he said the

statement, that his remark did not seem to be addressed to
any particular individual or group, and that his tone, although
loud, was no louder than that of the other people in the area.
Hess was convicted and he appealed.

The U. S. Supreme Court ruled (6-3) that Hess's words,
in this case, did not fall into any of the classes of words that
were denied First Amendment protection. Hess's remark
could not be punished as obscene or offensive under the ruling
in Cohen. Any suggestion that Hess' speech amounted to
"fighting words" could not withstand scrutiny. Even if, under
other conditions, this remark could be regarded as a personal
insult, the statement in this instance was not directed to any
specific person or group of persons, it could not be claimed
that he was advocating any action. And, without evidence
that his words were intended and likely to produce imminent
disorder, the words could not be punished for a "tendency to
lead to violence. " The conviction was overturned. In Hess
as in Bachellar and Cohen, the Court refused to punish "offensive words. "

Authority Retaliation

A dissenter frequently directs a communication against
some type of authority, who in turn responds by wielding
power against the dissenter. One such case involved retaliation against a government employee who criticized his superiors. Other cases concerned selective service reclassification of college students who protested the Vietnam War and
the draft. In these cases, communication rubbed authorities
in such a way as to provoke retaliation.

Arnett v. Kennedy 416 U. S. 134 (1974)

In 1969, Wayne Kennedy, a federal employee in the
Chicago regional office of the Office of Economic Opportunity
(OEO), filed a grievance against a superior, charging him
with "deceit, incompetence, and dishonesty. " In 1971, he
charged a Division Chief with "managerial incompetence and
with attempting to discredit the employee's union. " Also, in
1971, Kennedy charged that officials of the OEO Regional Office "negotiated in bad faith" with representatives of Indian
organizations about grants of federal funds and accused some
OEO officials of "bribery and conflicts of interest. " Because
of these grievances against his superiors, Kennedy was

regarded as a troublemaker and was fired. He filed an administrative appeal with the Civil Service Commission and also initiated class action in the District Court charging that the procedures for removal of federal employees denied them procedural due process.

The court held that the regulations were "unconstitutionally vague" in failing to "furnish sufficiently precise guidelines as to what kind of speech may be made the basis of removal action," and ordered that Kennedy be reinstated with back pay. The Supreme Court reversed (6-3) the lower court's decision. The majority believed that the regulations authorizing removal of an employee for "such causes as will promote efficiency of the service" were not unconstitutionally vague or too broad because there are many circumstances in which public remarks by employees might reasonably justify dismissal for cause. This "cause" provision was viewed as adequately describing employee conduct for removal, as authorizing dismissal for speech as well as other behavior, and as excluding constitutionally protected speech. In this decision, the Court supported the doctrine of privilege. Under this doctrine, public employment is not considered a constitutional right. Any constitutional right can be restricted while a citizen is publicly employed. If a citizen accepts a public employment, he voluntarily accepts the possible forfeiture of his constitutional rights. So, under this doctrine, superiors in the civil service and the military service may fire or court-martial subordinates who criticize them or their methods. Wise employees will certainly learn to keep their mouths shut and thereby retain their jobs. The effect of the Arnett case may be to prevent the discovery of corrupt and inefficient superiors.

Wolff and Shortt v. Selective Service Local Board No. 66
372 F. 2d 817 (1967)

In 1967 the courts heard another case involving authority retaliation. During the mid-1960s college student antidraft groups sprang up around the United States in protest against the Vietnam War. Students expressed their personal dissent against the war and the draft in numerous ways. Sometimes, such actions brought retaliatory action from local draft boards. Peter Wolff and Richard Shortt were classified II-S because of their status as full-time students at the University of Michigan. On October 15, 1965, they participated in a demonstration to protest American involvement in Vietnam.

At the request of the New York City Director of Selective
Service, the local boards reclassified the two students I-A.
It was alleged that by participating in the demonstration the
students became "delinquents" by violating Section 12 of the
Universal Training Act by knowingly hindering or interfering
with the administration of the act. They appealed.

The court ruled for Wolff and Shortt; the local boards
had acted without justification. No regulation authorized a
draft board to declare anyone delinquent or to reclassify an
individual for violating Section 12. Yet, more importantly,
the court noted that a mere threat of sanctions may have the
result of destroying First Amendment rights as much as if
the sanctions were actually used. Indeed, "the effect of the
reclassification itself is immediately to curtail the exercise
of First Amendment rights." The mere threat of receiving
a I-A classification will tend immediately to silence dissent.
In this case, the court decided that the free speech rights to
criticize current policies must take precedence over the policy
of nonintervention in the Selective Service system.

Oestereich v. Selective Service Board No. 11
393 U. S. 233 (1968)
Gutknecht v. United States
396 U. S. 295 (1970)
Breen v. Selective Service Local Board No. 16
396 U. S. 460 (1970)

A nationwide draft card turn-in was scheduled to be
held on October 16, 1967. Thousands of persons attended a
rally on the Boston Common, followed by a march to the Ar-
lington Street Church where more than three-hundred young
men approached the pulpit either to burn their draft cards at
the altar candle or to deposit them in the collection plate.
Among these men stood a Wyoming-bred divinity student named
James Oestereich. Meanwhile, in the midwest, twenty protestors tried to deliver their cards to the authorities in Minne-
apolis; when the U. S. Marshal refused to accept them, the
protestors dropped the cards at his feet. One of the twenty
was a full-time activist named David Gutknecht. Exactly one
month later, forty young men participated in a turn-in sponsored by the Boston Resistance at the Old West Methodist
Church. Among them was an undergraduate music student
named Timothy Breen. As a result of their actions, the three
young men were either reclassified or moved up in the draft-
call list by their local draft boards. All sued on the grounds

that their free speech had been violated and that the punitive
use of the draft was unconstitutional.

The U. S. Supreme Court, in the opinion written by
Justice Douglas, ruled (6-3) in Oestereich that "Once a person
registers and qualifies for a statutory exemption we find no
legislative authority to deprive him of that exemption because
of conduct or activities unrelated to the merits of granting or
continuing that exemption." In this case, the "conduct of a
local board ... is basically lawless." The local draft board
rulings against Gutknecht and Breen were likewise vacated.
However, it should be noted that the Court did not absolve
draft resisters. Possession of both the Registration Certificate and the Notice of Classification remained duties required
by the Selective Service regulations, and willful failure to
perform those duties remained punishable under Section 12 of
the Universal Training Act. The Court did not indicate that
turning in a draft card constituted a legally protected form
of speech. In fact, in light of the O'Brien decision, to be
considered next, the opposite conclusion seems warranted.

SYMBOLIC SPEECH

At an ever-increasing rate during the past two decades,
dissent has incorporated the use of symbols. In such cases,
the meaning is less obvious than with pure speech and print.
The U. S. Supreme Court, in a series of relatively recent
decisions, has been presented an opportunity to decide whether
"symbolic speech" warrants the umbrella of First Amendment
protection.

Symbol Desecration

The Vietnam War divided the American people as much
as any event in the preceding century. Many Americans who
opposed the war had to choose between loyalty to the policy
of the government and to the soldiers fighting and dying in
support of that policy, and their own personal, deep belief
that the United States policy was wrong, immoral, and likely
to fail. Some outspoken opponents of the war chose to record
their opposition through the act of burning their draft cards.
This form of symbolic communication, through desecration of
a symbol, posed a significant question for the Court: was
"symbolic speech" subject to First Amendment protection,
and if so, to what extent?

United States v. O'Brien 391 U. S. 367 (1968)

      According to the Universal Military Training and Service Act, American men, upon reaching the age of eighteen, must register with a local draft board. The registrant is then assigned a Selective Service number and issued a registration certificate. In 1965, a congressional amendment made it a criminal act to forge, alter, or in any way knowingly to destroy or mutilate a selective service certificate. On March 31, 1966, David Paul O'Brien and three colleagues burned their draft cards on the steps of the South Boston Courthouse. A crowd, including several FBI agents, witnessed the event. In front of the crowd, O'Brien produced the charred remains of his draft card which, with his consent, were photographed. O'Brien was arrested. At his trial, O'Brien admitted that he had burned the card. He argued that he burned his certificate publicly in an effort to influence others to adopt his antiwar beliefs. O'Brien also claimed that the federal law prohibiting the knowing destruction of draft cards was unconstitutional because it was enacted to abridge freedom of speech. He was convicted.

      Before the U. S. Supreme Court, O'Brien contended that his act of burning his draft card was protected "symbolic speech" within the First Amendment. The Court rejected the view (7-1) that a limitless variety of conduct could be labeled "speech" whenever the person engaging in it intended to express an idea. The Court also noted that even if the communication element in O'Brien's action justified the application of the First Amendment, it did not necessarily follow that the destruction of a registration certificate was constitutionally protected. In the past, the Court had held that when "speech" and "non-speech" elements were combined in the same course of conduct, a sufficiently important governmental interest in regulating the "non-speech" element justified incidental limitations on First Amendment freedoms. The power of Congress to classify and conscript manpower for military service was an important governmental interest "beyond question." Congress could establish a system of registration and could require such individuals to cooperate in the system. According to the Court, the system was valuable in four ways: 1) the registration certificate served as proof that the individual described on the certificate had registered for the draft; 2) information supplied on the certificate facilitated communication between registrants and local boards; 3) the certificate served as a reminder that registrants must notify the board of any change in address and status; and 4) the system included clearly valid prohibitions against the alteration, forgery, or misuse of the certificates. The Court concluded that it was essential for America to have a system for raising armies that functioned with maximum efficiency. The availability to each registrant of his Selective Service Certificate furthered the smooth and proper functioning of the system.

In 1970, following considerable protest against the draft during the previous decade, a presidential commission recommended that the United States establish all-voluntary military forces. In January, 1973, following the signing of a cease-fire agreement terminating American involvement in Vietnam, the U. S. adopted an all-volunteer system.

Street v. New York 394 U. S. 576 (1969)

During the civil rights and Vietnam War protests, the American flag was the most prominent national symbol that was subjected to desecration. These situations again raised the issue of whether "symbolic speech" falls within the protection of the First Amendment. The Court had an opportunity to grapple with this issue in Street. On the afternoon of June 6, 1966, Sidney Street was listening to the radio in his Brooklyn apartment when he heard that civil rights leader James Meredith had been shot by a sniper in Mississippi. He said to himself, "They didn't protect him, " and then took from his dresser drawer a forty-eight-star American flag which he had displayed on national holidays and carried it to a street corner where he burned it. A police officer stopped his patrol car and found the burning flag. He noticed that Street was talking to a small group of people. As the officer approached, he heard Street say, "We don't need no damn flag, " and when the officer asked Street if he burned the flag, Street replied, "Yes, that is my flag; I burned it. If they let that happen to Meredith, we don't need an American flag. " Street was charged with the crime of malicious mischief for having willfully and unlawfully defiled and burned the American flag, in violation of the New York Penal Law. Street was subsequently convicted and given a suspended sentence.

When the case reached the U. S. Supreme Court, a majority of justices felt (5-4) that Street might have been punished for his words as well as the act of burning the flag. As a result, they inquired as to whether Street's words offered any justification for such a conviction. According to the Court, no governmental interest would be furthered by punishing

Street's words. First, Street was not inciting the public to commit unlawful acts. Street simply recommended that the country should, at least temporarily, abandon one of its national symbols. The Fourteenth Amendment clearly restricts the states from punishing anyone who publicly advocates peaceful change in societal institutions. Second, Street's words were not so inflammatory as to provoke others to retaliate physically against him. Even though the words might excite some individuals, they are not "fighting words, " that is, words which are "likely to provoke the average person to retaliation, and thereby cause a breach of peace. " Third, Street's words were not offensive, and so they did not necessitate protecting the sensibilities of passers-by. Any shock effect of the remarks stemmed from the ideas and not the words. The Constitution forbids outlawing "the ideas themselves, " even if they may be offensive to their hearers. Fourth, Street's speech was within constitutionally guaranteed freedom to differ with the existing order. His contemptuous remarks about the flag were not punishable for showing improper respect for the national emblem. Overall, the majority felt that they were unable to uphold the conviction because it could have been based upon a form of expression which, even though distasteful, was protected by the Constitution.

The minority justices decided the case on a distinctly different basis. In their view, Street was convicted for his act of burning the flag, not for his words. In the minority opinion of Chief Justice Earl Warren, "I believe that the States and the Federal government do have the power to protect the flag from acts of desecration and disgrace. " Justice Abe Fortas felt,

> One may not justify the burning of a house, even if it is his own, on the ground, however sincere, that he does so as a protest. One may not justify breaking the windows of a government building on that basis. Protest does not exonerate lawlessness. And the prohibition against flag burning on the public thoroughfare being valid, the misdemeanor is not excused merely because it is an act of flamboyant protest.

In this case, the minority held that the act for which Street was convicted, burning the flag, was not protected by the First Amendment. The majority took the position that the conviction may have been based on Street's words, which were protected. But, the majority opinion avoided consideration of whether the act of flag burning was "symbolic speech" deserving of First Amendment protection.

People v. Radich 308 N. Y. S. 2d 846 (1970)

A year after Street, the courts heard another case of symbol desecration. In 1967, Stephen Radich, the proprietor of an art gallery in New York City, offered for sale several pieces of sculpture which expressed opposition to the Vietnam War. The sculptures prominently displayed the U. S. flag in the form of the male sexual organ, erect and protruding from the upright portion of a cross; in the form of a human body hanging from a yellow noose; and wrapped around a bundle resting upon a two-wheeled vehicle which resembled a gun caisson. Radich called the sculptures "protest art." He was arrested and charged with violating the New York flag desecration law. The Court ruled that the sculptures clearly cast the flag into dishonor--at least the penis and noose sculptures. Furthermore, the court noted that the clear legislative purpose of the flag desecration statute was to prevent breach of the peace. The Court compared the treatment of the flag in this case with that in Street.

> Here, the expression, if less dramatic, was given far wider circulation and, in consequence, perhaps, a measureable enhancement of the likelihood of incitement to disorder, by the placement of one of the constructions in a street display window of defendant's gallery on Madison Avenue in the City of New York, and the exhibition and exposure for sale of the companion pieces in the public gallery and mercantile establishment within. Implicit in the invitation to view was the opportunity thereby afforded to join in the protest, or in counterprotest, with the consequent potential of public disorder....

The Court concluded that the legitimate public interest which the New York statute was designed to protect was threatened by Radich's "protest art." His conviction was upheld.

Smith v. Goguen 415 U. S. 566 (1974)

Four years later, the Court further developed its position regarding flag desecration. Valarie Goguen wore a small flag sewn on the seat of his blue jeans. He was convicted of

violating the Massachusetts flag misuse statute. The U. S.
Supreme Court noted (6-3) that "Flag wearing in a day of relaxed clothing styles may be simply for adornment or a ploy
to attract attention. However, careless uses of the flag constitute unceremonial treatment that many people may regard
as contemptuous. " The Court realized that the Massachusetts
legislature did not intend to make criminal every informal and
unceremonious use of the flag. But the law "fails to draw
reasonably clear lines between the kinds of unceremonial treatment that are criminal and those that are not. " So the Massachusetts flag misuse statute was unconstitutionally vague and
over-broad. Speaking for the minority, Justice William Rehnquist found marginal elements of "symbolic speech" in Goguen's
display of the flag, but argued that this was not protected expression. Forbidding desecration of a unique national symbol
was a legitimate right of Massachusetts and took precedence
over "abstract, scholastic interpretations" of the First Amendment. In Goguen, the Court majority affirmed that not all
unusual usage of the flag could be banned. However, they did
not consider the First Amendment issue of whether flag wearing constituted protected "symbolic speech. "

Spence v. Washington 418 U. S. 405 (1974)

On May 10, 1970, Harold Spence displayed a privately
owned U. S. flag from his apartment window in Seattle. A
large peace symbol was affixed to both sides of the flag with
removable tape. Three police officers saw the flag and approached Spence. He said, "I suppose you are here about the
flag. I didn't know there was anything wrong with it. I will
take it down. " Spence allowed the officers to take the flag.
He was arrested under a Washington law which prohibited improper display of the flag. Spence admitted that he put the
peace symbol on the flag and publicly displayed it as a protest
against the invasion of Cambodia and the Kent State University
killings. He intended to associate the flag with peace rather
than war or violence. He was convicted.

The U. S. Supreme Court reversed (6-3) the conviction.
Application of the Washington statute to Spence infringed upon
protected expression. The Court noted that the flag was owned
privately, displayed on private property, and displayed without breach of the peace. The context in which this "symbol"
was used for purposes of legitimate expression became important to the Court. The majority concluded that "given the protected character of his [Spence's] expression and in light of

the fact that no interest the State may have in preserving the physical integrity of the privately owned flag was significantly impaired on these facts, the conviction must be invalidated. " Rehnquist's dissent stressed that the First Amendment allows state restriction on activity when such restrictions further an important interest. In this case, the state's interest was preserving the "physical integrity of the flag" and "preserving the flag as an important symbol of nationhood and unity. " Again, Rehnquist acknowledged the presence of "symbolic speech, " but denied such activity First Amendment protection. However, in Spence, the Court protected a form of "symbolic" expression when no state interest was impaired. For the most part though, as evidenced by such cases as O'Brien, Street, and Smith, the Court has been unwilling to take the position that actions such as draft card burning or flag desecration are in fact "symbolic speech, " and, more importantly, that such actions are subject to constitutional protection. The Court is clearly more willing to protect "pure speech" than "symbolic speech. "

Display Symbols

Over the past few decades, a popular form of dissent involves displaying a "symbol" of protest in some prominent location, thereby calling attention to the focal point of the protestor's dissatisfaction. Buttons, arm bands, uniforms, license plates, even a clothesline, have been the "symbols" of dissent used to protest various causes. The Courts have been called upon to define the specific regulations which control the displaying of such symbols of dissent.

Stromberg v. California 283 U. S. 359 (1931)

In 1931, the U. S. Supreme Court decided that California could not outlaw flying a red flag merely as a symbol of opposition to organized government. This decision paved the way for the displaying of dissent symbols. Yetta Stromberg, a nineteen-year-old female member of the Young Communist League, supervised a summer camp for ten- to fifteen-year-old children in the San Bernardino mountains. Each day, she led the children in their study of history and economics. She also directed the children in a daily ritual which involved raising a red flag and pledging allegiance "to the worker's red flag, and to the cause for which it stands; one aim throughout our lives, freedom for the working class. " A library was main-

tained at the camp which contained several pieces of communist propaganda. The books contained incitements to violence
and armed uprisings and urged "the indispensability of a des-
perate, bloody, destructive war as the immediate task of the
coming action. " Stromberg admitted ownership of the books
but testified that none of the materials was brought to the attention of the children and that no word of violence, anarchism, or
sedition was used in her teaching.

Under a California law, police officials charged that
Stromberg did willfully and unlawfully display a red flag in a
public place as a symbol "of opposition to organized government and as an invitation and stimulus to anarchistic action
and as an aid to propaganda that is and was of a seditious
character. " Miss Stromberg was convicted even though it was
unclear which of the three criteria against displaying a red
flag--1) as a symbol of opposition to organized government,
2) as an invitation to anarchistic action, or 3) as an aid to
propaganda of a seditious character--constituted the basis for
the conviction. At trial, the judge had indicated that Stromberg should be convicted if the flag was displayed for any one
of the three purposes. The U. S. Supreme Court reversed
(7-2) on the ground that if Stromberg had been convicted for
flying the flag as a symbol of opposition to organized government, her First Amendment freedom of speech had been violated.

People v. Stover 12 N. Y. 2d 462 (1963)

In a case heard thirty-two years later, the Courts
placed restrictions on dissent symbols. Mr. and Mrs. Webster Stover lived in a pleasant and built-up residential district
in Rye, New York. In 1956, the Stovers put up a clothesline,
filled with old clothes and rags in their front yard as a form
of "peaceful protest" against the high taxes imposed by the
city. During each of the five following years, they added another clothesline to record their continued dissatisfaction with
the taxes. In 1961, six lines, filled with tattered clothing, old
uniforms, underwear, rags, and scarecrows, were strung
across the yard. In August, 1961, the city passed an ordinance prohibiting the erection and maintenance of clotheslines
in a front or side yard. City permits could be applied for.
The Stovers applied, but when their request was turned down,
they kept the clothesline up. They were arrested, tried, and
convicted. They appealed. The Court noted that the prohibition against "clotheslines is designed to proscribe conduct which

offends the sensibilities and tends to depress property values. "
Furthermore, the prohibition bears no necessary relationship
to the dissemination of ideas or opinions. So the Stovers were
not entitled to violate it "by choosing to express their views
in the altogether bizarre manner which they did. "

Burnside v. Byars 363 F. 2d 744 (1966)

In Burnside, the Court examined the display of buttons
by high school students. Early in the 1964 school year,
Montgomery Moore, Principal of the Booker T. Washington
High School of Philadelphia, Mississippi, noticed that a number of his students were wearing "freedom buttons" obtained
from the headquarters of the COFO (Council of Federated Organizations). The button contained the wording "One Man One
Vote" around the perimeter, with SNCC (Students Nonviolent
Coordinating Committee) inscribed in the center. The students wore the buttons as a means of silently expressing an
idea, and to urge the members of their community to exercise their civil rights. Moore announced to the student body
that they were not permitted to wear the buttons. They were
given a chance to remove the buttons but a few students kept
them on and were sent home. Three days later, thirty to
forty children displayed the buttons. Moore assembled the
children, reminded them of the regulations, and gave them
the choice of removing the buttons or being sent home. Most
went home. Moore sent a letter to the parents of his students and received the cooperation of all but Mrs. Burnside
and two other ladies who brought an injunction against the
school. The Court ruled for Mrs. Burnside. School officials
cannot ignore expressions of feelings with which they do not
wish to contend. They cannot infringe upon their students'
rights to free and unrestrained expression, when, as in this
case, the wearing of "freedom buttons" did not hamper the
regular conduct of school activities.

Tinker v. Des Moines Independent Community School District 393 U. S. 503 (1969)

In 1969, the Court reinforced Burnside in another case
involving the display of symbols by students. In December,
1965, some school children of the Des Moines school district,
encouraged by their parents, decided to wear black armbands
to school prior to the Christmas holiday to protest American
involvement in Vietnam. The principals of the Des Moines

schools became aware of the plan to wear armbands and, on December 14, they adopted a policy that any students wearing an armband to school would be requested to remove it, and if they refused, they would be suspended until they returned without the armband. All students were made aware of this regulation. On December 16, Mary Beth Tinker, a student in junior high school, and Christopher Eckhardt, a high school student, wore black armbands to school. John Tinker, a high school student, wore his armband the next day. During the same week, Paul Tinker, a second-grader, and Hope Tinker, a fifth-grader, wore armbands. They were asked to remove the armbands. When they refused they were sent home and suspended from school until they would return without their armbands. They did not come back until after New Year's day. The fathers of the students brought suit for an injunction which would restrain the school administrators from disciplining their children.

The U. S. Supreme Court decided (7-2) that the wearing of an armband in order to express views is an act of symbolic communication that is within the protection of the First Amendment. In this case, students exercising First Amendment rights collided with the rules of the school authorities. In the majority opinion prepared by Justice Abe Fortas, the wearing of armbands was entirely divorced from actually or potentially disruptive behavior by the students engaging in the protesting act. In this case, the school administration had sought to punish a few students for silent, passive expression of their dissent of the war. Just a few of the eighteen thousand students in the school system wore the armbands and only five students were suspended. There was no evidence of any disruption or disorder. The students never interfered with the work of the school or with the rights of other students. According to the Court, the act of wearing an armband is closely akin to "pure speech." The School administration cannot ban an act of "pure speech" simply because it might cause discomfort or unpleasantness. No other symbols were excluded. Students were allowed to wear political buttons, and some wore the Iron Cross, a symbol of Nazism. School officials sought to ban only one symbol, and without any indication that it was necessary to avoid substantial interference with the work of the school. Such a ban was not constitutionally permissible.

Schacht v. United States 398 U. S. 58 (1970)

In this case, the Court reinforced its liberal interpre-

tation of freedom of expression.   Daniel Jay Schacht was one
of a group of three people who took part in a skit as part of
a larger peaceful antiwar demonstration at the Houston Armed
Forces Induction Center.   Schacht and his colleagues prepared
a script and rehearsed their roles at least once.   The skit
was designed to show undesirable aspects of the American
presence in Vietnam.   For the skit, Schacht was dressed in
a military uniform and cap.   A second person was wearing
"military colored" coveralls.   The third person was outfitted
in typical Viet Cong apparel.   The first two men carried wa-
ter pistols.   They would yell, "Be an able American, " and
then they would shoot the Viet Cong.   The pistols expelled a
red liquid which, when it hit the victim, gave the impression
that he was bleeding.   Once the victim fell down the other
two walked up to him and exclaimed, "My God, this is a
pregnant woman. "   This skit was reenacted several times between 6:30 and 8:30 on the morning of December 4, 1967.
Schacht was indicted for wearing the uniform of the armed
forces without authority.   Schacht defended his conduct in
court on the ground that he was authorized to wear the uniform under a law which provides that "while protraying a
member of the Army, Navy, Air Force, or Marine Corps,
an actor in a theatrical or motion picture production may wear
the uniform of that armed force if the portrayal does not tend
to discredit that armed force. "   Schacht argued that he wore
the army uniform as an actor in a theatrical production which
was performed several times in front of the Houston Induction
Center.   Nevertheless, he was convicted.

In a unanimous decision the U. S. Supreme Court held
(8-0) that the part of the law which stipulated that dramatic
portrayal is only lawful if it "does not tend to discredit that
armed force" was an unconstitutional abridgment of freedom
of speech.   The Court thereby overturned Schacht's conviction.
However, three members of the Court in a separate concurring opinion pointed out that "theatrical production" in which
a military uniform is permitted must be restricted to a setting where viewers realize that they are "watching a make-
believe performance. "   If this had been supported by a Court
majority, Schacht would not have been engaged in a "theatrical
production" and could have been found guilty.

Wooley v. Maynard 430 U. S. 705 (1977)

The Maynard case presents a unique twist on display.
Rather than dissenting through the act of showing a symbol,

the Maynards dissented by covering their license plate.
George Maynard and his wife, members of the Jehovah's
Witnesses religion, covered over that portion of their automobile license plate stamped with the New Hampshire state
motto, "Live Free, or Die." The couple found the motto
repugnant to their moral and religious beliefs. Maynard was
charged with violating a New Hampshire statute that makes it
a misdemeanor to knowingly obscure the figures or letters on
any license plate. Maynard sued. The case reached the U.S.
Supreme Court.

The Court sided (6-3) with Maynard. First, the Court
reaffirmed that First Amendment protection includes the right
to speak freely as well as the right to refrain from speaking
at all.

> A system which secures the right to proselytize
> religious, political, and ideological causes must
> also guarantee the concomitant right to decline to
> foster such concepts. The right to speak and the
> right to refrain from speaking are complementary
> components of the broader concept of individual
> freedom of mind.

Second, the Court considered the interests claimed by the
state in requiring people to display the state motto. The
state claimed that such display of the motto facilitated the
identification of passenger vehicles. The Court decided that
the license plates contain "a specific configuration of letters
and numbers, which makes them readily distinguishable from
other types of plates, even without reference to state motto."
The State also argued that requiring the display of the state
motto promotes appreciation of history and state pride. The
Court reasoned that the State's interest in disseminating an
ideology "cannot outweigh an individual's First Amendment
right to avoid becoming the courier for such messages." New
Hampshire could not require Maynard and his wife to display
the state motto upon their automobile plates.

The lesson of Maynard, Schacht, Tinker, and Stromberg
is that "display" is a form of "symbolic speech" which is
entitled to First Amendment protection. O'Brien, Street,
Radich, and Goguen suggest that the level of protection given
to "desecration" as a form of "symbolic speech" remains a
question mark. Clearly, the U.S. Supreme Court has acknowledged the right to "display" symbols of dissent while remaining reluctant to award "desecration" the same status.

Bibliography

Books

Bosmajian, Haig A., ed. Dissent: Symbolic Behavior and Rhetorical Strategies. Boston: Allyn and Bacon, 1972.

_____. The Principles and Practice of Freedom of Speech. Boston: Houghton Mifflin, 1971.

Chafee, Zechariah, Jr. Free Speech in the United States. Cambridge: Harvard University Press, 1954.

Konvitz, Milton R., ed. Bill of Rights Reader: Leading Constitutional Cases. 5th ed. Ithaca: Cornell University Press, 1973.

Articles

Martin, Philip L. "The Improper Discharge of a Federal Employee by a Constitutionally Permissible Process: The OEO Case," Administrative Law Review 28 (Winter, 1976), 27-39.

Pearlstein, Mark. "The 'Fighting Words Doctrine' as Applied to Abusive Language Toward Policemen," DePaul Law Review 22 (Spring, 1973), 725-36.

Ragan, Fred D. "Justice Oliver Wendell Holmes, Jr., Zechariah Chafee, Jr., and the Clear and Present Danger Test for Free Speech: The First Year, 1919," Journal of American History 58 (June, 1971), 24-45.

Shea, Thomas F. "Don't Bother to Smile When You Call Me That--Fighting Words and the First Amendment," Kentucky Law Journal 63 (1974-75), 1-22.

"Spence v. Washington: Smith v. Goguen: Symbolic Speech and Flag Desecration," Columbia Human Rights Law Reserve 6 (Fall/Winter, 1974-75), 535-50.

Strong, Frank R. "Fifty Years of 'Clear and Present Danger': From Schenck to Brandenburg--and Beyond," Supreme Court Review (1969), 41-80.

Thayer, Ted J. "Freedom of Speech and Symbolic Conduct:

The Crime of Flag Desecration, " Arizona Law Review 12 (Spring, 1970), 71-88.

"Threatening the President: Protected Dissenter or Potential Assassin, " Georgetown Law Review 57 (February, 1969), 553-72.

Tucker, Angula Gay. "Arnett v. Kennedy: Restrictions on Public Employee's Freedom to Criticize, " Free Speech Yearbook: 1976, 31-6.

Wall, Joseph E. "Fighting Words or Free Speech?" North Carolina Law Review 50 (February, 1972), 382-90.

Ware, Russell M. "The Black Armbands Case--Freedom of Speech in the Public Schools, " Marquette Law Review 52 (Winter, 1969), 608-13.

Cases

Abrams v. United States 250 U. S. 616 (1919)

Arnett v. Kennedy 416 U. S. 134 (1974)

Bachellar v. Maryland 397 U. S. 564 (1970)

Bond v. Floyd 385 U. S. 116 (1966)

Brandenburg v. Ohio 395 U. S. 444 (1969)

Breen v. Selective Service Local Board No. 16 396 U. S. 460 (1970)

Burnside v. Byars 363 F. 2d. 744 (1966)

Chaplinsky v. New Hampshire 315 U. S. 568 (1942)

Cohen v. California 403 U. S. 15 (1971'

Debs v. United States 249 U. S. 211 (1919)

DeJonge v. Oregon 299 U. S. 353 (1937)

Dennis v. United States 341 U. S. 494 (1951)

Feiner v. New York 340 U. S. 315 (1951)

Gitlow v. New York 268 U. S. 652 (1925)

Gooding v. Wilson 405 U. S. 518 (1972)

Gutknecht v. United States 396 U. S. 295 (1970)

Hess v. Indiana 414 U. S. 105 (1973)

Lewis v. New Orleans 415 U. S. 130 (1974)

Noto v. United States 367 U. S. 290 (1961)

Oestereich v. Selective Service Board No. 11 393 U. S. 233
    (1968)

People v. Radich 308 N. Y. S. 2d. 846 (1970)

People v. Stover 12 N. Y. 2d. 462 (1963)

Scales v. United States 367 U. S. 203 (1961)

Schacht v. United States 398 U. S. 58 (1970)

Schenck v. United States 249 U. S. 47 (1919)

Smith v. Goguen 415 U. S. 566 (1974)

Spence v. Washington 418 U. S. 405 (1974)

Street v. New York 394 U. S. 576 (1969)

Stromberg v. California 283 U. S. 359 (1931)

Terminiello v. Chicago 337 U. S. 1 (1949)

Tinker v. Des Moines Independent Community School District
    393 U. S. 503 (1969)

United States v. O'Brien 391 U. S. 367 (1968)

Watts v. United States 394 U. S. 705 (1969)

Whitney v. California 274 U. S. 357 (1927)

Wolff & Shortt v. Selective Service Local Board No. 66
    372 F2d. 817 (1967)

CHAPTER III

ASSEMBLY

America certainly is a nation of joiners. Everywhere
people gather together to form associations aimed at achieving
political, religious, racial, social, or economic purposes.
People join groups to attain objectives they cannot achieve
acting alone. The rights and privileges of assembly are important to students of communication law because interest
groups of various sizes, scopes, and functions are a predominant aspect of American life. In this chapter, the freedoms
of and limitations on assembly are examined under two head-
ings: association (which concerns the gathering, uniting, or
joining of people) and petition (which involves pleading for, or
making a cause known to others).

ASSOCIATION

Government may restrict or prohibit associations that
band together for criminal or immoral purposes. Government
may also place limitations on associations when such action is
required to maintain public peace and order. It is, however,
generally realized that a fundamental factor in a constitutional
democracy is the right of persons to join in religious, political, and labor associations. Yet, for many years in the
United States, that right was not evident in constitutional law.

Freedom to Join

The freedom to join together and organize groups was
omitted by the framers of the Bill of Rights because of the
fear that associations were harmful to the country's well-
being. Influenced largely by the thinking of James Madison,
the framers sought to control factions. The constitutional
guarantee of freedom to associate was not included. Not until

1958 did the Court acknowledge association as a constitutional freedom.

National Association for the Advancement of Colored People v. Alabama 357 U. S. 449 (1958)

The case involved the Alabama branch of the National Association for the Advancement of Colored People. The NAACP, first chartered by the State of New York in 1909 as a nonprofit membership corporation designed to secure the elimination of racial barriers, opened local branches in Alabama in 1918. It had fifty-eight branches and a membership of nearly fifteen thousand in that state by 1956. In the early 1950s, the NAACP, at both the national and state levels, waged successful battles for the civil rights of black citizens. In 1954, the organization won a major victory in Brown v. Board of Education, a school desegregation case. In 1955-56, the Association played a vital role in the Montgomery bus boycott. Southern politicians soon thereafter designed a strategy which crippled the energy of the NAACP. Southern officials challenged the existence of the organization, thereby forcing the Association to fight for its own life, leaving it little energy to continue its civil rights program.

Like several other states, Alabama had a statute which required foreign corporations to qualify prior to doing business in the state by filing the corporate charter with the Secretary of State and designating a place of business and an agent. The law provided fines for a corporation, as well as criminal prosecution of the officers of a corporation, which failed to qualify. The Alabama NAACP never complied with the qualification statute because it considered itself exempt. In 1956, the Attorney General of Alabama claimed that the NAACP had recruited members and solicited donations within the state, had opened a regional office and several affiliates in Alabama, had given financial aid and furnished legal advice to black students trying to enter the state university, and had backed a boycott of the bus lines in Montgomery to force the seating of passengers without regard to race. The Attorney General alleged that the NAACP did business in Alabama without complying with the qualification statute. He sought a judgment forbidding the NAACP from engaging in further activities within Alabama. In practice, he sought to oust the NAACP from the state.

During state court proceedings, the NAACP admitted to the actions in the complaint, but maintained that those activities

did not subject it to the qualification requirements. The
NAACP was ordered to produce records and papers, including
the names and addresses of the members of the Association
in the state. The NAACP produced all the records, including
members who were employed or held official positions, but
refused to produce the membership lists. The NAACP
claimed that Alabama could not compel the surrender of the
lists. The group was held in contempt and fined $10,000.
The verdict stipulated that the fine could be reduced if the
lists were provided within five days. Otherwise, the fine
would be increased to $100,000. Within five days, the NAACP
submitted all data except the membership lists, maintaining
that Alabama could not constitutionally force submission of
those lists. The NAACP moved to vacate the contempt citation. The motion was denied, and the fine was increased to
$100,000. The NAACP appealed.

The U.S. Supreme Court unanimously ruled that the
NAACP had the right to protect the membership lists on behalf of the private interests of its members. According to
Justice John Harlan, writing for the Court, the due process
clause of the Fourteenth Amendment protects the freedom to
associate for the advancement of beliefs and ideas pertaining
to political, social, economic, cultural, or religious matters.
According to the Court, compelled disclosure of affiliation
with groups engaged in advocacy may constitute an effective
restraint on freedom of association. Under the circumstances, compelled disclosure of NAACP Alabama membership
would likely adversely affect the ability of the Association to
pursue the goals which it has the right to pursue. The civil
contempt judgment and the $100,000 fine were reversed.

Bates v. City of Little Rock 361 U.S. 516 (1960)

Four years later, the Court reaffirmed its recognition
of the right to associate in the case of Bates v. City of Little
Rock. Cities in Arkansas were authorized to levy a license
tax on any individual or corporation engaging in any "trade,
business, profession, vocation or calling" within their corporate limits. The city of Little Rock had for some years imposed annual license taxes on a broad variety of businesses,
occupations, and professions. Charitable organizations were
exempted from paying the taxes. In 1957, Little Rock amended the occupation license tax ordinance so that upon request,
any organization had to supply the city clerk the official name
of the organization, its headquarters or regular meeting place,

the names of the members and officers, the purpose of the organization, a statement as to dues and contributions, and an affidavit stating whether the organization was subordinate to a parent organization.

Upon request, Daisy Bates, the custodian of the records of the Little Rock NAACP, supplied the city with some of the required information. She did not, however, divulge the names of the organization's members and contributors. She claimed that disclosure of the names would lead to harassment, economic reprisal, and perhaps even bodily harm, because of local anti-NAACP sentiment. Bates was arrested and tried for refusing to furnish city officials with the list of names. At Bates' trial, evidence was presented which showed that several former members of the local NAACP had declined to renew their membership because of the ordinance. There was also evidence of harassment and threats of bodily harm to NAACP members. Yet Bates was convicted and fined. She appealed.

The U.S. Supreme Court unanimously affirmed that "it is now beyond dispute that freedom of association for the purpose of advancing ideas and airing grievances is protected by the Due Process Clause of the Fourteenth Amendment from invasion by the States." In this case, as in NAACP v. Alabama, the Court noted that "compulsory disclosure of the membership lists of the local branches of the National Association for the Advancement of Colored People would work a significant interference with the freedom of association of the members." The Court said that such a significant encroachment upon personal freedom could be justified only in cases where the state could prove a compelling interest. Such an interest was lacking in this case. There was no clear and relevant correlation between the city's power to impose occupation license taxes and the compulsory disclosure of membership lists of the local NAACP chapter.

Gibson v. Florida Legislative Investigation Committee
372 U.S. 539 (1963)

A similar case, which further strengthened the freedom to associate, involved litigation between the Florida Legislative Investigation Committee and the Miami branch of the NAACP. In 1956, the Florida legislature began investigating the NAACP. A subpoena was issued to obtain the entire membership list of the Miami branch. The NAACP refused. On appeal, the

Florida Supreme Court held that the committee could not compel production and disclosure of the entire membership list of
the organization, but could require the custodian of records to
bring them to the hearings. The committee could refer to
them to determine whether specific persons, otherwise identified as or suspected of being Communists, were NAACP members. Reverend Theodore Gibson, president of the Miami
branch, appeared before the committee on November 4, 1959.
Gibson admitted that he was custodian of the membership records. He testified that the local group had about 1,000 members. Gibson, however, told the committee that he had not
brought the records with him and said he would not produce
them for the purposes of answering questions concerning membership in the NAACP. He did, however, volunteer to answer
such questions on the basis of his own personal knowledge.
When given the names and shown photographs of fourteen individuals previously identified as Communists, Gibson said he
could associate none of them with the NAACP. Gibson refused
to produce his own organization's membership lists on the
ground that to supply the lists to the committee would interfere with the free exercise of Fourteenth Amendment association rights of actual and prospective members of the NAACP.
Gibson was given a hearing before a state court, was judged
in contempt, and was sentenced to six months in prison and
fined $1,200 or, for failure to pay, an additional six months'
imprisonment. He appealed.

The U. S. Supreme Court reversed (5-4). The Court
noted that the "summary of the evidence discloses the utter
failure to demonstrate the existence of any substantial relationship between the NAACP and subversive or Communist
activities." Furthermore, no claim was made "that the
NAACP or its Miami branch was engaged in any subversive
activities or that its legitimate activities have been dominated
or influenced by Communists." The Court concluded "that
groups which themselves are neither engaged in subversive or
other illegal or improper activities, nor demonstrated to have
any substantial connections with such activities, are to be protected in their rights of free and private association." Justices Harlan, Clark, Stewart, and White dissented because
they felt the decision seriously limited the power of a legislature to investigate the Communist Party and its activities. According to the minority, "The net effect of the Court's decision is, of course, to insulate from effective legislative inquiry and preventive legislation the time-proven skills of the
Communist Party in subverting and eventually controlling legitimate organizations." The Court's majority, however, sided

with the First Amendment argument of the NAACP and upheld the right of association.

Containment and Control

Over the past half-century, certain groups have posed real and imagined threats to the security of the United States. Fearful of the potential danger such groups posed, the government dealt with them through a policy of containment and control--sometimes officially sanctioned by legislation, and at other times unofficially carried out by agencies of the government. In 1944, the United States Supreme Court upheld an executive action which contained Japanese-American citizens through a policy of exclusion.

Korematsu v. United States 323 U. S. 214 (1944)

On December 7, 1941, Japanese bombers attacked U. S. military bases at Pearl Harbor in Hawaii. As a result of several military victories in 1942, Japan extended her area of control to include an area from the Aleutian Islands south to the Solomon Islands, and from Wake Island west to Burma. At this time, about 112,000 persons of Japanese ancestry lived on the Pacific Coast of the United States. The government, through Executive Order 9066, declared that "the successful prosecution of the war requires every possible protection against espionage and against sabotage to national-defense material, national-defense premises, and national-defense utilities." Subsequently, the government issued Civilian Exclusion Order No. 34, which directed that after May 9, 1942, all Japanese-Americans should be excluded from the West Coast. Fred Toyosabubo Korematsu, a Japanese-American, was convicted for remaining in San Leandro, California, in defiance of the order. Korematsu was placed on probation for five years. He appealed.

The U. S. Supreme Court upheld (6-3) the conviction. According to the Court, the act which permitted the internment was necessary under the war powers of Congress and the Executive. In the opinion of the Court, written by Justice Black, Korematsu was not excluded because of his race but because military authorities feared an invasion on the West Coast and felt certain security measures were necessary. There was evidence of disloyalty on the part of some Japanese-Americans and the military experts considered that the need for action was great.   Thus, in upholding the exclusion policy, the Court perceived the issue as encompassing military danger rather than social prejudice.

Communist Party v. Subversive Activities Control Board
367 U. S. 1 (1961)

The Communist Party was also a target of the government's efforts at containment and control.   The Communist Party of the United States was founded in 1919.   Its major period of growth was during the Depression of the 1930s, when membership may have reached 100,000.   Membership declined because of Soviet World War II policy and the exposé of Joseph Stalin's crimes in the 1950s.   In the mid-1970s Party leaders claim to have about 15,000 members.   Even though the Party has had little influence through the years, the government has maintained an intense interest in containing the growth of membership, identifying the persons affiliated with the organization, and controlling the activities of Communist Party members in the United States.

In 1950 the Korean War started.   This conflict between Communist and non-Communist forces provided agitation for drastic action against the Communist Party.   In 1950 Congress passed the McCarren Act over President Harry Truman's veto.   Under the act, each Communist-action or Communist-front organization was required to register with the Attorney General, giving the names and addresses of the officers, a financial statement, and, in the case of Communist-action groups, the names and addresses of all members.   The Communist Party did not register, so the Attorney General petitioned the Subversive Activities Control Board to require the Party to register as a Communist-action organization.   After extensive hearings, the board ordered the Party to register. The Party appealed.

In June, 1961, eleven years after initiation of the proceeding, the U. S. Supreme Court upheld (5-4) the order.   In the majority opinion by Justice Felix Frankfurter, the act was merely regulatory, not prohibitory, and the requirement to file the membership list was "demanded by rational interests high in the scale of National Concern. "   According to Frankfurter,

Where the mask of anonymity which an organization's members wear serves the double purpose of

protecting them from popular prejudice and of enabling them to cover over a foreign-directed conspiracy, infiltrate into other groups, and enlist the
support of persons who would not, if the groups were
revealed, lend their support ... it would be a dis-
tortion of the First Amendment to hold that it prohibits Congress from revealing the mask.

On this basis the Court upheld the requirement to file the
membership list, whereas in NAACP v. Alabama such a requirement was overturned. Indeed, the freedom to associate
is subject to reasonable limitations and regulations. Requiring disclosure of membership lists is a reasonable regulation,
if it is not aimed at prohibiting a particular group.

Konigsberg v. State Bar of California 366 U. S. 36 (1961)

In another case that same year the Court again emphasized that the right to associate is not absolute. Raphael
Konigsberg, a 1953 graduate of the University of Southern
California Law School, refused to answer questions before the
California State Committee of Bar Examiners relating to his
membership in the Communist Party. He affirmed his dis-
belief in the violent overthrow of the government and stated
that he was never knowingly a member of any organization
which advocated such action. California denied Konigsberg
admission to the California bar. He appealed.

The U. S. Supreme Court ruled (5-4) against Konigsberg.
Using the balancing test, they felt the state's interest outweighed the free speech considerations in this case.

Baird v. State Bar of Arizona 401 U. S. 1 (1971)

A case with similar facts but a different result involved
Sara Baird, a 1967 graduate from the law school at Stanford
University. Baird took and passed the Arizona bar examination. Among the questions she answered was one which insisted that she reveal all organizations with which she had been
associated since she became sixteen years old. Baird answered
this question to the satisfaction of the Arizona Bar Committee.
She was also asked to state whether she had ever been a member of the Communist Party or any organization "that advocates overthrow of the United States Government by force or
violence. " When she refused to answer this question, the

Committee declined to recommend her admission to the bar.
She appealed.

The U. S. Supreme Court ruled (5-4) that Baird did not
have to answer the question.   In Arizona it is perjury to answer the bar committee's questions falsely, and perjury is
punishable as a felony.   In effect, Baird was asked in the examination to make a guess as to whether any organization to
which she ever belonged "advocates overthrow of the United
States Government by force or violence. "   The Court majority
felt that the First Amendment protected an applicant to the
state bar from being subjected to a question potentially haz-
ardous to her liberty.   The majority also noted that the First
Amendment prohibits a state from excluding a person from a
profession solely because she is a member of a particular
political organization.   The Court minority based its opinion
on the Konigsberg reasoning: a state's insistence that a person
answer questions about membership in the Communist Party
outweighs any deterrent effect upon freedom of speech and
association.   In Baird, however, the Court majority, on balance, weighted the issue in favor of First Amendment freedoms.

United States v. Robel 389 U. S. 258 (1967)

As has been demonstrated, the Communist Party historically has not enjoyed favored status among American political parties, to say the least.   During the 1960s the stigma
of association with communism was reduced.   In 1967 the
Court extended freedom of association in the case of United
States v. Robel.   The case involved a 1950 act which banned
Communist Party members from working for the government.
Section 5 of the Subversive Activities Control Act of 1950 prohibited members of Communist-action groups from working in
any defense facility.   Eugene Robel, a member of the Communist Party, was employed as a machinist at the Seattle, Wash-
ington shipyard of Todd Shipyards Corporation.   In 1962 the
Secretary of Defense designated the shipyard as a "defense
facility. "   On May 21, 1963, an indictment was filed charging
Robel with a violation of the law.   The case reached the U. S.
Supreme Court.

The Court ruled (7-2) that Section 5 was an unconstitutional abridgment of the right of association protected by the
First Amendment.   The section indiscriminately prohibited all
members of Communist-action organizations from working for
the government.   This amounted to preventing employment

because of guilt by mere association. According to the opinion written by Chief Justice Earl Warren, it was "precisely because that statute sweeps indiscriminately across all types of associations with Communist-action groups, without regard to the quality and degree of membership, that it runs afoul of the First Amendment. "

Communist Party of Indiana v. Whitcomb
414 U. S. 441 (1974)

Seven years later, the Court struck another blow for the freedom of association by banning an Indiana loyalty oath. The Communist Party of Indiana applied for a place on the Indiana ballot for the 1972 general election. The application was rejected for failure to submit an oath stating that the Party did not advocate the overthrow of the local, state, or national government by force or violence. The Party appealed.

The Supreme Court unanimously agreed that the loyalty oath violated free speech guarantees. Indiana could not proscribe advocacy, except where such advocacy attempts to incite or produce imminent lawless action and is likely to produce such action. For purposes of granting access to the ballot, a group advocating violent overthrow as abstract doctrine was not necessarily advocating unlawful action. The Court noted that "the right to associate with the political party of one's choice is an integral part" of protected First Amendment rights. In essence, the Court rejected the Election Board's claim that "at least for purposes of determining whether to grant a place on the ballot, any group that advocates violent overthrow as abstract doctrine must be regarded as necessarily advocating unlawful action. "

Government efforts to contain and control groups, thereby limiting the right of association, have been interpreted fairly consistently by the U. S. Supreme Court. In early cases, Korematsu, Communist Party, and Konigsberg, the Court decided, on balance, that the nation's interests warranted the limits placed on association. In the more recent cases, Robel, Baird, and Communist Party of Indiana, the Court reaffirmed that guilt by mere association and forbidding advocacy of violent overthrow as mere abstract doctrine contradict First Amendment guarantees. Clearly, the Court's perception of the threat that certain groups, notably the Communist Party, pose for the nation, has diminished over time.

Right to Solicit Members

Essential to the freedom of association is the right to solicit members for an organization. But unrestrained solicitation can lead to door-to-door canvassing on behalf of fraudulent causes at almost any time of the day. In order to protect its citizens from such invasions of personal privacy, localities have passed measures restricting the right to solicit. The courts have had to weigh the rights of soliciting membership against the right to be left undisturbed.

Cantwell v. Connecticut 310 U. S. 296 (1940)

One of the earliest cases dealing with this issue was Cantwell v. Connecticut. The Cantwells, a father and two sons, were arrested for conducting door-to-door religious solicitation on behalf of Jehovah's Witnesses in a predominantly Catholic neighborhood in New Haven. They were convicted of violating a Connecticut statute which required any person soliciting for a religious cause to file an application for a certificate of approval with the welfare secretary, who then decided whether the cause was "a bona fide object of charity" and whether it conformed to "reasonable standards of efficiency and integrity. " The penalty for violating the law was a $100 fine or thirty days' imprisonment, or both.

The U. S. Supreme Court unanimously decided that the statute was not regulatory but prohibitory, because it allowed a state official to ban religious solicitation from the streets of Connecticut entirely. Once a certificate of approval was issued by the state welfare secretary, solicitation could proceed without any restriction whatsoever under the statute. And once a certificate was denied, solicitation was banned. The Court ruled that the statute in effect established a prior restraint on First Amendment freedoms. If a state wanted to protect its citizens against door-to-door solicitation for fraudulent "religious" or "charity" causes it could constitutionally enact a regulation directed at that problem. The Court noted that a state could regulate religious solicitation in the same way that it regulates other types of solicitation. For example, a state could restrict the time of day during which solicitation may occur, or could grant a householder the right to terminate the solicitation by demanding that the visitor leave the premises. The state may not, however, force people to submit to licensing of religious speech. The broad sweep of the Connecticut law infringed on First Amendment rights. The Cantwells' convictions were declared unconstitutional.

Thomas v. Collins 323 U. S. 516 (1945)

Five years later, a divided Court strengthened the right to solicit members. A Texas statute prohibited labor union organizers from soliciting members unless they first obtained an organizer's identification card from a state official. Union organizers had to carry their cards whenever conducting solicitation and to produce them upon request. R. J. Thomas, an officer of the United Automobile, Aircraft, and Agricultural Implements Workers (UAW), traveled to Pelly, Texas to deliver a union organizing speech. The state attorney general obtained a restraining order enjoining Thomas from soliciting any union memberships. Confronted with this injunction, Thomas appeared as scheduled and made a point of soliciting his entire audience, and one listener in particular, to join the U. A. W. He was immediately arrested and convicted of contempt of court for violating the order. He appealed.

The U. S. Supreme Court reversed (5-4) the conviction on the ground that solicitation could not effectively be separated from general speech-making. The Court majority argued that when a union organizer went beyond mere speech and advocacy to the solicitation of monies, "he enters a realm where a reasonable registration or identification requirement may be imposed" because the state has an interest in protecting its citizens against fraud and financial loss. But in this case Thomas had not engaged in fundraising. The Texas statute impermissibly infringed on Thomas' freedom to express his beliefs and to urge others to join the union. Court dissenters felt that Thomas was in Texas to pursue his professional vocation as union organizer. As an agent for a business corporation, Thomas was subject to the licensing power of the state. Thomas would have been free to deliver a speech so long as he avoided solicitation of union memberships. In Thomas, however, the majority upheld his right to solicit members.

Staub v. Baxley 355 U. S. 313 (1958)

More than a decade later, the issue was raised again. The International Ladies' Garment Workers Union was trying to organize the employees of a manufacturing company located in Hazelhurst, Georgia. A number of the employees lived in nearby Baxley. On February 19, 1954, Rose Staub and Mamie Merritt, salaried employees of the Union, went to Baxley and, without applying for a permit, talked with several workers at their homes about joining the Union. A Baxley ordinance made

it a crime to solicit members for any organization that required the payment of dues without first procuring a permit
from city officials. The two women were approached by the
Chief of Police, who questioned them about their activities.
Staub and Merritt said they were talking to women employees
about organizing. Later that day a meeting was held at one
of the workers' houses where Staub talked to some workers.
She claimed that joining the Union would be beneficial, and
that the weekly dues would be 64 , payable after the employees were organized. She urged the women to get other workers to join; blank membership cards were distributed for that
purpose. On the same day, the Chief of Police served a sum-
mons to Staub requiring her to appear in court three days later. She was charged with "soliciting members for an organization without a Permit & License. " Staub was not accused of
any act against the peace and order of Baxley, nor was she
charged for any specific thing she said to the employees of the
company. She was simply charged with soliciting members
for an organization without a permit. Staub was convicted and
sentenced to imprisonment for thirty days or to pay a fine of
$300. She appealed.

The U. S. Supreme Court reversed (7-2). The Baxley
ordinance made enjoyment of the constitutionally guaranteed
freedom of speech contingent upon the discretion of the mayor
and the city council, thus constituting a prior restraint upon
freedom of speech. The Baxley statute provided no definitive
standards or other controlling guidelines governing the action
of the city officials regarding the granting or withholding of a
permit. The city officials were free to act as they wished.
The Baxley ordinance was an unconstitutional prior restraint
upon free speech. In Staub, as in Cantwell and Thomas, the
Court supported the right to solicit members for an association.

Right to Meet Publicly

An important facet of the freedom of association is the
right to meet publicly. Most cities have ordinances which stipulate the conditions under which such public meetings may be
held. Some of these ordinances have been upheld while others
have been overturned by the courts. A few are examined in
this section.

Hague v. Committee for Industrial Organization 307 U. S. 496 (1939)

In Jersey City, the Director of Public Safety was authorized to grant permits for parades and public assemblies on the streets or in public buildings and parks. This public official could refuse to issue a permit "for the purpose of preventing riots, disturbances or disorderly assemblage. " The C. I. O. was repeatedly refused permits for its organizers to arrange meetings to speak in behalf of the union movement on the grounds that the individuals requesting permits were Communists. The same individuals were denied the right to distribute pamphlets and the right to rent a hall for a public meeting. Policemen stopped C. I. O. representatives as they entered the city, seized literature in their possession and, in some cases, arrested them. The individuals against whom these actions were taken denied that they were Communists and claimed that their only aim was to describe for workers their rights under the National Labor Relations Act and explain why they should join the C. I. O. The Union obtained an injunction from a federal court against the enforcement of the city's ordinance.

Before the U. S. Supreme Court, Mayor Frank Hague argued that the city's ownership of streets and parks was as absolute as an individual's ownership of a home, with subsequent power to exclude persons from the use of such places. The Court noted that streets and parks have always been used for public assembly, communicating ideas between citizens, and discussing public issues. The right had been practiced since ancient times. Yet the right to meet in streets and parks is not absolute. It may be regulated in the public interest. It must be exercised so as not to interfere with general comfort, convenience, peace, and order. However, the right must not, in the guise of regulation, be abridged or denied. Uncontrolled official suppression of the right cannot be substituted for the city's duty to maintain order. The New Jersey ordinance allowed city officials arbitrarily to consent to or withhold permission for public meetings, and thus violated the rights of citizens. The Court judged the ordinance unconstitutional on its face because it did not make comfort or convenience in the use of streets and parks the criterion for official action. In Hague, the Court determined (5-2) that freedom to disseminate information concerning the provisions of the National Labor Relations Act, to assemble peaceably for discussion of the Act, and to discuss the opportunities and advantages offered by the Union, was a privilege protected against state abridgement by the Fourteenth Amendment.

Cox v. New Hampshire 312 U. S. 569 (1941)

As already noted, however, the state may regulate the usage of streets and parks in the public interest. In a 1941 case, the Court agreed that the control of parades or processions can be a legitimate state concern. Sixty-eight members of Jehovah's Witnesses along with twenty other people met at a hall in Manchester on Saturday night, July 8, 1939, in order to participate in an information march. The people were divided into four or five groups which proceeded to different parts of the city's business district. The small groups lined up in single-file fashion and marched along the sidewalks. Each marcher carried a sign reading "Religion Is a Snare and a Racket" and, on the other side, "Serve God and Christ the King." Some marchers carried banners on which was printed "Fascism or Freedom. Hear Judge Rutherford and Face the Facts." The marchers also handed out leaflets announcing a meeting, to be held at a later time, which would be open to the public free of charge. Most were arrested and convicted for violating a New Hampshire statute prohibiting a "parade or procession" upon a public street without a special permit. During the trial, the State pointed out that 26,000 people normally pass by one of the intersections where the defendants marched every hour on a typical Saturday night. Although no technical breach of the peace occurred, the State claimed that the marchers had interfered with normal sidewalk travel. No permit was sought for the march, even though the Witnesses knew that one was required.

The U. S. Supreme Court unanimously held the New Hampshire statute valid on the ground that a state may prevent serious interference with normal usage of streets and parks.

> The authority of a municipality to impose regulations in order to assure the safety and convenience of the people in the use of public highways has never been regarded as inconsistent with civil liberties but rather as one of the means of safeguarding the good order upon which they ultimately depend.

The Court noted that the obvious advantage of a permit system was to give opportunity for proper policing of the event. The New Hampshire statute was upheld because it served to fix time and place and thereby avoided confusion with overlapping processions, and minimized the risk of disorder. Most importantly, the statute did not grant the permit board arbitrary "power"; its discretion had to be exercised with uniformity of method and treatment. The Jehovah's Witnesses would have been, if after an investigation it was found that the convenience of the public in the use of the streets would not be unduly disturbed, granted a permit. In such cases, a change in time, place, and manner might be necessary to avoid disturbance.

Kunz v. New York 340 U. S. 290 (1951)

A decade later, the Court sharpened its opinion on the matter. New York City adopted an ordinance which made it illegal for an individual to hold a public worship meeting on the streets without first obtaining a permit from the city police commissioner. Carl Jacob Kunz, an ordained Baptist minister who spoke under the auspices of the Outdoor Gospel Work, had been preaching for about six years He claimed it was his belief and obligation to "go out on the highways and byways and preach the word of God. " In 1946 he applied for and received a permit to preach on the streets of New York City. The permit was good only for the calendar year for which it was issued. In November, 1946, his permit was revoked after a hearing before the police commissioner on the ground that Kunz had ridiculed and denounced Catholics and Jews at his worship meetings. Kunz applied for a permit in 1947, and again in 1948, but both times his request was "Disapproved" with no reason for the rejection given. On September 11, 1948, Kunz was arrested for speaking at Columbia Circle in New York City without a permit. Kunz was convicted and fined $10.

The U. S. Supreme Court held (8-1) the ordinance invalid, a prior restraint on First Amendment rights. The police commissioner refused to issue the permit on the ground that a permit had been previously revoked "for good reasons. " However, there was no mention in the ordinance of conditions under which a permit application could be refused. The law thus allowed the commissioner to exercise discretion in rejecting applications on the basis of his personal interpretation. The commissioner had discretionary power to control in advance the right of persons to speak on religious matters on the streets of New York. The ordinance lacked appropriate standards to guide the action of the city police commissioner.

Niemotko v. Maryland 340 U. S. 268 (1951)

Another case involving the regulation of public property was Niemotko v. Maryland. Daniel Niemotko, a member of the Jehovah's Witnesses, at the invitation of other members of the religious group, scheduled Bible talks in the public park in Havre de Grace, Maryland. Although there was no ordinance prohibiting or regulating the use of this park, it had been the custom for organizations and individuals desiring to use it to obtain a permit from the Park Commissioner. In conformity with this practice, the Jehovah's Witnesses requested the permission of the Park Commissioner to use the park on four consecutive Sundays in June and July, 1949. Permission was refused. The petitioners were told that an Elk's Day ceremony would take place on the first Sunday, but were given no explanation for refusal on the other three Sundays. They held their meeting anyway. There was no evidence of disorder or threats of violence. Niemotko, who opened the meeting, was arrested by police, brought to trial on a disorderly conduct charge, convicted, and fined $25 and costs. Niemotko appealed.

The U. S. Supreme Court unanimously concluded that the use of the park was denied because of the city council's disagreement with the views of the Jehovah's Witnesses. The city allowed other religious groups to use the park. To allow expression of religious beliefs by some, and to deny the same privilege to others merely because their views are unpopular, is a denial of equal protection of the law. The freedoms of speech and religion are entitled for firmer protection than that which can accrue from the whims or personal opinions of local government officials. According to Chief Justice Fred Vinson, it "thus becomes apparent that the lack of standards in the license issuing 'practice' renders that 'practice' a prior restraint in contravention of the Fourteenth Amendment, and that the completely arbitrary and discriminatory refusal to grant the permits was a denial of equal protection." The conviction was overturned.

Poulos v. New Hampshire 345 U. S. 395 (1953)

A similar case was heard two years later. As in Kunz, the Court again made it clear that ordinances giving local officials excessive discretion were unconstitutional. A Portsmouth city ordinance banned any "theatrical, or dramatic presentation," "parade or procession upon any public street or way," or "open air public meeting," unless a license was obtained from the city council. William Poulos, a Jehovah's Witness, applied for and was refused a permit for a religious meeting. Poulos and his colleagues attempted to hold the meeting in a public park without a license. When arrested for violating the law, Poulos defended himself on the basis that the council's license denial constituted an abridgment of his First Amendment freedoms. He was convicted and fined $20. On appeal, the New Hampshire Supreme Court held the ordinance valid on its face. Poulos' remedy against the discriminatory refusal of city officials to grant the permit was to seek a court order to force issuance of the permit. The court held that Poulos had violated the law when he ignored the denial of the license and attempted to hold the meeting anyway. Poulos appealed to the U. S. Supreme Court.

The Court noted that the Portsmouth ordinance laid down no standards whatsoever by which the granting or denial of permits was to be regulated. The law granted local officials unlimited discretion in deciding which applications for public meetings would be granted. But the New Hampshire Supreme Court had avoided this issue by construing the ordinance in a very narrow manner. According to the state court, the ordinance gave local authorities no discretion in refusing permits. Rather, the ordinance instructed them to process all permit applications and to regulate the issuance of licenses only when necessary to avert congestion in the public parks. The ordinance, thus construed, was valid as a "ministerial," traffic-management ordinance. It was not a discretionary law. The Court accepted (7-2) the construction of the ordinance which had been applied by the state court. The Court conceded that procedural delay was quite likely but decided that the law did not impose an unconstitutional prior restraint. The majority, in the opinion of Justice Stanley Reed, concluded that there is a defense only if the ordinance is later declared invalid on its face. However, it is an offense to disobey a valid ordinance even if it can be proven that the ordinance was implemented in a discriminatory fashion. The Court affirmed the conviction.

Rockwell v. Morris 211 N. Y. 2d 25 (1961)

In 1961 a New York case again illustrated the reluctance of judges to give too much discretion to local officials. George Lincoln Rockwell, a self-styled American Nazi and a rabid racist, applied to the Commissioner of Parks on May 17, 1960, for a permit to use Union Square Park to deliver a public political address the following July 4th. The Park is located in New York City in a traffic and pedestrian-congested area which is also a transfer point for a number of rapid-transit lines. The Commissioner of Parks, Newbold Morris, denied the application without offering Rockwell an alternative time or place. Rockwell asked for a review of the decision. The appeal was denied because Rockwell had by speech and pamphlet accused more than two-and-a-half-million citizens of New York City, identifiable by their ethnic or religious classification, of being traitors. The Commissioner also denied hearing because "to loose self-confessed advocates of violence upon a community at a time and place where it is inevitable that public disorder and riot will occur" is not within the Constitution. The Commissioner argued that he had the power, constitutionally, to refuse a permit to anybody whose activities would create serious disorder. Such action constituted a clear and present danger.

The New York state court reversed. First, there was no competent way the Commissioner could arrive at the conclusion that Rockwell's proposed speech would create disorder. It was upon this basis that the application had been denied. Second, the city ordinance mandates that whenever a permit is denied for any but commercial or private uses, an alternative suitable location and date must be offered to the applicant. This the Commissioner failed to do. Third, there is no power under the Constitution to impose prior restraint on the expression of views, unless it is clearly demonstrable that such expression will immediately and irreparably create injury to the public weal. A community cannot suppress a speaker through any prior restraint on the basis of hunches that what he did yesterday, he will do today. If the speaker incites others to immediate unlawful action he may be punished. He may be stopped when disorder actually occurs, but this should not be confused with unlawful action from others who intend unlawfully to suppress the speaker. The court concluded that the right of free expression is not to be entrusted to administrative previous restraint for contemplated violation of law. An actual incident of unprotected expression is subject to punishment after the fact.

From considering the cases in this section, it seems clear that there does, in fact, exist a right to meet publicly. In Hague, Kunz, and Niemotko, the Court overturned ordinances which allowed city officials to arbitrarily consent to or withhold permission for a public meeting. Specific standards are necessary to guide official action in determining whether permission will be granted or denied. In Rockwell, a state court overturned a license denial which was based on the inference that a proposed speech would necessarily disturb the public order. This constituted an unconstitutional prior restraint. Yet in Hague and Cox, the Court acknowledged that a state may regulate public meetings on streets and in parks to maintain public comfort, convenience, peace, and order. Such conditions must be clearly set forth in the ordinance. In Poulos, the Court determined that a person who ignores the denial of a request for a permit to hold a public meeting, and holds the assembly anyway, has no defense unless the ordinance is later declared invalid. Proof that a valid ordinance was applied in a discriminatory fashion does not offset the crime. In general, the right to meet publicly is guaranteed, but it may be regulated to provide comfort, convenience, peace, and order.

Access to Facilities

A vital prerequisite to freedom to associate is access to public facilities. Many Southern blacks were denied equal access to such facilities as lunch counters, recreational areas and libraries until progress was made in the courts early in the 1960s.

Garner v. Louisiana 368 U. S. 157 (1961)

One of the first such cases to test the constitutionality of segregated facilities was Garner v. Louisiana. John Garner and six other black college students went to a Kress Department Store where blacks were welcome as customers but were served food in a segregated area. The students sat down at the "whites only" lunch counter. The store manager told a waitress to inform the blacks that they could be served at the counter across the aisle. She did, but the blacks remained in their places. After being called by the manager, the police ordered the students to leave. When they refused, they were arrested and charged with disturbing the peace. They were tried and convicted, and subsequently sentenced to four months' imprisonment, three months of which would be suspended upon payment of a $100 fine. They appealed.

The U. S. Supreme Court overturned (9-0) the convictions for breach of the peace, noting, in the opinion of Chief Justice Earl Warren, that the facts indicated that the black students "not only made no speeches, they did not even speak to anyone except to order food; they carried no placards, and did nothing, beyond their mere presence at the lunch counter, to attract attention to themselves or others." According to the Court, "peaceful conduct, even though conceivably offensive to another class of the public, " could not be proscribed by a Louisiana breach of the peace law. There must be evidence that the individuals behaved in "some outwardly unruly manner. " The State presented no such evidence in this case.

It is interesting to note that the police, not an employee of the store, asked the students to leave. Also, the manager did not file a complaint; the police pressed charges. The lack of a complaint shows, first, that the store manager did not want to cause a disturbance and lose potential black customers. It also indicates that the manager did not feel there was a breach of the peace.

Peterson v. Greenville 373 U. S. 244 (1963)

In another case involving a Kress store, the Court again took a stand for civil rights. On August 9, 1960, ten black girls and boys entered the Kress store in Greenville, South Carolina, and sat down at the lunch counter to be served. The manager asked one of his employees to call the police, turn off the lights, and declare the lunch counter closed. When the police arrived, the manager announced that the counter was closed, and asked everyone to leave. The black youths, who had been sitting at the counter for five minutes, remained seated, and were immediately arrested. The manager did not request the police to arrest the youths; he asked the youths to leave because integrated service was "contrary to local customs" and in violation of a Greenville ordinance which required separation of the races in restaurants. The youths were convicted and fined $100 or, if unable to pay, they were to serve thirty days in jail.

The U. S. Supreme Court unanimously reversed the conviction, noting that "the evidence in this case establishes beyond doubt that the Kress management's decision to exclude petitioners from the lunch counter was made because they were negroes. " The ordinance in question has "determined that a person owning, managing or controlling an eating place is left with no choice of his own but must segregate his white and Negro patrons. " The Court concluded:

> When a state agency passes a law compelling persons to discriminate against other persons because of race, and the State's criminal processes are employed in a way which enforces the discrimination mandated by that law, such a palpable violation of

the Fourteenth Amendment cannot be saved by attempting to separate the mental urges of the dis-
criminators.

Lombard v. Louisiana 373 U. S. 267 (1963)

In 1963 the Court banned de facto segregation by a
Louisiana city. The case provided a logical counterpart to
Garner and Peterson. At about 10:30 in the morning on
September 17, 1960, one white and three black students entered the McCrory Five and Ten Cent Store in New Orleans,
Louisiana. They sat down at a refreshment counter at the
back of the store and asked for service. Although no sign so
indicated, the management operated the counter on a segregated basis, serving only white patrons. The restaurant manager
asked the students to leave, the black students because of
their race, and the white student because he was in the company of the blacks. When the students did not leave, the manager ordered that the counter be closed, and called the police
even though the students had caused no disturbance. When
police officers arrived, the manager went behind the counter
and, in a loud voice, asked the students to leave. When they
remained seated, they were arrested by the police, led out
of the store, and taken away in a patrol wagon. They were
tried and convicted for violating the Louisiana criminal mischief statute. They were sentenced to serve sixty days in the
parish jail, and to pay a fine of $350. They appealed.

The U. S. Supreme Court decided (8-1) that, even
though there was no state statute or city ordinance which forbade desegregation of the races in restaurant facilities, evidence of city coercion was present.

> A state, or a city, may act as authoritatively
> through its executive as through its legislative
> body.... As we interpret the New Orleans city
> officials' statements, they here determined that the
> city would not permit Negroes to seek desegregated
> service in restaurants. Consequently, the city must
> be treated exactly as if it had an ordinance prohibi-
> ting such conduct.

In Lombard, as in Peterson, the "convictions, commanded as
they were by the voice of the State directing segregated service," had to be reversed. Through "sit-in demonstrations,"
which were supported by the Court in Garner, Peterson, and

Lombard, the access of blacks to lunch counters was affirmed. Other efforts were directed toward desegregating parks.

Wright v. Georgia 373 U. S. 284 (1963)

One such attempt was made in Wright v. Georgia. The case involved the use of a public park by black children. Six black youths were playing basketball in Daffin Park in Savannah, Georgia, on the afternoon of Monday, January 23, 1961. Customarily, the Park was used only by whites, for recreation. The boys did not create any disturbance. They were arrested simply for playing basketball in the park, and were charged with assembling "for the purpose of disturbing the public peace." Upon conviction, one youth, Nathaniel Wright, was sentenced to pay a fine of $125, or to serve six months in jail. The other boys were sentenced to pay a fine of $100, or to serve five months in jail.

When the case arrived at the U. S. Supreme Court, the justices rejected the arguments of the state. First, it was contended that failure to obey the command of a police officer constituted a form of breach of peace. However, the Court maintained that a person cannot be punished for failing to obey the command of a police officer if that command is itself a violation of the Constitution. In this instance, the officer's action was unconstitutional because he tried to enforce racial discrimination in the park. Second, it was contended that the youths were guilty because their behavior was likely to cause a breach of peace by others. The Court maintained that the possibility of disorder by others cannot justify the exclusion of persons from a place where they have a constitutional right to associate. In Wright, the justices unanimously agreed that the regulations concerning play at the park were not posted, and the breach of peace statute failed to give adequate notice of prohibited conduct. Such an act violated due process guaranteed by the Fourteenth Amendment.

Watson v. Memphis 373 U. S. 526 (1963)

Another case dealing with the use of parks was Watson v. Memphis. In May, 1960, some black citizens of Memphis, Tennessee initiated a court action seeking immediate desegregation of municipal parks and other city-operated recreational facilities. In defense of its policy, Memphis officials pointed to the partial desegregation that had occurred and argued that

delay in following constitutional requirements was necessary.
The Court ordered the city to formulate, within six months,
a plan for further desegregation of the relevant facilities.

When the case reached the U. S. Supreme Court, the
justices examined the chronological timetable Memphis had
applied to desegregating facilities over the past decade. Memphis owned 108 developed parks, only 25 of which were de-
segregated at the time of the trial; 58 were restricted to use
by whites, and 25 to use by blacks. The City Park Commission operated other recreational facilities, most of which were
racially segregated. About two-thirds of the 61 city play-
grounds were reserved for whites only. All twelve of the
community centers were segregated; eight being available for
whites, four for blacks. Only two of the city golf courses
permitted play by blacks; the other five were restricted solely
to whites. The opinion in Watson, written by Justice Goldberg, noted that "we cannot ignore the passage of a substantial
period of time since the original declaration of the manifest
unconstitutionality of racial practices such as are here challenged, the repeated and numerous decisions giving notice of
such illegality, and the many intervening opportunities here-
tofore available to attain the equality of treatment which the
Fourteenth Amendment commands the States to achieve. " The
justices noted (9-0) that the criterion of "all deliberate speed"
in achieving desegregation did not justify indefinite delay in
eliminating racial barriers. Because Memphis failed to demonstrate any compelling reasons justifying the delay in desegregating the publicly owned and operated recreational facilities,
the Court demanded that the constitutional rights of the black
citizens be promptly restored.

Brown v. Louisiana 383 U. S. 131 (1966)

Another target of the "sit-in" tactic was the public
library. In 1966 the Court heard a case involving discrimination in library policy. The Audubon Regional Library serviced
towns located near Clinton, Louisiana. The library operated
two bookmobiles which served 33 schools in the area. One of
the bookmobiles was red; it served only white persons. A
blue bookmobile operated for black citizens. Printed on the
registration cards issued to blacks was the word "Negro. " The
card enabled the holder to obtain books, but only from the blue
bookmobile. A white person could receive service only from
the red bookmobile, or from a branch library. On March 7,
1964, Henry Brown, along with four other young black males,

entered the adult reading room of the library and requested the
book, The Story of the Negro by Arna Bontemps. Mrs. Katie
Reeves, the assistant librarian, checked the card catalog,
determined that the library did not have the book, and told
Brown that she would request the book from the state library.
He could then pick it up at the bookmobile or he could have the
book mailed to his home address. Mrs. Reeves expected that
the blacks would leave the library, but they remained. She
asked that they leave, but they did not. They stayed in the
library and said nothing.

The sheriff, who had been previously notified by the
Congress of Racial Equality (CORE) of a sit-in at the library,
arrived in about fifteen minutes. He asked the blacks to leave.
They remained and were promptly arrested. The library obtained a copy of the requested book and mailed it to Brown on
March 29, along with a card which read, "You may return the
book either by mail or to the Blue Bookmobile." On March
25, Brown was tried, convicted, and sentenced to pay $150
and costs, and in default thereof, to spend ninety days in jail.
Brown's friends were fined $35 and costs, or fifteen days in
jail. The complaint charged that they had congregated in the
public library "with the intent to provoke a breach of the peace
and under circumstances such that a breach of the peace might
be occasioned thereby" and that they had failed and refused "to
leave said premises when ordered to do so" by the librarian
and the sheriff.

This conviction was reversed (5-4) by the U. S. Supreme
Court. The majority opinion argued that Brown had, in fact,
intended to, and did, stage a peaceful and orderly protest
demonstration with no "intent to provide a breach of the
peace." He did and said nothing that was remotely provocative. He was entitled to the basic right of assembly and the
right for a redress of grievances. In the opinion of the minority justices, no provision of the Constitution was meant to
forbid any state from making it illegal to stage sit-ins or
stand-ups in public libraries for the purpose of objecting to
the public policies of the state. The minority feared that
powerful private groups might use this opinion as a license
to invade the peace and tranquility of libraries whenever they
disagreed with a state policy. The majority noted that a state
could regulate the use of the libraries, as well as other public facilities, but they could not do so in a discriminatory
fashion. The Louisiana practice of providing segregated facilities violated the law. In Brown, as in the other cases
cited in this section, the Court struck down a discriminatory

policy, and thereby facilitated association among black citizens in the United States. With access to public facilities affirmed, the freedom of association for blacks has indeed been enhanced.

Flower v. United States 407 U. S. 197 (1972)

Two recent cases considered the question of public access to military facilities for the purpose of distributing leaflets and/or making political speeches. John Thomas Flower, a regional Peace Education Secretary of the American Friends Service Committee, was arrested by military police while quietly distributing leaflets on New Braunfels Avenue within the limits of Fort Sam Houston, San Antonio, Texas. He had previously been barred from the post by order of the deputy commander because he attempted to distribute "unauthorized" leaflets. Flower was convicted under a federal law for reentering a military base in violation of an expressed order not to do so. He was sentenced to spend six months in prison.

The U. S. Supreme Court reversed (6-3) the conviction. The Court noted that the fort commander chose not to bar the public from the street where Flower was arrested. Vehicular and pedestrian traffic moved freely on New Braunfels Avenue. The Court explained,

> Under such circumstances the military has abandoned any claim that it has special interests in who walks, talks, or distributes leaflets on the avenue. The base commandant can no more order petitioner off this public street because he was distributing leaflets than could the city police order any leafleteer off any public street.

The Court concluded that the First Amendment protected Flower under these conditions.

Greer v. Spock 424 U. S. 828 (1976)

A related case came to the Court recently. In 1972, Dr. Benjamin Spock, a candidate of the People's Party for the office of President, and other minor party candidates for national public office applied to the commanding officer of Fort Dix to visit the Army post in order to distribute campaign literature and hold a meeting to discuss election issues with

servicemen and their families.   The commanding officer rejected the request.   It was common for civilian speakers to
address military personnel at Fort Dix on some subjects, such
as business management and drug abuse.   Clergymen participated in religious services at the post and visiting theatrical
and musical groups put on productions.   But base regulations
banned "demonstrations, picketing, sit-ins, protest marches,
political speeches, and similar activities" and permitted the
posting of handbills and the distribution of leaflets only with
prior written approval.   Spock sued to enjoin enforcement of
the regulations, contending a violation of First and Fifth Amendment rights.

     The Court supported (7-2) the policy of Fort Dix "of
keeping official military activities there wholly free of entan-
glement with partisan political campaigns of any kind. " Soldiers stationed at Fort Dix were free as individuals to attend
political rallies, out of uniform, and off base.   But the policy
of banning speeches was "wholly consistent with the American
Constitutional tradition of a politically neutral military establishment under civilian control. " Furthermore, "it is a policy
that the military authorities at Fort Dix were constitutionally
free to pursue. " Put simply, "the notion that federal reservations, like municipal streets and parks, have traditionally
served as a place for free public assembly and communication
of thoughts by private citizens is thus historically and constitutionally false. " The Court emphasized that the military
camp Fort Dix did not abandon any right to regulate traffic or
the distribution of leaflets, as did the camp in Flower.   In
that case, New Braunfels Avenue was considered a public
thoroughfare, and the military consequently abandoned any right
to ban civilian traffic.   No principle of access was established
in Flower; admittance to a military facility can be prohibited
under specific situations.

PETITION

     The First Amendment right of petition involves bringing
a grievance before a higher authority in the hope of obtaining
relief.   In the twentieth century, petition is a typical device
employed by labor, civil rights, anti-war, womens' rights,
and gay liberation groups, to name a few.   Some specific forms
of petition, and the controls placed over such activities, are
considered in the next section.

Right to Picket

Picketing is a tactic employed by American citizens in order to make objections known to others. The practice has long been associated with the labor movement as a form of protest against employers to improve wages and working conditions. Picketing has also been used by the civil rights movement to further the opportunities of black citizens. In several cases, the Supreme Court has been called upon to stipulate the specific conditions under which picketing is allowed.

Thornhill v. Alabama 310 U. S. 88 (1940)

One such case involved a violation of an Alabama law. Union organizer Byron Thornhill peacefully urged would-be strikebreakers to return home and not to cross the picket line. Thornhill was convicted of violating the Alabama anti-picketing law. The U. S. Supreme Court reversed the conviction and held that the right to picket enjoyed First Amendment protection. The specific Alabama anti-picketing statute was declared invalid because of two flaws: first, overbreadth, in that it proscribed activities which were constitutionally protected, as well as activities which were not; and second, vagueness, because the term "picket" was "nowhere delineated." The Court also noted that "the dissemination of information concerning the facts of a labor dispute must be regarded as within that area of free discussion that is guaranteed by the Constitution." The public discussion of the conditions in industry and the causes of labor disputes seems indispensable "to shape the destiny of modern industrial society."

Limitations on Picketing

According to the Court in Thornhill, peaceful picketing was "dissemination of information concerning a labor dispute," and was clearly entitled to protection as free speech by the Constitution. Soon thereafter the Court began to impose restrictions on picketing.

Giboney v. Empire Storage and Ice Co. 336 U. S. 490 (1948)

About 160 of the 200 retail peddlers who delivered ice door-to-door in Kansas City, Missouri were affiliated with the

American Federation of Labor. The Union wanted to persuade all the peddlers to join. However, most of the nonunion peddlers refused. In an effort to break down the resistance, the Union asked all wholesale ice distributors not to sell ice to non-union peddlers. Agreement was obtained from all distributors except Empire Storage and Ice Company, which refused to go along with the system. Consequently, the union picketed the Empire building. About eighty-five per cent of the truck drivers working for Empire's customers were union members. These drivers refused to deliver merchandise to and from Empire's place of business. If any of the drivers crossed the picket line they would have been fined or suspended by their union. The AFL action clearly violated Missouri antitrust law. The case reached the U. S. Supreme Court. Union lawyers argued that picketing should be allowed in this instance because the major objective of the Union was to improve wages and working conditions for the employees. The right to picket was legal. Any violation of Missouri law should, therefore, be dismissed because it was merely incidental to the primary, lawful purpose.

The Supreme Court disagreed. In a unanimous decision, the justices did not believe that labor unions possessed "a peculiar immunity from laws against trade restraint combinations." The Court did not believe unions were entitled to any special constitutional protection which was denied to all other people. In Giboney, the right to picket was restricted; the Union could not violate Missouri law by picketing a company in restraint of trade.

Hughes v. Superior Court of State of California in and for Costra County 339 U. S. 460 (1950)

In Hughes, the Court noted that picketing is not the equivalent of speech. John Hughes, acting on behalf of a group calling themselves "Progressive Citizens of America," demanded that Lucky Stores hire blacks at a Richmond, California grocery store as soon as white clerks quit, until the proportion of black to white clerks approximated the proportion of black to white customers. About fifty per cent of the customers at the store were blacks. Upon refusal of this demand, pickets systematically patrolled in front of the store. Lucky Stores obtained an injunction restraining the group from picketing. The group continued to picket the store, carrying placards reading: "Lucky Won't Hire Negro Clerks in Proportion to Negro Trade--Don't Patronize." The pickets were found guilty of contempt for "willfully disregarding" the injunction and were sentenced to imprisonment for two days and fined $20 each.

The U. S. Supreme Court made the point (8-0) that picketing and speech differ. The Court noted that "picketing, not being the equivalent of speech as a matter of fact, is not its inevitable legal equivalent. Picketing is not beyond the control of a State if the manner in which the picketing is conducted or the purpose which it seeks to effectuate gives ground for its dissallowance." In fact, states were "not required to tolerate in all places and all circumstances, even peaceful picketing by an individual." In Hughes, while the Court could not establish general guidelines or specific rules regulating picketing, it did determine that it could be restricted in this case. California was able to ban what it considered the evil of picketing to induce proportional hiring of the races.

Cameron v. Johnson 390 U. S. 611 (1968)

In Cameron, the Court continued to restrict picketing. A large rally to increase voter registration of blacks was held at the courthouse in Hattiesburg, Mississippi, on January 22, 1964. During the following months, blacks maintained a picket line every day except Sundays outside the courthouse. On April 8, the Governor signed an anti-picketing law. The pickets were warned to disperse but the picketing continued. Some were arrested and convicted. On May 18, John Cameron initiated action seeking a permanent injunction against the enforcement of the anti-picketing statute.

The U. S. Supreme Court held (7-2) that the statute was not unconstitutional on its face, either for vagueness or selective enforcement designed to harass a particular group. The Court upheld the constitutionality of the anti-picketing law.

American Radio Association, AFL-CIO v. Mobile Steamship Association 419 U. S. 215 (1974)

Another case dealing with the question of regulating picketing was heard in 1974. This case involved the issue of whether a state, in enforcing some public policy, could constitutionally prohibit peaceful picketing. During 1971, members of the maritime unions picketed against the Aqua Glory, a ship of Liberian registry. The picketing was designed to publicize

the undesirable effects on American seamen of foreign-flag
carriers which employ foreign crewmen at wages considerably
lower than those paid to American seamen. The nonviolent
and nonobstructive picketing was effective. Longshoremen and
other port workers refused to cross picket lines to load and
unload the ships. Mobile Steamship Association initiated an
action seeking an injunction against the pickets. A temporary
injunction was issued. The case reached the U. S. Supreme
Court.

The Court decided (5-4) that the picketing was for the
purpose of wrongfully interfering with the steamship companies'
business. They noted that a union official in charge of the
picketing had expressed hope that the union men would refuse
to cross the lines, that the port would become cluttered with
ships, and that the dock would thus close down. They believed that the case involved much more than expressive conduct informing the public of injuries suffered by the seamen.
The majority concluded that the jurisdiction of the Alabama
courts was not preempted by the National Labor Relations Act
and the courts could legally enjoin picketing. Such an action
did not violate First or Fourteenth Amendment rights, since
a state could, in the interests of a desirable public policy,
seek to preserve the status quo, pending final resolution of
a dispute.

Amalgamated Food Employees Union Local 590 v. Logan Valley Plaza 391 U. S. 308 (1968)

In the past decade, the Court has examined the question of whether picketing is permissible in privately-owned
shopping areas. A 1968 case is particularly noteworthy.
Logan Valley Plaza owned a large, newly developed shopping
center complex, located near Altoona, Pennsylvania. The
shopping center was totally separated from adjoining roads by
twelve to fifteen feet-wide earthen berms. On December 8,
1965, Weis Markets Inc. opened for business in the Plaza,
employing only nonunion workers. Weis Markets posted a
sign at the back of the building prohibiting trespassing or
soliciting by anyone other than its employees, on the porch
or parking lot. On December 17, members of Amalgamated
Food Employees Union, Local 590, started picketing the store.
They carried signs claiming that the workers were not "receiving union wages or other benefits. " The pickets were all
employees of Weis's competitors. During the next ten days,
an average of six pickets were constantly marching in the

parcel pickup area and the adjacent parking lot. Any congestion was sporadic and infrequent. The picketing was peaceful
at all times. On December 27, Logan instituted legal action.
The lower courts issued an order enjoining the Union from
picketing in the storeroom, porch, parcel pickup area, parking
lot, or entrances and exits leading to the parking areas. The
effect of the order was to force all picketing to be conducted
along the berms beside the roads outside the shopping center.

The U. S. Supreme Court noted (6-3) that there was no
proof that the picketing significantly interfered with the use of
the center by the general public. The Court also noted that
"the mere fact that speech is accompanied by conduct does not
mean that the speech can be suppressed under the guise of prohibiting the conduct. Here it is perfectly clear that the prohibition against trespass on the mall operates to bar all speech
within the shopping center." In his concurring opinion, Justice William Douglas said, "Picketing is free speech, plus,
the plus being physical activity that may implicate traffic and
related matters. Hence, the latter aspects of picketing may
be regulated." In short, Douglas claimed that a law or injunction which prohibited picketers from interfering with employees, deliverymen, and customers would be proper. The
Court concluded that a state cannot use its trespass laws to
exclude members of the public wishing to exercise their First
Amendment rights from so doing on premises which are freely
accessible and open to the public.

Lloyd Corp. , Limited v. Tanner 407 U. S. 551 (1972)

In this case, the Court considered the same issue taken
up in Logan Valley. Donald Tanner and four other young people distributed handbills in the interior mall of Lloyd Center
in Portland, Oregon. The handbills announced a meeting of
the "Resistance Community" to protest the draft and the Vietnam War. Since the Lloyd Center had a strict no-handbilling
regulation, security guards requested Tanner and his friends
to stop. They complied, but later claimed the action violated
their First Amendment rights. They started action.

The U. S. Supreme Court's majority opinion, written by
Justice Lewis Powell, rejected (5-4) a precedent set in Marsh
v. Alabama. According to the Court, Lloyd Center had not
been dedicated to public use and was open to the public only
for the specific purpose of carrying on business. The public
had been invited to shop, but there was "no open-ended invita-

tion to the public to use the Center for any and all purposes, however incompatible with the interests of both the stores and the shoppers whom they serve. " Lloyd Center did not lose its private character simply because the public used the center for the purpose of doing business. The majority also cited some fine distinctions to free Lloyd from the precedent set by Logan Valley. The facts were found to be sufficiently different. Logan Valley involved picketing of a store "so located in the center of a large private enclave as to preclude other reasonable access to store patrons. " In Logan Valley, the picketing was directed at a specific audience and concerned the use of the shopping center property. It had been upheld because of a lack of alternative opportunities for communicating the message to the intended audience. The Court said the handbilling in Lloyd Center was unrelated to any activity within the center, and Tanner had adequate alternative means of communication. The dissenters did not agree that the factual difference between topics--the Vietnam War and the draft, as opposed to activities of a store in a shopping center--should have differing constitutional implications. The majority, however, concluded that a privately-owned shopping center had the right to prohibit the distribution of handbills on its property when the handbilling is unrelated to the shopping center's operation. The Court in Lloyd did not overrule Logan Valley; rather, it based its decision on differences between the two cases.

Hudgens v. National Labor Relations Board
424 U. S. 507 (1976)

In a 1976 case, the Court clearly overruled Logan Valley. Striking employees of the Butler Shoe Company peacefully picketed the company's warehouse, and also all nine of its retail stores. When several employees showed up to picket Butler's store in the North DeKalb Shopping Plaza, located outside Atlanta, Georgia, the manager told them that they could not picket within the mall or parking lot. The picketers left, but the union filed an unfair labor practice complaint with the National Labor Relations Board against Scott Hudgens, the owner of the shopping center.

The U. S. Supreme Court, in the opinion of Justice Potter Stewart, argued (6-2) that if the young people "in the Lloyd case did not have a First Amendment right to enter that shopping center to distribute handbills concerning Vietnam, then the respondents in the present case did not have a First

Amendment right to enter this shopping center for the purpose
of advertising their strike against the Butler Shoe Company. "
The Court concluded "that under the present state of the law
the constitutional guarantee of free expression has no part to
play in a case such as this. "

In this section, Thornhill clearly demonstrated that
there is a right to picket, but ensuing cases placed limitations
on that right. In Giboney, the Court denied a union the right
to picket a company in restraint of trade. In Hughes, California was able to forbid picketing designed to obtain proportional
hiring of the races. In Cameron, the Court upheld a Mississippi anti-picketing law because there was no evidence that the
statute was selectively enforced so as to harass any particular
group. In Mobile Steamship, the Court allowed Alabama to
enjoin peaceful picketing in order to enforce a public policy.
And, in Lloyd and Hudgens, the Court set aside Logan Valley
by denying public picketing in privately-owned shopping centers. The right to picket exists, but under considerable restrictions.

Right to Demonstrate

Mass demonstration became a popular means of petition
in the 1960s. With the increase in the number of television
sets, leaders of aggrieved groups realized that any significant
event, no matter where it occurred, would immediately be
witnessed by a national audience. A mass demonstration, pro-
jected over national news media, brought a grievance that affected a few people to the attention of millions of American
citizens. Petitioners were thus assured of a national forum.

Edwards v. South Carolina 372 U. S. 229 (1963)

In the case of Edwards v. South Carolina, the Court
affirmed the right to demonstrate. The case involved a group
of black student protesters who were convicted of a breach of
peace. On the morning of March 2, 1961, 187 black high
school and college students, including James Edwards, met
at the Zion Baptist Church in Columbia, South Carolina. They
walked in separate groups of fifteen to the South Carolina
statehouse grounds, an area open to the general public. The
blacks wanted to submit a protest to the people and legislators
of South Carolina regarding current discriminatory practices
against blacks. The students were met on the statehouse

grounds by thirty police officers who informed the students that they could march on the grounds as long as they were peaceful. For the next half-hour the students walked in single file or two abreast in an orderly manner through the grounds. Some students carried signs bearing messages such as, "I am proud to be a Negro," and "Down with segregation." A crowd of 200-300 onlookers formed, and even though the crowd did not interfere with the pedestrian or vehicular traffic, the police told the students to disperse within fifteen minutes, or they would be arrested. The students refused to disband. Instead, they gathered together and sang "The Star Spangled Banner" and other patriotic and religious songs, while stamping their feet and clapping their hands. After fifteen minutes, they were arrested. The trial court convicted the students of a breach of peace, and imposed sentences ranging from a $10 fine or five days in jail, to a $100 fine or thirty days in jail. They appealed.

The U.S. Supreme Court ruled (8-1) that South Carolina infringed on the rights of the protesters. The students had a valid complaint in what they perceived to be the discriminatory laws against "Negro privileges." The students peaceably assembled. At no time was there an act of violence or the threat of violence on the part of the students. Police protection was always ample. Furthermore, the students were not convicted by a precise and narrowly drawn regulatory statute referring to specific conduct which should be limited. The protesters had not been arrested for violating a law regulating traffic, nor had they been arrested for violating a law concerning the periods during which the statehouse grounds were open to the public. They were convicted of peaceably expressing opinions that were opposed to the views of the majority of the community to the extent that they attracted a crowd of sufficient numbers to warrant police protection. But, the Court concluded that the Fourteenth Amendment does not permit a state to declare illegal the peaceful expression of unpopular views. The Court reversed the convictions.

Cox v. Louisiana 379 U.S. 536, 559 (1965)

Two years later the Court further strengthened the freedom to demonstrate. On December 14, 1961, twenty-three students from Southern University were arrested in downtown Baton Rouge for picketing stores which maintained segregated lunch counters. The next morning about two thousand students assembled at the old State Capital Building. Led by the

Reverend B. Elton Cox, a Field Secretary of CORE, they marched to the courthouse where the twenty-three students were jailed. Police officers agreed to allow a peaceful demonstration, provided the demonstrators stayed across the street, at least 101 feet from the courthouse steps. The students remained across the street. They sang songs and listened to a short speech by Cox in which he stated that the demonstration was a protest against the "illegal arrest" of the students. When it was lunch time, Cox urged his listeners to go out and eat, and called attention to the stores which had segregated lunch counters. The sheriff decided that the words were "inflammatory," ordered the gathering to disperse, and used tear gas to enforce his order. Cox was arrested the next day and charged with three offenses: "disturbing the peace," "obstructing public passages," and "court-house picketing." He appealed.

The U. S. Supreme Court overturned (9-0) the conviction for breach of the peace. The record showed "no conduct which the State had a right to prohibit as a breach of the peace." The entire meeting was orderly and not riotous; there were no "fighting words" and there was no justifiable fear that violence was ever about to ensue. The lower courts had interpreted the term "breach of the peace" in such a way as to allow persons to be punished merely for peacefully expressing unpopular views. The Court also overturned (7-2) the convictions for obstruction of public passages. The students had lined up across the street, thus blocking the sidewalk but not the street. The demonstration did not obstruct public passages. The Court also approved (5-4) courthouse picketing. The students had been convicted under a Louisiana statute which forbade picketing and parading in or near a courthouse with the "intent of interfering with, obstructing, or impeding the administration of justice, or with the intent of influencing any judge, juror, witness, or court officer in the discharge of his duties...." But in this case the students were given permission to demonstrate where they did, which was, in effect, an administrative determination that they were not "near" the courthouse. The sheriff's order to disperse could not legally revoke that determination. This was an abuse of discretion which, in the area of free expression, the Court would not allow. Yet, even though the Court allowed courthouse picketing because the marchers had permission in this case, the Court continued to examine the constitutionality of the Louisiana anti-picketing statute. In this case, the police interpreted "near" to mean across the street from the courthouse. Later, the police ordered the group to disperse, even though there

was no breach of the peace or obstruction of public passage-
ways. In this sense, the statute allowed the police unfettered
discretion in determining time and place limitations regarding
picketing. The Court declared the statute unconstitutional.

Gregory v. Chicago 394 U. S. 111 (1969)

The right to demonstrate was again reinforced in a 1969
case. Blacks in Chicago had become dissatisfied because Dr.
Benjamin Willis, Superintendent of Chicago's public school
system, was not moving speedily enough to desegregate the
public schools. While Mayor Richard Daley did not appear to
have legal authority to remove Dr. Willis, the group evidently
believed the Mayor could cause him to be removed, so they
directed their prodding toward the Mayor as well as against
Willis. A group of blacks began a march near the Chicago
Loop and walked in a peaceful and orderly fashion the five
miles to the neighborhood of Daley's home. A crowd of about
a thousand onlookers started shouting threats: "God-damned
nigger, get the hell out of here," and "Get out of here nig-
gers--go back where you belong or we will get you out of
here." Cars were stopped in the streets with their horns blow-
ing. Ku Klux Klan signs were observable, and people started
singing the Alabama Trooper song. Afraid that the crowd was
about to erupt, the police asked march leader Dick Gregory to
leave the area. When Gregory refused, he was arrested,
charged, and convicted of breaking the Chicago disorderly conduct law which provides: "All persons who shall make, aid,
countenance, or assist in making any improper noise, riot,
disturbance, breach of peace, within the limits of the city;
all persons who shall collect in bodies or crowds for unlawful
purposes, or for any purpose, to the annoyance or disturbance
of other persons; ... shall be deemed guilty of disorderly conduct, and upon conviction thereof, shall be severely fined not
less than one dollar nor more than two hundred dollars for each
offense. "

In a brief opinion, the U. S. Supreme Court reversed
the conviction (9-0), holding that the demonstration had been
peaceful and orderly, and that the conduct of the marchers was
protected by the First Amendment. The Chicago disorderly
conduct ordinance was considered too sweeping and vague. In
their concurring opinion, Justices Hugo Black and William
Douglas reaffirmed the idea that police may not stop a peaceful demonstration simply because a hostile crowd disagrees
with the protestors. Police may stop a demonstration only if

there is imminent threat of violence, and the police have ex-
pended all reasonable efforts to protect the demonstrators. In
this case, the trial court failed even to inquire as to whether
the imminent threat of violence existed, and whether the police
attempted to protect the demonstrators. Instead, it was sufficient to determine that the demonstrators were making improper noise, or collecting in crowds for unlawful purposes, or to
disturb other people. The jury was told to ignore the violence
committed by onlookers, and the behavior of police in response
to the actions of onlookers. It was possible that Gregory and
his followers were arrested simply because they collected in
crowds to the annoyance of other persons. They may have been
arrested and convicted simply because their behavior dis-
pleased onlookers. Such a possibility necessitated the reversal
of Gregory's conviction. In Gregory, as in Edwards and Cox,
the Court clearly supported the right of mass demonstration.

Limitations on Demonstration

In response to the numerous demonstrations that took
place during the 1960s cities passed new and/or invoked existing ordinances in order to prevent or control mass demonstrations. The ordinances also stipulated specific conditions and
procedures under which cities could limit demonstration.

Adderley v. Florida 385 U. S. 39 (1966)

In Adderley, the Court had to decide if the right to
demonstrate applied when demonstrators protested against private property. About two hundred students of Florida A & M
University at Tallahassee marched from the school to the county jail to protest against the arrests of other protesting students the day before. When the students arrived at the jail,
singing and clapping their hands, they began to block the jail
entrance, which was used by the sheriff to transport prisoners
from the jail to the court nearby. The sheriff notified the students that they should leave, and that if they refused they would
be arrested. Some students left, but Harriet Louise Adderley
and over 100 other students remained, and were arrested.
Adderley and 31 others were convicted of trespassing "with a
malicious and mischievous intent" upon the premises of the
county jail. They appealed.

The majority of the U. S. Supreme Court upheld (5-4)
the convictions because the protest was lodged against a jail,

traditionally closed to the public and built for security purposes. Unlike the precedent in Edwards, where the protest was
lodged against a public building, the students protested against
private property, and on that ground were subject to prosecution. In a dissenting opinion, Justice Douglas argued that
Edwards was applicable because a jailhouse, like an executive
mansion, courthouse, or statehouse, was a seat of government,
"whether it be the Tower of London, the Bastile, or a small
county jail. And when it houses political prisoners or those
whom many think are unjustly held, it is an obvious center for
protest. " The protest in this case should have been considered
as a petition for the redress of grievances, rather than an
incidence of trespass. In Adderley, however, the majority
upheld the convictions of students who protested against private
property.

Police Department of Chicago v. Mosley 408 U. S. 92 (1972)

In the early 1970s the Court decided two cases involving
demonstrations in front of school buildings. The first case,
heard in 1972, involved a Chicago ordinance which banned
picketing in front of a school. According to the ordinance,
enacted on March 26, 1968, any individual was guilty of disorderly conduct who "pickets or demonstrates on a public way
within 150 feet of any primary or secondary school building
while the school is in session and one-half hour before the
school is in session and one-half hour after the school session
has been concluded, provided, that this subsection does not
prohibit the peaceful picketing of any school involved in a labor
dispute. " Earl Mosley had frequently picketed Jones Commercial High School in Chicago for seven years prior to the passage of the statute. Usually by himself, Mosley would walk the
public sidewalk next to the school, carrying a sign that read:
"Jones High School practices black discrimination. Jones High
School has a black quota. " He was always peaceful, orderly,
and quiet. On April 4, the day the ordinance became effective, Mosley ended his picketing next to the school. He brought
action in court seeking injunctive relief. He argued that the
statute punished activity protected by the First Amendment,
and by exempting only peaceful labor picketing the statute denied him equal protection of the law.

The U. S. Supreme Court, in a unanimous opinion, held
that the ordinance was unconstitutional because it made an impermissible distinction between labor picketing and other peaceful picketing. The ordinance did not limit picketing in terms of

time, place, or manner, but rather in terms of subject matter. Such legislation is unconstitutional.

Grayned v. City of Rockford 408 U. S. 104 (1972)

The second case was also decided in 1972. Richard Grayned took part in a demonstration in front of West Senior High School in Rockford, Illinois. Black students at the school had presented their grievances to school administrators, but when the principal took no action a more public demonstration of protest was planned. On April 25, 1969, approximately two hundred students, their family members, and friends gathered next to the school grounds. The demonstrators marched around on a sidewalk about a hundred feet from the school building. Many carried signs which summarized the grievances: "Black Cheerleaders to cheer too"; "Black History with black teachers"; "Equal rights, Negro counselors. " Others, without placards, made the "power to the people" sign with their upraised and clenched fists. There were contradictory opinions about the peacefulness of the demonstration. Government officials claimed that the demonstrators baited policemen and made noise that was audible in the school so that hundreds of students were distracted from their school activities. Other witnesses claimed that the demonstrators were at all times quiet and orderly. In any event, the police warned the demonstrators, and then arrested 40 of them, including Grayned. Grayned was tried and convicted of violating two Rockford ordinances, the "anti-picketing" and the "anti-noise" ordinances. A $25 fine was imposed for each violation.

The U. S. Supreme Court found (9-0) that Rockford's anti-picketing ordinance, which provided that a person commits disorderly conduct if he knowingly "pickets or demonstrates on a public way within 150 feet of any primary or secondary school building while the school is in session ... provided that this subsection does not prohibit the peaceful picketing of any school involved in a labor dispute, " violated the equal protection clause of the Fourteenth Amendment for the same reasons as given in Mosley. The conviction on this ground was reversed. However, the Court affirmed the conviction (8-1) under the anti-noise ordinance which stipulated that no person shall willfully make any noise or diversion which disturbs the peace or good order of a school session or class. Grayned claimed that the ordinance was both vague and overbroad, and therefore unconstitutional. But the Court noted that the Rockford ordinance "punishes only conduct which disrupts or is about to disrupt normal school activities. " Peaceful picketing that does not interfere with the normal operation of the school is permitted. Also, the ordinance gives no authority to punish anyone because of what he says. Justice Thurgood Marshall, writing for the Court, continued his discussion of the ordinance:

> We recognize that the ordinance prohibits some picketing which is neither violent nor physically obstructive. Noisy demonstrations which disrupt or are incompatible with normal school activities are obviously within the ordinance's reach. Such expressive conduct may be constitutionally protected at other places or other times ... but next to a school, while classes are in session, it may be prohibited. The anti-noise ordinance imposes no such restriction on expressive activity before or after the school session, while the student-faculty audience enters and leaves the school.

In conclusion, the Rockford ordinance was upheld because it restricted particular activity at a specific time and place in order to protect the schools. Such regulation is consistent with the First and Fourteenth Amendments.

Walker v. Birmingham 388 U. S. 307 (1967)

In Walker, the Court faced a new issue: was a demonstrator required to obey an injunction, even though the ordinance upon which it was justified was actually unconstitutional? During the spring of 1963, sit-ins and parades were conducted by the black community to protest discrimination in Birmingham, Alabama. City officials secured affidavits stating that the demonstrators had trespassed upon private property, unlawfully picketed private places of business, congregated in mobs, and that this had caused an undue burden and strain upon the police power of the city. A circuit court granted a temporary injunction enjoining the leaders of the demonstrations from encouraging parades without a permit. The rights leaders applied for a permit, but City Commissioner Eugene "Bull" Conner replied, "No, you will not get a permit in Birmingham, Alabama, to picket. I will picket you over to city jail. " Despite Conner, and without any request that the court injunction be dissolved, demonstrations were held on Good Friday and Easter. Eight black ministers, including Wyatt Walker and Martin Luther King, Jr. , were arrested and held in contempt for leading the marches. They were sentenced to five days in jail and a $50 fine. They appealed, contending that the Birmingham law required permission from city administrators who had made it clear no permission would be granted.

The U. S. Supreme Court affirmed the convictions (5-4). The major reason for the decision was that initial obedience is required of even an unconstitutional court decree, like the injunction in this case, even though obedience is not required of an unconstitutional ordinance, as the Court noted in Poulos. The Court found against Walker because he disobeyed the injunction, even though the city ordinance was subject to considerable constitutional question. The majority of the Court thus concluded that an order of a lower court, which almost certainly would be reversed on appeal, must be obeyed by the parties subject to it until the order was set aside by a higher court.

Shuttlesworth v. Birmingham 394 U. S. 147 (1969)

In Shuttlesworth, the Birmingham ordinance was declared unconstitutional. On Good Friday afternoon in 1963, fifty-two black citizens, led by Reverend Fred L. Shuttlesworth and two other ministers, marched out of a Birmingham church to protest denial of civil rights to blacks in the city. The marchers did not interfere with pedestrians, nor did the traffic suffer any inconvenience. A group of observers developed and spilled over into the street, but not to the point of blocking traffic or obstructing vehicles in any fashion. After four blocks the marchers were stopped by the police and arrested for violating a Birmingham law which made it an offense to participate in a public demonstration without first obtaining a permit. Shuttlesworth was convicted and sentenced to ninety days in prison at hard labor, and an additional forty-eight days at hard labor for failing to pay a $75 fine and $24 in court costs. He appealed.

In the opinion of the U. S. Supreme Court (8-1), picketing and parading are means of expression which are entitled to First Amendment protection. The Birmingham ordinance violated those freedoms. The ordinance subjected "the exercise of First Amendment freedoms to the prior restraint of a license, without narrow, objective, and definitive standards to guide the licensing authority. " Such a practice is unconstitutional. The Court acknowledged the right of a state to prevent serious interference with normal use of streets and parks, but the Court condemned a licensing system which gave an admin-istrative official discretion to grant or deny a permit upon broad criteria unrelated to proper control of public places. The Court noted that Shuttlesworth had sent a telegram to Commis-sioner Conner asking for a permit to picket "against the injus-tices of segregation and discrimination." His request indicated the sidewalks where picketing would occur. The request was denied, Conner bluntly stating, "I insist that you and your peo-ple do not start picketing on the streets of Birmingham, Ala-bama." In applying the law, Conner made it clear that under no circumstances would the group of protestors be allowed to demonstrate in Birmingham. In Shuttlesworth, the U. S. Su-preme Court overturned the conviction of Reverend Shuttles-worth and found unconstitutional the Birmingham ordinance as a form of prior restraint which lacked ascertainable standards for the granting of permits.

Carroll v. President and Commissioners of Princess Anne County 393 U. S. 175 (1968)

Another important issue that arose in the late 1960s was whether a city could proscribe a demonstration without granting a hearing to the demonstrators. On July 6, 1966, the National States Rights Party, a white supremacist organi-zation, conducted a rally near the courthouse of Princess Anne, Maryland. The speeches vilified and insulted blacks and Jews and were amplified so they could be heard for sev-eral blocks. About sixty state policemen were brought in because of the tenseness of the crowd which grew to number about 125, one-fourth of whom were blacks. The rally broke up in the early evening with the promise that another gathering would be held the following night. However, the Princess Anne Commissioners obtained a ten-day restraining order to prevent another rally. The injunction was obeyed and at a trial at the end of ten days the court extended the restraint for a period of ten months. On appeal, the Court of Appeals affirmed the ten-day injunction, but reversed the ten-month ex-tension, holding that "the period of time was unreasonable, and that it was arbitrary to assume that a clear and present dan-ger of civil disturbance and riot would persist for ten months." Joseph Carroll, on behalf of the Party, sought U. S. Supreme Court review of the ten-day order. Though the ten-day period had long since passed, Carroll argued that the decree affected the willingness of officials in other Maryland counties to allow the group to hold rallies.

The Court reversed the state decision (9-0) and held that the ten-day injunction was unconstitutional. The proceedings which initially set up the ten-day injunction were ex parte, no notice being given to the States Rights Party to appear. The Carroll decision held that ex parte orders restraining marches or demonstrations are unconstitutional when it is possible to provide an opportunity for notice and hearing to the demonstrating group, and such opportunity prior to rendering the ex parte order had not been provided. Officials were clearly able, but not willing, to notify Carroll of the hearing on the injunction, since Carroll and his followers were in the county on that day. In this case, it should also be noted that the States Rights Party followed the stipulations of Walker. Party members abandoned their plan for the second rally and obeyed the terms of the ten-day injunction. Then they sought and obtained judicial review of its issuance and terms. And, in Carroll, the Court's ruling was favorable to the Party.

National Socialist Party of America v. Village of Skokie
432 U. S. 43 (1977)

A more recent decision reflects a much more divided Court on the issue of regulation of demonstrations. On April 29, 1977, the Circuit Court of Cook County, Illinois entered an injunction against the National Socialist Party of America which prohibited them from performing any of the following actions within the predominantly Jewish village of Skokie: marching, walking, or parading in the uniform of the National Socialist Party of America; displaying the swastika on or off their persons; distributing pamphlets which incite or promote hatred against persons of Jewish faith or ancestry or hatred against persons of any faith or ancestry, race or religion. The Party sued.

The U. S. Supreme Court decided (5-4) that the injunction deprived the marchers of First Amendment rights during the period of appellate review which, in normal course, may take a year or more to complete. If a state seeks to impose a restraint of this kind, it must provide strict procedural safeguards, including immediate appellate review. The case was remanded for further proceedings consistent with the Court's opinion.

Shortly thereafter, Frank Collin, leader of the National Socialist Party, announced a plan for his group to march in Skokie on July 4. The Court of Appeals refused to hear the case, however, until July 8, and subsequently banned the march. On April 6, 1978, the Court of Appeals overturned Skokie ordinances which forbade groups that preached hatred or wore military-type uniforms to march or to pass out "hate literature," and which required a group to have $300,000 in liability insurance. The Court, however, upheld an ordinance requiring a group to apply for a permit thirty days before a march. The Nazis were granted a permit to march in Skokie on June 25. They were also granted permission to demonstrate in Chicago in July. In the face of threatened reprisals, the Nazis decided not to march in Skokie, but, instead, to demonstrate in Chicago. That event gained nationwide publicity for the Nazi cause.

This section contains a discussion of cases involving demonstration. In Edwards, the Court acknowledged the right to demonstrate. Cox and Gregory involved state ordinances which treated breach of peace in a broad and sweeping fashion. Shuttlesworth involved an ordinance which functioned as a prior restraint and lacked ascertainable standards for granting permits. In these cases, the Court struck down the ordinances and affirmed the right to demonstrate. In other cases, the Court limited the conditions under which demonstration is permissible. In Adderley, the Court restricted demonstration on private property. Grayned placed restrictions on noisy demonstrations near a school which disturbed a class. Walker stipulated that an unfairly levied injunction must be obeyed; when that was done in Carroll, the Court upheld the right to demonstrate. Carroll also confirmed the right of marchers to a hearing. In Skokie, the Court ruled that when a state imposes a restraint on a march, strict procedural safeguards, including immediate appellate review, must be provided. The right to demonstrate is clearly established, but within clearly defined controls established by the U. S. Supreme Court.

Bibliography

Books

Fellman, David. The Constitutional Right of Association. Chicago: University of Chicago Press, 1963.

Horn, Robert A. Groups and the Constitution. New York: AMS Press, 1971.

Kalven, Harry, Jr. The Negro and the First Amendment. Chicago: University of Chicago Press, 1965.

Konvitz, Milton R.   Expanding Liberties: Freedom's Gains in Postwar America.   New York: Viking Press, 1966.

Articles

Alpert, Robert.   "Lloyd v. Tanner: Handbilling Within a Shopping Mall Not Directed at a Store Is Not Protected by the First Amendment Unless No Adequate Alternative Location Exists, " New York University Review of Law and Social Change 3 (Winter, 1973), 70-82.

Blasi, Vince.   "Prior Restraints on Demonstrations, " Michigan Law Review 68 (August, 1970), 1481-1574.

Boccarosse, Ralph N.   "Lloyd Corporation v. Tanner: Expression of First Amendment Rights in the Privately Owned Shopping Center--A Re-evaluation by the Burger Court, " Catholic University Law Review 22 (Summer, 1973), 807-29.

Fellman, David.   "Constitutional Rights of Association, " Supreme Court Review (1961), 74-134.

Haiman, Franklyn S.   "The Rhetoric of the Streets: Some Legal and Ethical Considerations, " Quarterly Journal of Speech 53 (April, 1967), 99-114.

Lambeth, Evelyn J.   "Hudgens v. NLRB: A Final Definition of the Public Forum?" Wake Forest Law Review 13 (Spring, 1977), 139-59.

Law, Robert E.   "Lloyd v. Tanner: Death of the Public Forum?" University of San Francisco Law Review 7 (April, 1973), 582-95.

Perlman, Gilbert T.   "The Public Forum from Marsh to Lloyd, " American University Law Review 24 (Fall, 1974), 159-203.

Cases

Adderley v. Florida 385 U. S. 39 (1966)

Amalgamated Food Employees Union Local 590 v. Logan Valley Plaza 391 U. S. 308 (1968)

American Radio Association, AFL-CIO v. Mobile Steamship
Association 419 U. S. 215 (1974)

Baird v. State Bar of Arizona 401 U. S. 1 (1971)

Bates v. City of Little Rock 361 U. S. 516 (1960)

Brown v. Louisiana 383 U. S. 131 (1966)

Cameron v. Johnson 390 U. S. 611 (1968)

Cantwell v. Connecticut 310 U. S. 296 (1940)

Carroll v. President and Commissioners of Princess Anne
County 393 U. S. 175 (1968)

Communist Party of Indiana v. Whitcomb 414 U. S. 441 (1974)

Communist Party v. Subversive Activities Control Board 367
U. S. 1 (1961)

Cox v. Louisiana 379 U. S. 536, 559 (1965)

Cox v. New Hampshire 312 U. S. 569 (1941)

Edwards v. South Carolina 372 U. S. 229 (1963)

Flower v. United States 407 U. S. 197 (1972)

Garner v. Louisiana 368 U. S. 157 (1961)

Giboney v. Empire Storage & Ice Co., 336 U. S. 490 (1948)

Gibson v. Florida Legislative Investigation Committee 372
U. S. 539 (1963)

Grayned v. City of Rockford 408 U. S. 104 (1972)

Greer v. Spock 424 U. S. 828 (1976)

Gregory v. Chicago 394 U. S. 111 (1969)

Hague v. Committee for Industrial Organization 307 U. S. 496
(1939)

Hudgens v. National Labor Relations Board 424 U. S. 507
(1976)

Hughes v. Superior Court of State of California in and for
Costra County 339 U. S. 460 (1950)

Konigsberg v. State Bar of California 366 U. S. 36 (1961)

Korematsu v. United States 323 U. S. 214 (1944)

Kunz v. New York 340 U. S. 290 (1951)

Lloyd Corp., Limited v. Tanner 407 U. S. 551 (1972)

Lombard v. Louisiana 373 U. S. 267 (1963)

Marsh v. Alabama 326 U. S. 501 (1946)

National Association for the Advancement of Colored People v.
Alabama 357 U. S. 449 (1958)

National Socialist Party of America v. Village of Skokie 432
U. S. 43 (1977)

Niemotko v. Maryland 340 U. S. 268 (1951)

Peterson v. Greenville 373 U. S. 244 (1963)

Police Department of Chicago v. Mosley 408 U. S. 92 (1972)

Poulos v. New Hampshire 345 U. S. 395 (1953)

Rockwell v. Morris 211 N. Y. 2d. 25 (1961)

Shuttlesworth v. Birmingham 394 U. S. 147 (1969)

Staub v. Baxley 355 U. S. 313 (1958)

Thomas v. Collins 323 U. S. 516 (1945)

Thornhill v. Alabama 310 U. S. 88 (1940)

United States v. Robel 389 U. S. 258 (1961)

Walker v. Birmingham 388 U. S. 307 (1967)

Watson v. Memphis 373 U. S. 526 (1963)

Wright v. Georgia 373 U. S. 284 (1963)

CHAPTER IV

ACADEMIC FREEDOM

The concept of academic freedom concerns the liberty to investigate, evaluate, interpret, present, and discuss facts related to any and all fields of learning. The concept has been traditionally related, however, almost exclusively to the faculty members of colleges and universities. According to Arthur O. Lovejoy, founder of the American Association of University Professors,

> Academic freedom is the freedom of a teacher or researcher in higher institutions of learning to investigate and discuss the problems of his science and to express his conclusions, whether through publication or the instruction of students, without interference from political or ecclesiastical authority, or from administrative officials of the institution in which he is employed, unless his methods are found by qualified bodies of his own profession to be clearly incompetent or contrary to professional ethics.

Sidney Hook describes academic freedom as "the freedom of professionally qualified persons to inquire, discover, publish, and teach the truth as they see it in the field of their competence." This freedom "is subject to no control or authority except the control or authority of the rational methods by which truths or conclusions are sought and established in these disciplines."

The concept of academic freedom employed in this chapter is quite broad. For our purposes, academic freedom involves the intellectual liberty to enable an educational institution to perform effectively the functions of teaching, learning, and research. Academic freedom certainly affects the rights of faculty, both inside and outside of the institution. A faculty member is not required to remain silent in order to

preserve his or her position. Outside the academic environment, a teacher has rights just like other citizens. Academic
freedom also concerns the interests of students, administrators, and the entire community, not just those of teachers.
Academic freedom relates to all educational institutions, not
just colleges and universities. It is, however, not absolute;
it is subject to controls. In this chapter, several issues are
considered on which the courts have been asked to make decisions affecting the nature and scope of academic freedom.

ADMINISTRATIVE CONTROLS

Over the years, various sources of influence have attempted to place controls on classroom subject matter, materials, methods, and activities. Teachers, parents, administrators, and even state legislatures have had their attempts
at control ultimately judged by the courts.

Curriculum

The curriculum includes all the subjects offered by an
educational institution. Two of the earliest efforts at curriculum control, each of which involved a substantial controversy,
grew out of the teaching of German as a foreign language,
and the use of a textbook which contained a discussion of the
theory of evolution.

Meyer v. Nebraska 262 U.S. 390 (1923)

Bartels V. Iowa; Bohning v. Ohio 262 U.S. 404 (1923)

During and immediately following World War I, some
legislatures as well as some local school boards set out to
forbid the teaching of the German language. For example, on
April 9, 1919, Nebraska passed a statute which prohibited any
person from teaching any subject in the curriculum in any
language other than English. The act also stipulated that languages other than English could be taught only after a pupil
successfully completed the eighth grade. Any person who violated the act was subject to a fine and imprisonment. The
language prohibition was especially harmful to some German
parochial schools which used German extensively in their curricular programs. Robert Meyer, an instructor at Zion
Parochial School, was convicted of teaching German to a ten-
year-old boy. He appealed.

The U. S. Supreme Court determined (7-2) that a state could require that instruction be spoken in the English language, but it may not forbid the teaching of subjects that would not injure the health or morals of the school children. In this case, it was felt that mere knowledge of the German language could not reasonably be considered harmful. Actually, it had been regarded as helpful and even desirable in the past. The foreign-born population of the United States was proportionately large. Several communities routinely used foreign languages. Consequently, students would be hampered from becoming the most useful citizens in their communities if they were deprived of the use of a foreign language. The Court found the Nebraska law unconstitutional, arguing that it violated the instructor's right to teach and the parents' right to hire a teacher for their children. Later that year, the Court declared similar state laws unconstitutional in Iowa and Ohio.

Epperson v. Arkansas 393 U. S. 87 (1968)

The Court was also concerned with state interference in the teaching of human evolution. In 1925, Tennessee passed a "monkey" law which forbade the teaching of Darwin's theory of evolution in the classroom. The constitutionality of the act was upheld in the famous Scopes Trial in 1927 (154 Tenn. 105). It was not until more than thirty years later that Tennessee repealed this anti-evolution law under which John T. Scopes had been convicted. In 1928, with the continued upsurge of interest in "fundamentalist" religious fervor that took place during the 1920s, Arkansas adopted a law which made it illegal for a teacher in any state-supported school "to teach the theory or doctrine that mankind ascended or descended from a lower order of animals" or "to adopt or use in any such institution a textbook that teaches" this theory. A violation was considered a misdemeanor, and any guilty teacher faced dismissal from his or her position within the Arkansas school system.

The textbook which had been used for decades in the teaching of biology at Little Rock Central High School did not contain a section on the Darwinian theory. Then, in 1965, the school administration, acting upon the recommendation of the biology instructors, adopted a text which had a chapter which set forth "the theory about the origin ... of man from a lower form of animal." Susan Epperson, a tenth grade biology teacher, was confronted with the new textbook dilemma. She was instructed to use the new book, but to do so would be a criminal offense which could subject her to dismissal from her teaching position. Epperson instituted court action seeking a declaration that the Arkansas statute was illegal and a decree ordering the officials of the Little Rock School system to re-frain from dismissing her if she used the textbook. The court held that the statute violated the Fourteenth Amendment be-cause it constituted a State interference with the freedom of speech and thought. Specifically, the statute "tends to hinder the quest for knowledge, restrict the freedom to learn, and restrain the freedom to teach. " On appeal, the Arkansas Supreme Court reversed the decision. In a two-sentence opin-ion, the court upheld the State's power to specify the curri-culum in public schools.

The U. S. Supreme Court unanimously held that the statute violated the First and Fourteenth Amendments of the Constitution. First, the First Amendment's command is to protect the fundamental rights of free speech and inquiry which are nowhere more vital than in the educational system. In this case, the State had prevented teachers from discussing the theory of evolution. Second, the government must be neu-tral in matters of religion. In this case, the State prohibited a particular view for the sole reason that it conflicted with a specific religious opinion, namely, the belief that Genesis of-fered the exclusive source of doctrine concerning the origin of human beings. The Court struck down the Arkansas anti-evolution act.

School Rituals

Two school rituals that were practiced frequently, in some cases daily, during the first few decades of the twentieth century were saluting the flag and saying a prayer. During the 1940s the U. S. Supreme Court first upheld, then overturned the flag salute ritual. Two decades later, the Court declared that school prayer exercises violated the Constitution.

Minersville School District v. Gobitis 310 U. S. 586 (1940)

The first of these cases involved two grade school pu-pils, Lillian and William Gobitis, aged twelve and ten years, who were expelled from the Minersville, Pennsylvania, public schools for refusing to pledge allegiance to the United States flag as part of a daily school ritual. The local Board of

Education required both teachers and pupils to participate in the exercise. The Gobitis family, as members of Jehovah's Witnesses, viewed the Bible as the supreme authority. The children had been raised to believe that saluting or pledging allegiance to the flag was forbidden by command of scripture. The Gobitis children were of mandatory school attendance age. Thus their parents had to place them in private schools. Walter Gobitis, the father, initiated suit for relief of the financial burden he experienced in educating his children. He sought to enjoin the school from continuing to require participation in the flag-salute as a condition of his children's attendance at the Minersville school.

The U. S. Supreme Court was faced with the issue of weighing the liberty of conscience against the power of school authorities. The Court decided (8-1) not to challenge the authority of the Minersville education system, which claimed that the flag salute was an effective means of promoting patriotism. The Court felt that granting an exemption from the flag salute to dissidents "might introduce elements of difficulty into the school discipline," and "might cast doubts in the minds of the other children which would themselves weaken the effect of the exercise." In Gobitis, the Court upheld the flag salute exercise as a required ritual.

West Virginia State Board of Education v. Barnette
319 U. S. 624 (1943)

Following the Gobitis decision, the West Virginia legislature amended its laws to require all public schools to offer instruction in history and civics "for the purpose of teaching, fostering, and perpetuating the ideals, principles, and spirit of Americanism, and increasing the knowledge of the organization and machinery of the government." On January 9, 1952, the West Virginia Board of Education passed a regulation requiring that the flag salute become "a regular part of the program of activities in the public schools," and that all teachers and students "shall be required to participate in the salute honoring the Nation represented by the flag." The Board declared that any student failing to comply with the policy would be expelled. During the period of expulsion, the student would be considered "unlawfully absent" and legally considered a delinquent. The child's parents were liable to prosecution, and if convicted, were subject to be fined not more than $50 and jailed for not more than thirty days. A group of Jehovah's Witnesses refused to obey the West Virginia statute because it

conflicted with their religious belief in a literal application of
Exodus, which commands that "Thou shalt not make unto thee
any graven image, or any likeness of anything...." The Witnesses view the flag as an "image" within this biblical decree.
Some children refused to salute the flag and were expelled from
school. Their parents were prosecuted, and the students were
threatened with punishment as criminal juveniles.

The U. S. Supreme Court noted (8-1) that there was no
claim by the West Virginia Board of Education that remaining
passive during a flag salute created any clear and present
danger that would justify the compelling of the salute. In arriving at the decision, the Court examined similarities and
differences between this case and Gobitis. The majority opinion, written by Justice Robert Jackson, noted four specific
differences. First, in Gobitis, the Court supported the idea
that a government must necessarily be stronger than the liberties of its people. In Barnette, the Court preferred individual freedom of mind over officially disciplined uniformity.
Second, in Gobitis, the Court felt that to interfere with educational decisions would make the Supreme Court the school
board for the nation. In Barnette, the Court ruled that while
boards of education have vital functions, none may be performed
in violation of the Constitution. Third, in Gobitis, the Court
reasoned that the field of education was an area in which the
court had no competence and that the controlling influence
should rest with legislatures and the public. In Barnette, the
Court ruled that the rights of free speech and press, and the
right to worship, are not subject to political debate or public
votes. Fourth, Gobitis supported the view that "national unity
is the basis of national security," and that school authorities
have a right to determine the means of attaining that unity. In
Barnette, the majority did not question the right of officials
to try to instill national unity, but they questioned whether the
compulsion was an appropriate means of achieving national
unity. According to the Court, "To believe that patriotism will
not flourish if patriotic ceremonies are voluntary and sponta-
neous instead of a compulsory routine is to make an unflatter-
ing estimate of the appeal of our institutions to free minds."
The Court set aside the mandatory flag salute exercise.

Engel v. Vitale 370 U. S. 421 (1962)

School prayer was another issue that came before the
U. S. Supreme Court. The Board of Regents of New York, a
governmental agency empowered with broad control over the

public school system, composed a prayer which was published as part of the "Statement of Moral and Spiritual Training in the Schools. " They commented: "We believe that this state- ment will be subscribed to by all men and women of good will, and we call upon all of them to aid in giving life to our pro- gram. " Soon thereafter, the Board of Education of Union Free School District No. 9, New Hyde Park, New York, directed the school principals to have the prayer said aloud by every class at the beginning of the every school day. The prayer was: "Almighty God, we acknowledge our dependence upon Thee, and we beg Thy blessing upon us, our parents, our teachers, and our country. " Parents of ten pupils initiated action in the courts, claiming that use of this prayer in the public schools violated their religious beliefs and practices, and those of their children. They insisted that the requirement violated the First Amendment, which stipulates that Congress shall make no law respecting an establishment of religion.

The New York Court of Appeals upheld the authority of New York to use the Regent's prayer as part of daily school operations so long as the schools did not require pupils to join in the prayer contrary to their own wishes or those of their parents. Teachers could not comment on the participation or nonparticipation of any student. Student nonparticipation could take the form of either remaining silent or being excused en- tirely from the prayer; they could meet in another room or arrive for school a few minutes later than other students. The schools could work out their own specific rules for nonpartici- pation.

The U. S. Supreme Court, however, decided (6-1) that the public school system's encouragement of the Regent's prayer constituted an action which contradicted the establish- ment clause of the First Amendment. Recital of a prayer was a religious activity; this prayer activity constituted an estab- lishment. The majority of the Court ruled that it was not anti-religious to determine that the government should refrain from writing official prayers. That sort of activity should be left to the people or to their ministers.

School District of Abington Township v. Schempp; Murray v. Curlett 374 U. S. 203 (1963)

One year later, the Court faced the "prayer" issue again. On each school day between 8:15 and 8:30, religious exercises were held at Abington Senior High School. The exercises were broadcast into each homeroom through a public address system. They were supervised by a teacher, and were presented with the help of students enrolled in the school's radio and television workshop. One student would read ten verses of the Bible which he or she had selected from any version; in fact, the King James, the Douay, and the Revised Standard versions had been used, as well as the Jewish Holy Scriptures. This was followed by a recitation of the Lord's Prayer. The exercises closed with the flag salute and any announcements of interest for that day. Participation in the exercises was voluntary; students could absent themselves from the room or, if they wanted, they could remain in the room and not participate in the exercises. During the exercises, there were no biased statements, no questions asked, and no comments of an interpretative nature. These exercises complied with a Pennsylvania law which required that "at least ten verses from the Holy Bible shall be read, without comment, at the opening of each public school on each school day." Any student could be excused from the exercise, with the written request of his or her parent. Edward Lewis Schempp, his wife Sidney, and their children, Roger and Donna, were members of the Unitarian Church in Germantown. The Schempps initiated action in the courts, arguing that their rights under the establishment clause of the First Amendment had been violated. Schempp contended that certain religious doctrines expressed by a literal reading of the Bible contradicted religious beliefs held by the Schempp family. Schempp considered having his children excused from the exercises, but decided against it because he believed that the relationship between his children and their teachers would be adversely affected. The case came to the U. S. Supreme Court.

Murray was a companion case. In 1905, the Board of School Commissioners of Baltimore adopted a rule which provided for the holding of religious services at the beginning of the school day. The services consisted of the "reading, without comment, of a chapter in the Holy Bible and/or use of the Lord's Prayer." Madalyn Murray and her son, William J. Murray, III, both professed atheists, brought suit, alleging that even though William had been excused from the readings, his rights as a student and Mrs. Murray's rights as a taxpayer had been violated. Murray contended that the exercise "threatens their religious liberty by placing a premium on belief as against non-belief and subjects their freedom of conscience to the rule of the majority." Espousal of a belief in God as the basis for all moral and spiritual values rendered Murray's beliefs "sinister, alien, and suspect," and tended to question "their morality, good citizenship and good faith."

The U. S. Supreme Court ruled (8-1) that both the establishment and the free exercise clauses of the Constitution were violated. The establishment clause is violated when a law seeks either the advancement or the inhibition of religion. In these particular cases, the states required the selection and reading of religious prayers at the opening of the school day. These exercises were considered as part of the curricular activities of the students, and were held in a school building under the supervision of teachers. Such an exercise is a religious ceremony, and violates the establishment clause. The free exercise clause withdraws from legislative authority the exertion of any restraint on the free exercise of religion. The clause acknowledges the value of religious training, but it also recognizes the right of every person to choose his or her own religious exercises, free of any state compulsion. A violation of this statute involves coercion against an individual in the practice of religion. The clause secures religious liberty by civil authority. According to the Court, even though the free exercise clause prohibited laws that deny the right of free exercise to anyone, it did not intend that a majority could use state legislative machinery to practice their beliefs. In their decisions in Schempp and Murray, as in Engel, the Court supported the concept of "neutrality" on the part of government regarding the area of religious rituals in the public schools.

Teacher Fitness

An area in which legislative investigative committees have attempted to exert some administrative control over the academic scene is teacher fitness. In some instances, the tendency of teachers to plead the Fifth Amendment, or in other ways to refuse to testify before a legislative investigating committee, was regarded as proof of both their moral unfitness and disloyalty.

Slochower v. Board of Higher Education 350 U. S. 551 (1956)

In a 1956 case, the Court dealt with a harsh municipal employee policy. Section 903 of the New York City Charter stipulated that whenever a city employee claimed the Fifth Amendment privilege against self-incrimination to avoid answering a question related to his employment conduct, "his term or tenure of office ... shall terminate." Harry Slochower, an Associate Professor of German at Brooklyn College,

was called to testify before the Internal Security Subcommittee
of the U. S. Senate. He stated that he was not a member of
the Communist Party. He indicated complete willingness to
answer all questions about his associations or political beliefs
since 1941, but refused to answer questions about his associations during 1940-41 on the ground that his answers might tend
to incriminate him. Slochower was suspended and his position declared vacant. He brought suit.

The U. S. Supreme Court ruled (5-4) for Slochower,
arguing that summary dismissal denied due process of law.
The New York law translated an employee's claim of Fifth
Amendment privilege "into a conclusive presumption of guilt.
Since no inference of guilt was possible from the claim before
the federal committee, the discharge falls of its own weight
as wholly without support. " The Court went on to note that
the state had broad powers in the hiring and firing of its employees. It might have been shown, after a proper inquiry,
that Slochower's continued appointment would operate against
the interests of the state. However, no such investigation was
held. New York's action against Slochower was overturned.

Beilan v. Board of Public Education 357 U. S. 399 (1958)

In another case dealing with guilt by association, the
Court once again ruled for the plaintiff. On June 25, 1952,
Herman A. Beilan, a teacher of twenty-two years in the Philadelphia Public School System, was called to the Superintendent's office and was asked whether he had been the Press
Director of the Professional Section of the Communist Political
Association in 1944. Beilan consulted an attorney, returned to
the office and declined to answer. The Superintendent made it
clear that he was investigating "a real question of the fitness
of Beilan to be a teacher. " Beilan refused to answer "questions of this type. " The School Board started dismissal proceedings and on January 9, 1954 dismissed Beilan for "incompetency" by a vote of fourteen to one. He appealed.

The U. S. Supreme Court found (5-4) that the questions
asked by the Superintendent were relevant to the issue of a
teacher's fitness to serve. When Beilan accepted the teaching
position, he agreed to be frank, candid, and cooperative in
answering questions related to his fitness to teach. The Court
ruled that Beilan was removed not for his Fifth Amendment
plea or his membership in the Communist Party, but because
his refusal to answer questions asked by his employer consti-

tuted evidence of unreliability and incompetency.   Actually, in both Slochower and Beilan, the Court affirmed the power of city authorities to inquire into a teacher's fitness.   In Slochower, city action was overturned because summary dismissal occured without a proper, extensive investigation.   In both decisions, however, the Court stood clearly against penalizing a teacher for invoking the Fifth Amendment, but did not ban endeavors to investigate teacher fitness.

Adler v. Board of Education 342 U. S. 485 (1952)

Another method of evaluating teacher fitness involved the close screening of the membership of teachers in certain organizations.   The New York Feinberg Law, passed in 1949, noted the existence of extensive communist infiltration into the public school system.   The law required that the Board of Regents make a list of all organizations which advocate, advise, teach, or embrace the doctrine that government should be overthrown by force, violence, or any other unlawful means. Membership of a teacher in a listed organization constituted prima facie evidence for disqualification from holding a teaching position in the New York School system.   In the case of Irving Adler, the U. S. Supreme Court, for the first time, reviewed a statute specifically applicable to the associational rights of teachers.

The Supreme Court thought it was clear that teachers had the right to assemble, speak, think, and believe as they wanted.   It was equally clear that if teachers did not choose to work on the reasonable terms laid down by the proper New York authorities, they were at liberty to retain their beliefs and associations, and go elsewhere.   Justice Sherman Minton's opinion for the majority upheld the right of a state to oversee the associational habits of teachers.

> A teacher works in a sensitive area in a school room. There he shapes the attitude of young minds towards the society in which they live.   In this, the state has a vital concern.   It must preserve the integrity of the schools.   That the school authorities have the right and the duty to screen the officials, teachers, and employees as to their fitness to maintain the integrity of the schools as a part of ordered society cannot be doubted.

The Court acknowledged that an individual's associates as well

as his or her conduct can properly be considered in determining fitness and loyalty. A person's reputation is shaped
in part by his or her past and current associations. The
Court knew of no rule which prevented a state, when determining the fitness and loyalty of teachers, "from considering
the organizations and persons with whom they associate." The
Court's majority (6-3) seemed to support the idea that citizens
who enter the field of public education can be forced to sacri-
fice some civil liberties.

Wieman v. Updegraff 344 U. S. 183 (1952)

In the same year that the Court heard Adler, it decided
another case involving a state statute which limited the associational rights of teachers. An Oklahoma statute required
that all state employees take a loyalty oath as a condition of
employment. The oath required that employees pledge to support and defend the constitutions of the United States and of
the state of Oklahoma, and to swear that they were not pres-
ently a member of the Communist Party or any organization
that advocates the overthrow of the government by force or
violence. Exactly which groups were proscribed was determined by a list which had been compiled by the United States
Attorney General before the passage of the Oklahoma act.
Some members of the faculty and staff of Oklahoma Agricultural and Mechanical College failed, within the thirty days
permitted, to take the oath. Paul Updegraff, a citizen and taxpayer, brought suit to prevent state officials from paying those
employees who had not taken the oath. The specific issue
raised in this case, because of the provisions of the Oklahoma
act, was "whether the due process clause permits a state in
attempting to bar disloyal individuals from its employ to exclude persons solely on the basis of organizational membership, regardless of their knowledge concerning the organizations to which they had belonged." Under the Oklahoma statute, the fact of membership alone disqualified a teacher from
employment.

The U. S. Supreme Court found (8-0) that membership
could be innocent. A person might have joined a forbidden
organization unaware of its activities and purposes. Also, at
the time of affiliation, a group itself may be innocent and may
only later turn toward illegitimate ends. Conversely, an organization that was formerly subversive, and so designated on
the list, may have subsequently rejected such influences. The
Court found that the oath denied due process because "the fact
of association alone determines disloyalty and disqualification;

it matters not whether association existed innocently or know-ingly. "

Shelton v. Tucker; Carr v. Young 364 U. S. 479 (1960)

A 1960 case involved a different legislative method for controlling the associations of teachers. An Arkansas law compelled every teacher, as a condition of employment in a public school, to file annually an affidavit listing every organ-ization to which he or she had belonged within the past five years. The statute also indicated that no public monies could be paid to any person who failed to file an affidavit. Filing a false statement was subject to a fine and the loss of the indi-vidual's teaching license. B. T. Shelton had been employed in the Little Rock Special School District for twenty-five years. In the spring of 1959 he was notified that, before he could be employed for the 1959-60 school year, he had to file the affidavit listing all his memberships over the previous five years. He declined to file the affidavit and his contract for the next school year was not renewed. The other petitioners in this case were Max Carr, an associate professor at the University of Arkansas, and Ernest T. Gephardt, a teacher at Central High School in Little Rock. Each refused to file the required affidavit. Both were advised that their failure to comply with the law would result in the curtailment of their employment. Shelton, Carr, and Gephardt initiated court action which ultimately reached the high Court.

Citing Adler, the Court affirmed that "there can be no doubt of the right of a state to investigate the competence and fitness of those whom it hires to teach in its schools. " The Court ruled (5-4), however, that the Arkansas law was "un-limited and indiscriminate. " The law required a teacher to list "every conceivable kind of associational tie--social, pro-fessional, political, avocational, or religious, " many of which might "have no possible bearing upon the teacher's occupa-tional competence or fitness. " In Shelton, even though the government's purpose was substantial, the means of achieving that purpose stifled personal liberty. The Court held the act unconstitutional because its "comprehensive interference with associational freedom" went beyond what could be justified in the exercise of a state's "inquiry into the fitness and compe-tency of its teachers. "

Cramp v. Board of Public Instruction of Orange County,
Florida 368 U. S. 278 (1961)

The loyalty oath was a method of checking specific
memberships of teachers. During the 1960s the Court struck
down several statutes which established such oaths. One involved a Florida statute which required each state employee to
take a written oath in which he swore that he had never lent
his "aid, support, advice, counsel or influence to the Communist Party. " In 1959, an employee was discharged for failure
to subscribe to the oath. After David Cramp had been employed
for more than nine years as a public school teacher in Orange
County, it was discovered that he had never taken the oath.
When requested to do so, he refused. He asked for a judgment
declaring the oath requirement unconstitutional.

The U. S. Supreme Court, in a unanimous decision,
noted that the issue was whether a state could compel employees to swear to a loyalty oath. The Court, pointing to
the ambiguity of the Florida act, stated that anyone who takes
the oath had to swear that they have never lent their "aid, " or
"support, " or "counsel, " or "influence, " to the Communist
Party.

> What do these phrases mean? In the not too distant
> past the Communist Party candidates appeared regu-
> larly and legally on the ballot in many state and local
> elections. Elsewhere the Communist Party has on
> occasion endorsed or supported candidates nominated
> by others. Could one who had ever cast his vote
> for such a candidate safely subscribe to this oath?
> Could a lawyer who had ever represented the Com-
> munist Party or its members swear with either con-
> fidence or honesty that he had never knowingly lent
> his counsel to the Party? Could a journalist who had
> ever defended the constitutional rights of the Com-
> munist Party conscientiously take an oath that he had
> never lent the Party his support? Indeed, could any-
> one honestly subscribe to this oath who had ever sup-
> ported any cause with contemporaneous knowledge
> that the Communist Party also supported it?

The Court concluded that "The very absurdity of these possi-
bilities brings into focus the extraordinary ambiguity of the
statutory language. " In this case, while the Court found the
language of the Florida act unconstitutionally vague, it did not
confront the more general issue of the constitutionality of
loyalty oaths.

Baggett v. Bullitt 377 U. S. 360 (1964)

A similar case came before the Court in 1964. All teaching personnel at the University of Washington were required by the Board of Regents to: 1) swear allegiance to the Constitution, laws, and institutions of the United States and of the state of Washington, and 2) disclaim membership in the Communist Party or any other subversive organization. Lawrence Baggett and sixty-three other members of the faculty, staff, and student body brought an action seeking a court judgment declaring unconstitutional the statute which required the execution of the oath.

The U. S. Supreme Court held (7-2) the loyalty oath unconstitutional because the language of the statute on which the oath was based was unduly vague, uncertain, and broad. In fact, the statute was subject to the same sort of inquiry posed by the Court in Cramp. The Court concluded that the statute forbade conduct in terms so vague that men of common intelligence had necessarily to guess at its meaning and understandably differ as to its application.

Keyishian v. Board of Regents 385 U. S. 589 (1967)

In 1967 the Court again demonstrated its reluctance to decide conclusively whether loyalty oaths were legitimate. In 1962 the University of Buffalo was merged into the State University. Thereupon, teachers at the University of Buffalo became state employees, and their continued employment was conditioned upon their willingness to sign the Feinberg certificate, indicating that they were not Communists and that if they had ever been one, they had communicated that fact to the President of the University. Harry Keyishian, an instructor in English, refused to sign the certificate. Keyishian's one-year contract was not renewed. He brought action to determine the constitutionality of the law.

The U. S. Supreme Court found (5-4) that the New York statute swept overly-broad into association which could not be proscribed. Disqualification arising from proof of mere membership could be rebutted, but only by a denial of membership, a denial that the organization advocated the overthrow of the government by force, or a denial that the teacher had knowledge of such advocacy. Proof of nonactive membership or a showing by the teacher of the absence of any intent to further unlawful aims could not be used against dismissal. The Court

found the act invalid because it proscribed mere knowing membership without any showing of specific intent to further the
unlawful aims of the Communist Party.

Whitehill v. Elkins 389 U. S. 54 (1967)

The final case to be considered in this section involved
the Maryland loyalty oath. Howard Whitehill was offered a
teaching position with the University of Maryland. However,
he refused to take an oath pledging that he was "not engaged in
one way or another in the attempt to overthrow the Government
of the United States, or the State of Maryland, or any political
subdivision of either of them, by force or violence." The
question of this oath's constitutionality reached the Supreme
Court.

The Court was concerned with the ambiguity of the act.
The justices asked,

> Would a member of a group that was out to overthrow
> the Government by force or violence be engaged in
> that attempt in one way or another within the meaning
> of the oath, even though he was ignorant of the real
> aims of the group and wholly innocent of any illicit
> purpose? We do not know; nor could a prospective
> employee know, save as he risked a prosecution for
> perjury.

The Court ruled (6-3) that "the continuing surveillance which
this type of law places on teachers is hostile to academic
freedom." The Court then overturned the Maryland loyalty
oath.

In all cases cited in this section, the Court seemed to
support the general right of a city or state legislature to inquire into the fitness of its public school teachers. But the
Court has been very rigid as to the specific means that tests
of fitness may include. In Slochower and Beilan, the Court
opposed any effort to penalize a teacher for merely invoking the
Fifth Amendment. In Wieman, an Oklahoma law was found to
violate due process because it did not acknowledge that association with a subversive organization might be innocent. In
Shelton, an Arkansas statute was declared unconstitutional because it required a teacher to reveal associational ties that
could have no bearing whatsoever upon a teacher's fitness.
Finally, in Cramp, Baggett, Keyishian, and Whitehill, the

Court overturned compulsory loyalty oaths. Such oaths, as a condition of employment, were so ambiguous that a person of average intelligence would have to guess at their meaning. It does appear, however, that the Court would support state inquiry into teacher fitness if conducted in a legal manner; that is, without ambiguity, discrimination, or overbreadth.

Campus Speakers

During the late 1960s and early 1970s several cases were decided by state courts which involved campus bans on outside speakers. In these cases, the courts consistently struck down university regulations that were vague or overbroad, and thereby helped to strengthen the freedom of expression and association on college and university campuses.

Dickson v. Sitterson 415 F. 2d 228 (1969)

In 1966, Paul Dickson, a student at the University of North Carolina, and thirteen other persons protested against section 1207 of the 1963 North Carolina Session Laws, commonly referred to as the "speakers ban" law. The law, regulating visiting speakers, forbade state-supported colleges or universities from allowing any person to use its facilities who: 1) was a known member of the Communist Party, 2) was known to advocate the overthrow of the constitutions of the United States or of North Carolina, or 3) had pleaded the Fifth Amendment in refusing to answer any question with respect to communist or subversive connections or activities, before a legislative committee, judicial tribunal, or executive or administrative board. Early in 1966, Frank Wilkinson and Herbert Aptheker were invited to speak on campus under the sponsorship of the Students for a Democratic Society (SDS). Wilkinson had previously pleaded the Fifth Amendment in refusing to answer questions asked him by a California Legislative committee. Aptheker was the Director of the American Institute for Marxist Studies, a communist organization. The Chairman of the Board of Trustees, Governor Dan Moore, denied permission to SDS. Moore said, "it should be obvious to everyone that the invitation under consideration was made in an effort to create controversy for the sake of controversy and not for any legitimate educational purpose." The invitations were made anyway. The SDS members requested permission to have the guest speakers admitted on campus, but a sharply divided student-faculty advisory committee recommended that permission not be granted. Wilkinson subsequently gave his talk on a side-walk, but was asked by some students to give it later that evening in Carroll Hall Auditorium. At 7:30 Wilkinson arrived at the auditorium and was asked to leave by a policeman. He did so. A week later Aptheker was to speak and was similarly told to leave by a police officer. Aptheker delivered his talk outside university property but was unable to be heard over the sounds of traffic. After being denied permission once again, the SDS members sued, claiming the law was unconstitutional.

The U.S. District Court said that universities and colleges have the right to promulgate and enforce rules governing the appearance of all guest speakers. No one has an absolute right to speak on campus. Yet, the court ruled that the North Carolina law and the regulations adopted by the Board of Trustees were facially unconstitutional because of vagueness. The effect of the law was to prohibit rather than regulate. The first provision concerning "known party members" came under attack because it failed to identify who the member was known by, and to what extent. The second provision failed to distinguish between advocacy of doctrine and advocacy combining force or violence. Any statute which forbids an act in terms so vague that men of common intelligence must guess at its meaning and application violates the due process clause of the Fourteenth Amendment. The third provision failed to clearly define "subversive connections" and violated the intent of the Fifth Amendment itself, by invoking sanctions for the exercise of the privilege. For these reasons, the North Carolina regulation was overturned.

Stacy v. Williams 306 F. Supp 963 (1970)

Later that year, a U.S. District Court extended freedom of speech by similarly declaring a speaker regulation as vague and exceeding constitutionally permissible limits on speech. Two similar cases were consolidated for the trial. One was instituted by student members of the University of Mississippi chapter of the Young Democratic Clubs of Mississippi (YDCM), the Institute of Civics, and the University of Mississippi chapter of the American Association of University Professors. They complained about the denial by the Board of Trustees of a request for a campus speech by Aaron Henry at a special civic program. The other case was also instituted by student representatives of the YDCM. They complained of refusal of a request for a campus address by Charles Evers in support of the Hubert Humphrey-Edmund Muskie 1968 Democratic presidential ticket.

The court acknowledged that the freedoms of speech and assembly occupied a "preferred position" among constitutional liberties but they "may not be exercised on public property without regard to its primary usage." However, the court attacked the discriminatory effect of the Mississippi regulation. Speaker regulations, by their very nature, are prior restraints, and must be narrowly drafted so as to suppress only that speech which presents a "clear and present danger" of substantive evil. The substantive evil must be extremely serious and the degree of imminence extremely high before utterances could be banned. Moreover, the distinction must be made between advocacy of action and advocacy of doctrine. The court admitted that the Board had rule-making power, but said that the power was not constitutionally exercised in this particular instance. The court then fashioned a set of rules which would govern campus speaker policy at the University of Mississippi until such time as the Board would formulate its own acceptable set of standards. The court limited the issuance of invitations to outside speakers according to six provisions: 1) any request had to be made by a bona fide student or faculty group, 2) no invitation could be sent without prior written permission from the head of the school, 3) any request had to include, in writing, the name of the sponsoring group, the proposed date, time, and location, the expected size of the audience, and topic of the speech, 4) a request could only be denied by the head of an institution if the proposed speech would constitute a clear and present danger to orderly operation, 5) a campus review committee, composed of three faculty and two students, would hear the appeal of an aggrieved sponsoring group; further appeal could be sought through the courts, and 6) upon approval of the speaker, the sponsoring organization had to, in writing, signify whether the invitation was accepted, and when. These rules would be applicable to later state cases involving the regulation of campus speakers.

Molpus v. Fortune 311 F. Supp 240 (1970)

The case of Molpus v. Fortune involved action by a student group to obtain an order requiring the University of Mississippi to grant permission to invite a speaker on campus. The rules set forth in Stacy were still in effect, since the Board of Trustees had not acted to formulate any rules

governing campus speakers. David Molpus and other members of the University of Mississippi chapter of the Young
Democratic Clubs of Mississippi (YDCM) requested permission
to invite Tyronne Gettis, President of the student body at
Mississippi Valley State College, to speak on campus. Gettis
had previously led a student revolt at the State College. The
request was denied by Chancellor Porter Fortune. The Chancellor believed that Gettis' appearance would constitute a clear
and present danger to the institution's orderly operation because of the likelihood that Gettis would advocate damage to
school property, seizure of buildings, forcible interference
with regularly scheduled classes, or campus disorder of a
violent nature. A second request was also rejected. A suit
was filed to obtain a temporary restraining order requiring the
University to grant permission for Gettis to speak.

The court argued that the burden of proof in this case
rested with university officials to show clearly that Gettis'
speech would constitute a clear and present danger. Even
though Gettis had a questionable reputation, the evidence did
not show he ever destroyed property or harmed any person.
The question of whether Gettis' appearance would constitute a
clear and present danger depended on whether he would advocate disorder or violence and urge the group to imminent lawless action. The court noted that Gettis had proposed to limit
his speech to a discussion of the crisis at the State College
as viewed by him as a student leader. Since it did not appear
that Gettis would advocate campus disorder of a violent nature,
it was unlikely that a "reasonable probability" of a clear and
present danger existed. University officials were directed to
approve the request.

Brooks v. Auburn University 296 F. Supp 188 (1969)

In another state case the court overturned a strict Auburn University speaker regulation because of vagueness and
overbreadth. The court noted that the guidelines used by President Harry M. Philpott constituted blatant political censorship.
The situation began when a written request for $650 to pay
Reverend William Sloan Coffin to speak on campus was approved by the university's Public Affairs Seminar Board, and
Coffin was invited to speak on campus. Philpott, however,
would not allow Coffin to appear. Prior to the invitation, Auburn had no written or orally announced policy regarding campus speakers. Several speakers, including George and Lurleen
Wallace, and Whitney Young, appeared at university expense

during the previous several years. Philpott argued that Coffin would not be allowed because he might advocate breaking the law, and because he was convicted recently for conspiracy to counsel and aid young men in resisting the Vietnam draft. Philpott personally established a written set of guidelines for issuing invitations to outside speakers: 1) speakers should be selected on the basis of their contribution to the goals of the university, 2) no invitations would be extended to those who advocated disregard for the laws or the violent overthrow of the government, and 3) the university would make every attempt to present opposing viewpoints on controversial issues. Larry Brooks and seven other students and faculty members at Auburn sought a preliminary injunction restraining the university from interfering with Coffin's scheduled appearance.

The court noted that there was no evidence that Coffin's appearance would unduly interfere with the discipline or orderly operation of Auburn: "In short, the basic reasons Dr. Philpott advances in support of his decision are based upon a philosophical concept and his decision in this matter constitutes a philosophical decision." Prior restraints on speech cannot be made unless there is a clear and present danger to the university. According to the court, the university could not withhold funds for no constitutionally acceptable reason, as a censorship device. Also, the President of the university could not regulate the content of ideas students may hear. Finally, the criminal prosecution against the speaker could not be used as a justification to prohibit his appearance. The court stressed that "there is no relationship between a speaker's criminal conviction--especially one on appeal--and the value of his words to the listener." More importantly, however, the court objected to Philpott's unabashed censorship of views that "Auburn could not sanction." The court concluded, "In plain words these regulations must fall because they constitute blatant political censorship." President Philpott's regulations were not only vague, but dangerous as well.

Duke v. State of Texas 327 F. Supp 1218 (1971)

Two years later, another speaker regulation was overturned. Herb Ninness, a student at North Texas State University, asked Elizabeth Duke and David Haylon to speak at a rally to protest military activities in Southeast Asia. The student senate passed a resolution supporting the rally. Ninness requested formal authorization to allow the rally to be held but the President's Cabinet denied the request, claiming that it was not "sponsored" by the Senate or any other recognized campus organization. The senators then passed a resolution sponsoring the rally. By this time the administration was actively seeking an injunction against Duke and Haylon. Around noon on February 17, 1971, the rally began, but shortly thereafter a temporary restraining order was served on Mrs. Duke. Both she and Haylon spoke and were subsequently arrested for contempt. They appealed, arguing that the university's security regulations concerning speakers were overly vague.

The court decided that the university's outside speaker regulations only partially conformed to the standards approved in Stacy. The regulations were condemned for the following reasons: 1) they did not have a provision providing that a request for an outside speaker not acted on in four days will be granted, 2) they did not adequately define impermissible advocacy, 3) they placed the responsibility for any violation of law arising from a meeting with an outside speaker on the sponsoring organization and its members, rather than on the speaker, 4) they failed to clarify which administrative officer was to approve an invitation for a speaker, 5) there was no evidence of any student-faculty review committee, and 6) there was reason to doubt whether the university policies, and the forms necessary to implement them, were adequately available to the students and the general public. Furthermore, the court objected to the language of the campus regulations: specifically, "persons having no legitimate business" and "an undesirable person." The court then noted "that the emphasized words do not give the fair notice of proscribed conduct required by the Due Process Clause and that they give unbridled discretion to administrative officers...." In overturning the regulations, the court noted that there was no evidence that either Duke or Haylon had made any "significant contribution to allegedly disruptive activity." The temporary restraining order and the resulting contempt convictions were declared constitutionally invalid.

In this section, the cases of Dickson, Stacy, Molpus, Brooks and Duke all contain the same theme: university regulations on outside speakers that are unduly vague or overbroad will be overturned by the courts. Even though the courts recognize the legitimate interest of universities in providing an educational atmosphere free from discord and violence, the regulations themselves must be sufficiently precise. Any system of prior restraints is viewed with caution. Any denial of the exercise of speech, or of listening as in Molpus, must be based on substantial proof that a clear and present danger to the orderly operation of the university would be engendered. Regulations must be drafted so as to give the minimum of discretion to those who will implement them. In Stacy, the court formulated a set of rules which constitute acceptable guidelines that a college or university might follow in regulating campus speakers.

Banned Books

During the past few decades, groups have attempted to remove certain books from school classrooms and libraries. In the 1950s super-patriotic organizations compiled lists of "undesirable" books which, supposedly, expressed a communistic philosophy or which contained subversive ideas. In the 1960s civil rights groups sought to keep from school children any books that pictured minority groups in an unfavorable light. In the 1970s parents and school boards seek to censor "obscene" and "vulgar" books.

Even though efforts to ban "offensive" books have been commonplace in U. S. history, few such instances have reached the courts. The case considered next, however, sheds some light on the U. S. Supreme Court's position on banning books from school libraries.

Presidents Council, District 25 v. Community School Board No. 25 409 U.S. 998 (1972)

A novel entitled Down These Mean Streets, by Piri Thomas, was purchased by the librarians of three junior high schools in School District 25 in Queens, New York. The book describes, in graphic detail, sexual activities and drug uses that are a part of everyday life for residents of Spanish Harlem. The scene is very depressing. The book was ordered to acquaint the predominantly white, middle-class youth of Queens with the problems of their contemporaries who live in this environment. Some parents objected to the book, and after a public meeting the School Board voted five-to-three to ban it from the libraries. Later, the Board allowed the book to remain on the shelves for direct loan to any parent who wanted his children to read it. No child could borrow it directly. A suit was initiated by a principal, a librarian, and some parents and children who all sought to have the Board's resolution declared unconstitutional and the book placed in circulation.

Before the U. S. Court of Appeals, the Board contended that a book with such vivid accounts of sordid and perverted occurrences was not good for junior high students. The court upheld the authority of the Board for selection of library holdings. The court noted that the action of the Board did not preclude the teacher from discussing the book in class or from assigning it for outside reading. A parent may borrow it if he wants his child to read it. The Board did not violate any First Amendment freedoms. The court set forth the following position:

> The ensuing shouts of book burning, witch hunting, and violation of academic freedom hardly elevate this intramural strife to first amendment constitutional proportions. If it did, there would be a constant intrusion of the judiciary into the internal affairs of the school. Academic freedom is scarcely fostered by the intrusion of three or even nine federal jurists making curriculum or library choices for the community of scholars.

In 1972, the U. S. Supreme Court, with Justice Douglas writing a strong dissent, denied certiorari. It would appear then, that the Court lent its approval to a school board's decision to ban a book from a school library.

STUDENT RIGHTS

During the second half of the 1960s an intense effort took place to convert educational institutions into agencies of social and political action. Many citizens in the community were shocked at this trend to move the school away from its traditional role as an apolitical place of learning and scholarship. A central issue within this setting was the extent to which students could organize and protest specific interests. Occasionally, the courts became the final determiner of student rights.

Armbands and Buttons

In some cases, the courts had to decide whether students could wear bands or buttons at school. In the classic case of Tinker, the U. S. Supreme Court set forth some ideas that were debated in later state court decisions.

Tinker v. Des Moines Independent Community School District
393 U. S. 503 (1969)

The specific facts of this case were discussed in Chapter II. School children were suspended for refusing to remove black armbands they were wearing to protest American involvment in Vietnam. The parents sued, seeking an injunction which would restrain school officials from punishing their children.

The U. S. Supreme Court noted (7-2) that school officials do not hold absolute power over the students. Under the Constitution, students are "persons," and they cannot be treated as "closed-circuit recipients of only that which the State chooses to communicate." In the majority opinion, Justice Fortas argued,

> Schools exist to carry out educational benefits at several levels one of which involves the interpersonal communication among the students. Whenever a student is at school no matter what the hour or the activity that student is free to express his or her views as long as they do not materially and substantially interfere with the operation of the school.

In this instance, no such interference was evident. The Court thus acknowledged that students have common rights of expression within the educational institution.

Guzick v. Drebus 431 F. 2d 594 (1970)

One year later, a federal court commented on the Tinker decision. On March 11, 1969, Thomas Guzick, Jr., a seventeen-year-old eleventh-grade student at Shaw High School, and another student appeared at the principal's office. They brought with them a supply of pamphlets which advocated attendance at a Chicago antiwar demonstration. The boys were denied permission to distribute the pamphlets, and were also instructed to remove the buttons which both were wearing. The legend on the buttons was:

> April 5 Chicago
> GI - Civilian
> Anti-War
> Demonstration
> Student Mobilization Committee

Guzick said that his lawyer told him that a United States Supreme Court decision entitled him to wear the button in school. The principal suspended the boys and advised them that the suspension would continue until they removed the buttons. The other student complied and returned to school. Guzick started action, asking that he be allowed to attend school wearing the button, that it be declared he had a constitutional right to do so, and that damages of $1,000 be assessed for each day of school he missed as a result of the principal's order.

The court differentiated this case from Tinker. In Guzick, the principal applied a long-standing rule; the wearing of buttons, badges, scarves, and other means whereby the wearers identified themselves as supporters of a particular cause, or which contained messages unrelated to education, were prohibited. Support for the high-school athletic teams, the drama club, or the like, were allowed. The rule had been uniformly enforced. The rule was established because buttons were thought to encourage division among students; they identify the wearer as a member of a particular group or the supporter of a particular cause. This, it was claimed, sets a student apart from other students wearing different buttons, or those without buttons. It magnifies the differences between students, emphasizes these differences, and polarizes the students into separate, distinct, and unfriendly groups. In recent years, black and white students had attempted to wear buttons expressing racially inflammatory messages. For these reasons, Shaw High officials enforced the anti-button rule. On the other hand, Tinker involved a situation where school authorities did not prohibit the wearing of all symbols of political or controversial significance--only the black armbands worn in opposition to the Vietnam War.

Also distinguishing Tinker from Guzick were the respective settings. No potential racial collisions were evident in Tinker, whereas the changing racial composition of Shaw High School from all white to seventy per cent black made the no-symbol rule considerably more important for maintaining order. According to the court, enforcing this unoppressive rule would serve the goal of meaningful integration of the public schools. The court concluded,

> We must be aware in these contentious times that America's classrooms and their environs will lose their usefulness as places in which to educate our young people if pupils come to school wearing the

badges of their respective disagreements, and provoke confrontations with their fellows and their
teachers.   The buttons are claimed to be a form of
speech.   Unless they have some relevance to what
is being considered or taught, a school classroom
is no place for the untrammeled exercise of such
rights. . . .

The anti-button policy at Shaw High School was upheld.

Printed Matter

During the years of protest against racial discrimination in America and participation in the war in Southeast Asia,
students utilized various forms of printed material.   Leaflets,
posters, pamphlets, even school newspapers were employed in
the interest of specific causes.   Accordingly, most schools
formulated regulations which governed the use of printed matter.

Eisner v. Stamford Board of Education 440 F. 2d 803 (1971)

On November 18, 1969, the Board of Education of
Stamford, Connecticut, adopted the following policy:

> The board of education desires to encourage freedom
> of expression and creativity by its students subject
> to the following limitations:
> No person shall distribute any printed or written
> matter on the grounds of any school or in any school
> building unless the distribution of such material shall
> have prior approval by the school administration.
> In granting or denying approval, the following
> guidelines shall apply.
> No material shall be distributed, which, either by
> its content or by the manner of distribution itself,
> will interfere with the proper and orderly operation
> and discipline of the school, will cause violence or
> disorder, or will constitute an invasion of the rights
> of others.

Some students at Rippowam High School in Stamford wanted to
distribute a mimeographed newspaper as well as other printed
literature which they had prepared.   They brought suit.

First, the court reaffirmed "the oft-stressed and carefully worded dictum in the leading precedent, Tinker ... that
protected speech in public secondary schools may be forbidden
if school authorities reasonably 'forecast substantial disruption
of or material interference with school activities. '" In evaluating the specific Stamford regulations, the court in Eisner
noted that "the policy criteria by which school authorities may
prevent students from distributing literature on school property
departs in no significant respect from the similarly very general and broad instruction of Tinker itself. " In general, the
Eisner court held that prior restraints requiring official approval before distribution of underground student newspapers
were constitutional. The court stressed that requiring the
prior submission of publications must be accompanied by elabo-
rate procedural safeguards.

The court then declared the Stamford policy unconstitutional and spelled out three specific deficiencies. First, it
failed to provide an expeditious review procedure. The policy
prescribed no period of time in which school officials had to
decide whether or not to permit distribution. To be valid, a
regulation must prescribe a definite brief period within which
review of submitted material will be completed. Second, the
policy failed to specify to whom and how material may be submitted for clearance. Without such specifications, students
are unreasonably prevented from distributing any written material because the statement leaves them ignorant of clearance
procedures. Finally, the proscription against "distributing"
material without prior consent was unconstitutionally vague.
The term "distributing" could mean nothing more than one
student passing to a fellow student a copy of a newspaper or
magazine, for example, Time or Newsweek. If students were
required to secure prior approval before passing notes to each
other in the hallways, or exchanging newspapers among themselves, "the resultant burden on speech might very likely outweigh the very remote possibility that such activities would
ever cause disruption. " Because of the three specific procedural deficiencies, the court enjoined enforcement of the Stamford policy for regulating printed matter.

Fujishima v. Board of Education 460 F. 2d 1355 (1972)

In Fujishima, the court disagreed with the Eisner
court's interpretation of Tinker. Section 6-19 of the rules of
the Chicago Board of Education provided that "No person shall
be permitted ... to distribute on the school premises any

books, tracts, or other publications ... unless the same shall
have been approved by the General Superintendent of Schools. "
Burt Fujishima and Richard Peluso were seniors at Lane
Technical High School. They were suspended for four and
seven days respectively for distributing about 350 copies of
The Cosmic Frog, an "underground" newspaper that they published. The papers were distributed free of charge both before
and between classes and during lunch breaks. Robert Balanoff, a sophomore at Bowen High School, was suspended for
two days for giving another student an unsigned copy of a
petition calling for "teach-ins" regarding the Vietnam War.
The exchange occurred in a school corridor between classes.
A few months later, Balanoff was suspended for five days for
distributing leaflets about the war to between fifteen and twenty
students. This distribution took place during a fire drill,
while the students were in their assigned places across the
street from the school. The three high school students,
Fujishima, Peluso and Balanoff, sought relief in the courts.

     The Chicago Board of Education argued that section
6-19 was constitutionally permissible because it did not require approval of the content of a publication before it could
be distributed. However, according to the court, that was
neither what the rule said nor how the schools had previously
interpreted it.

> The Superintendent must approve 'the same,' which
> refers back to 'any books, tracts, or other publica-
> tions. ' The superintendent cannot perform his duty
> under the rule without having the publication sub-
> mitted to him. The principals believed the rule
> requires approval of the publication itself: the Fuji-
> shima and Peluso suspensions were for 'distribution
> of unauthorized material in the school'; the Balanoff
> suspensions were for 'distribution of unauthorized
> materials in the school building' and for 'distributing
> unapproved literature in class during fire drill. '

Because section 6-19 required prior approval of publications,
it was declared unconstitutional as a prior restraint in violation of the First Amendment. The judges then expressed their
belief that the Eisner court erred "in interpreting Tinker to
allow prior restraint on publication--long a constitutionally
prohibited power--as a tool of school officials in 'forecasting'
substantial disruption of school activities. "

     Tinker in no way suggests that students may be

required to announce their intentions of engaging in
certain conduct beforehand so school authorities may
decide whether to prohibit the conduct.   Such a concept of prior restraint is even more offensive when
applied to the long-protected area of publication.

According to the court in Fujishima, the Tinker forecast rule
was designed as a formula for determining when the requirements of school discipline justify punishment of students for
exercise of their First Amendment rights.   It was not a ration-
ale "for establishing a system of censorship and licensing designed to prevent the exercise of First-Amendment rights. "

In Fujishima, the court declared section 6-19 unconstitutional.   The court did, however, indicate that the Chicago
Board of Education could promulgate "reasonable, specific
regulations setting forth the time, manner and place in which
distribution of written materials may occur. " In adopting a
set of regulations, the Board had the burden of telling students
when, how, and where they may distribute literature.   The
Board may then punish students who violate the regulations.
The Board may also establish a provision punishing students
who publish and disseminate any obscene or libelous materials
on school grounds.

In Tinker, the Court upheld the right of students to
express their opinions as long as they do not interfere with
the operation of the school.   Yet, because of the vagueness
of the Tinker formula describing exactly what constitutes interference and disruption, state courts applied Tinker inconsis-
tently in Guzick, Eisner, and Fujishima.

Dickey v. Alabama State Board of Education 273 F. Supp 613
(1967)

The remaining cases in this section concern the First
Amendment rights of college and university students.   In
April, 1967, Dr. Frank Rose, President of the University of
Alabama, came under attack by Alabama state legislators for
his refusal to censor the University of Alabama student publication, Emphasis 67, A World in Revolution.   The publication
carried excerpts from the speeches of Bettina Aptheker, a
Communist who gained notoriety at the University of California, and Stokely Carmichael, President of the Student Nonviolent Coordinating Committee.   To provide a balanced view of
a "world in revolution, " Emphasis carried articles by notable

anti-revolutionists such as General Earl G. Wheeler, Chairman of the Joint Chiefs of Staff. In the face of public criticism by some state legislators, Dr. Rose took a public stand in support of the right of the academic freedom of students. Criticism of Dr. Rose for this position by certain state legislators became rather intense. State newspapers publicized the controversy to such an extent that it became a matter of public interest throughout Alabama.

During the early part of the 1966-67 school year, Gary Clinton Dickey, a full-time student at Troy State College, was chosen as an editor of the student newspaper, The Tropolitan. Dickey determined that the paper should take a position in regard to the Emphasis controversy. He prepared and presented to the faculty advisor an editorial supporting the position taken by Dr. Rose. He was instructed not to publish the editorial. A policy at Troy State, "Adam's rule," prohibited any editorials in the school paper that were critical of the Governor or the Alabama legislature. Dickey published the editorial. Because he acted contrary to the advice of the faculty advisor and Troy State President Adams, he was accused of "willful and deliberate insubordination." On this basis, Dickey was denied admission to Troy State College beginning with the fall quarter of 1967.

The court noted that a state cannot force a college student to forfeit his constitutionally protected right of freedom of expression as a condition for his attending a state-supported institution. The court ruled that the action taken by Troy State College was unconstitutional, and was therefore rescinded.

Papish v. Board of Curators of the University of Missouri
410 U.S. 667 (1973)

In a 1973 case, the Court considered the rights of students and the issue of obscenity. Barbara Papish, a graduate student in Journalism at the University of Missouri, was expelled for distributing a newspaper "containing forms of indecent speech." The newspaper, Free Press Underground, had been sold on campus for more than four years. The particular issue in question was unacceptable for two reasons. First, on the front cover the publishers had reproduced a political cartoon depicting a policeman raping the Statue of Liberty and the Goddess of Justice. The caption read, "With Liberty and Justice for All." Secondly, the issue contained an article entitled "Mother-Fucker Acquitted," which discussed the trial and acquittal on an assault charge of a New York City youth who was a member of an organization known as "Up Against the Wall, Mother-Fucker. " Following a hearing, the Student Conduct Committee found that Miss Papish had violated the General Standards of Student Conduct which required students "to observe generally accepted standards of conduct" and specifically prohibited "indecent conduct or speech. " Her dismissal was affirmed first by the Chancellor and then by the Board of Curators. She was not given credit for a course in which she achieved a passing grade during that semester. She claimed that the dismissal violated the First Amendment.

Before the U.S. Supreme Court, the main issue was whether the material was obscene. In a minority report, Chief Justice Warren Burger argued that "To preclude a university or college from regulating the distribution of such obscene materials does not protect the values inherent in the First Amendment; rather, it demeans those values. " William Rehnquist held that the public use of the word "mother-fucker" is "lewd and obscene. " The Court majority (6-3), however, felt that neither the political cartoon nor the headline story could be labeled as constitutionally obscene or otherwise unprotected. The university was ordered to award Miss Papish any course credits she earned for the semester and to reinstate her as a student in the graduate program.

Organization

The right and ability of students to form associations was fundamental for conducting effective protests during the 1960s and 1970s. School officials formulated regulations designed to control the membership and activities of campus groups. In 1972 a case dealing with this issue reached the U.S. Supreme Court.

Healy v. James 408 U.S. 169 (1972)

In 1969, unrest prevailed on numerous college campuses. Vandalism, arson, seizure of buildings, and demonstrations were commonplace. Records and files were rampaged. Some colleges and universities shut down altogether. A major force in the student activism of the period was Students for a Democratic Society (SDS). In September, 1969, students at Central Connecticut State College (CCSC), a state-supported institution, attempted to organize a local chapter of

SDS. Following the requirements of the college, the students filed a request with the Student Affairs Committee for official recognition as a campus organization. The request listed three purposes for the organization: 1) to provide "a forum of discussion and self-education for students developing an analysis of American society, " 2) to serve as "an agency for integrating thought with action so as to bring about constructive changes, " and 3) to provide a "coordinating body for relating the problems of leftist students" with other interested groups on campus and in the community. The Student Affairs Committee expressed concern that the group might become associated with the national SDS organization. The students, however, stated that their group would remain completely independent of any national organization. By a vote of six to two the committee approved the application and recommended to Dr. F. Don James, President of the College, that the organization be given official recognition. The committee recommendation warned the SDS that immediate suspension would be considered if the group's activities interfered with the privacy of other students or caused the destruction of property.

Several days later, President James rejected the recommendation and issued a statement denying official campus recognition to the proposed SDS group. He indicated that the organization's philosophy was opposed to CCSC's policies, that the group's independence from the national organization was doubtful, and that approval should not be granted to a group that "openly repudiates" the school's dedication to academic freedom. The group's survival was almost impossible without official recognition. The members were not allowed to place announcements regarding meetings or other activities in the student newspaper. They could not post notices on campus bulletin boards. Most important, they were forbidden the use of campus facilities for holding meetings. The members of the organization initiated suit in the courts.

The U. S. Supreme Court, in a unanimous opinion, noted that freedom of association had long been implicit in the freedoms of speech, assembly and petition. In this case, the denial of official recognition burdened and abridged that right of association. First Amendment principles were clearly denied to the group, but since the Court could not decide from the record whether the students were willing to abide by reasonable campus regulations, the case was remanded for reconsideration. By way of instruction, the Court stated that a college administration could impose a requirement that the group affirm in advance its willingness to obey reasonable

campus laws, as a condition for official recognition. Participation in the internal life of a college community may be denied
to an organization that reserves the right to violate any valid
campus regulation.

Due Process

Two cases heard by the U. S. Supreme Court in 1975
established the right to due process in disciplinary actions
taken by authorities against students.

Goss v. Lopez 419 U. S. 565 (1975)

Dwight Lopez and other high school students from Columbus, Ohio, were suspended from school for misconduct for
up to ten days without a hearing. The suspensions occurred
during a period of widespread student unrest during February
and March of 1971. The students brought action against the
school officials on the grounds that the Ohio statute permitting
such suspensions was unconstitutional.

The U. S. Supreme Court upheld (5-4) a lower court
finding that the students were denied due process of law because they were "suspended without hearing prior to suspension
or within a reasonable time thereafter." The Ohio regulations
were unconstitutional in permitting such suspensions. School
officials were ordered to remove all references to the suspensions from school records. In its decision, the Court made
it clear that students facing temporary suspension qualified for
protection of the due process clause. Even in the instance of
suspension of ten days or less, the student must be given oral
or written notice of the charges against him, and if he denies
them, an explanation of the evidence the officials have and an
opportunity to present his side of the case. The Court indicated
that in the vast majority of such cases the disciplinarian could
informally discuss the allegations with the student minutes after
it had occurred. In the Court's opinion, however, "The Clause
requires at least these rudimentary precautions against unfair
or mistaken findings of misconduct and arbitrary exclusion
from school."

Wood v. Strickland 420 U. S. 308 (1975)

The due process rights of students were extended by

the Court one month later. Peggy Strickland and Virginia Crain, tenth-grade students at Mena (Arkansas) Public High School, were expelled for violating a school regulation prohibiting the use or possession of intoxicating beverages at school activities. The girls "spiked" the punch served at a meeting of an extra-curricular school organization attended by parents and students. The meeting took place without incident. The girls admitted their involvement to the teacher, and a few days later to Principal P. T. Waller. He suspended them from school for a maximum two-week period; but after a meeting of the school board, the girls were expelled for the remainder of the semester. The students brought suit against the school officials, claiming that their expulsion infringed upon their right to due process. The Court of Appeals found that the students' rights to "substantive due process" were denied since the decision about expulsion was made on the basis of no evidence that the regulation had been violated.

The U. S. Supreme Court ruled (9-0) that the lower court erred on this issue, and returned the case to the appropriate court. But, the Court also decided (5-4) that a school board member is not immune from liability for damages "if he knew or reasonably should have known that the action he took within his sphere of official responsibility would violate the constitutional rights" of the student, or "if he took the action with the malicious intention to cause a deprivation of constitutional rights or other injury to the student. " In their decision, the Court minority wondered whether Wood, by enhancing the possibility of personal liability, would discourage qualified persons from continuing "in the desired numbers to volunteer for service in public education. "

During the decade of Vietnam War protest, the U. S. Supreme Court heard five major cases involving student rights. In all the cases, the Court upheld the academic freedom of students. In Tinker, the Court acknowledged the right of students to express their views as long as they do not cause substantial disruption or material interference with school activities. In Papish, the Court ruled that the dissemination of ideas, no matter how offensive to good taste, cannot be forbidden on a university campus simply in the name of "decency. " In Healy, the right of students to associate was generally upheld, even though the Court did determine that the university could require an organization to abide by reasonable campus rules. Goss held that before students could be suspended from public schools, they must be given notice of

charges and an opportunity to defend themselves. In Wood,
the Court added that in a student suit against school administrators for violation of civil liberties, the administrators were
not entitled to good faith immunity if they reasonably should
have known that their acts violated the student's constitutional
rights.

FACULTY RIGHTS

In 1915, a handful of scholars founded the American
Association of University Professors (AAUP) to advance the
standards, ideals, and welfare of higher education faculty.
In its "1940 Statement of Principles on Academic Freedom
and Tenure," the organization claimed that a teacher is entitled
to: 1) full freedom in research and in publication of the results, 2) freedom in the classroom in discussing his subject,
and 3) freedom from institutional censorship or discipline when
he communicates as a citizen. The most important function
of the AAUP, over the years, has been to work to have its
policies on such matters as tenure, proper notice, grievance
procedures, extramural statements, and political activity of
professors observed by the country's educational institutions.
When a violation of AAUP principles regarding academic freedom occurs or is alleged, the organization investigates the
situation and, when necessary, censures the institution and
its administration. Most institutions wish to avoid this, so a
real or even an implied threat of censure is usually sufficient
to promote the interests of academic freedom. The AAUP,
however, lacks legal force, such as that held by the courts.
Accordingly, the judicial system has shaped numerous policies
regarding teaching methods, expression of views, and due process.

Teaching Methods

To what extent should a faculty member have freedom
to select classroom materials? Can a school board, principal,
or parent censor certain materials, prohibit particular assign-
ments, or ban specific teaching methods? While a U. S. Supreme Court precedent is not available, the lower courts have
shed some light on this issue.

Keefe v. Geanakos 418 F. 2d 359 (1969)

On the opening day of school in 1969, Robert Keefe

gave to each student in his English class at Ipswich (Massachusetts) High School a copy of the September, 1969 Atlantic
Monthly magazine and assigned the students to read the first
article. Keefe discussed the article, and focused on the word
"mother-fucker," which was used in the piece. Keefe explained
the word's origin and context, and the reasons the author had
included it. Keefe also stated that any student who found the
assignment distasteful could have an alternative one. The next
evening Keefe was called to a meeting of the school committee
and asked to defend his use of the offending word. Following
his explanation, a majority of the committee asked him informally if he would agree not to use it again in the classroom.
He replied that he could not, in good conscience, agree.
Thereafter, Keefe was suspended, and it was proposed that he
should be discharged. He brought action.

The court first analyzed the assigned article, "The
Young and the Old," by Robert J. Lifton, psychiatrist and professor at Yale Medical School. With regard to the word itself, the court thought it was known to many students in the
senior year of high school and was used by young radicals and
protesters from coast to coast. The point of the article rejected, rather than approved, the word's use. The court
agreed that no proper study of the article could avoid consideration of the word. The question facing the court was whether
a teacher may, for educational purposes, quote a "dirty" word,
or whether the shock is too great for high school seniors to
stand. The court noted the lack of judicial precedent on this
issue, and then went on to state that the public regulation of
classroom speech in "the present case demeans any proper
concept of education. The general chilling effect of permitting
such rigorous censorship" was dangerous. Finally, the court
found that no less than five books containing the word in question were available in the school library. It was difficult "to
think that any student could walk into the library and receive
a book, but that his teacher could not subject the content to
serious discussion in class." In light of such inconsistency,
the court supported Keefe's use of the article for his class
assignment.

Parducci v. Rutland 316 F. Supp 352 (1970)

One year later, the question of curriculum control was
raised again. On April 21, 1970, Marilyn Parducci assigned
to her junior English classes a story entitled Welcome to the
Monkey House. The story, a comic satire by Kurt Vonnegut,

was selected to give the students a better understanding of one particular genre of western literature, the short story. The following morning, Parducci was called to Principal Rutland's office for a conference with him and the associate superintendent for the school system. Both administrators expressed their displeasure with the content of the story, which they described as "literary garbage," and with the "philosophy" of the story, which they construed as condoning, if not encouraging, "the killing off of elderly people and free sex." They were concerned that three of Parducci's students had asked to be excused from the assignment and that several disgruntled parents had called to complain. They then admonished Parducci from using the story in any of her classes. Parducci expressed bewilderment at their interpretation of and attitude toward the story. She still considered it to be a good literary work and said she thought that she had a professional obligation to teach the story.

On May 6, the School Board notified Parducci that she had been dismissed from her job for assigning materials which had a "disruptive" effect on the school and for refusing "the counseling and advice of the school principal." The School Board also said that one of the bases for her dismissal was "insubordination," by reason of a statement that she made to the principal that "regardless of their counseling" she "would continue to teach the eleventh-grade English class at the Jeff Davis High School by the use of whatever material" she wanted "and in whatever manner" she thought best. The principal made it clear that Parducci's teaching ability was not an issue; he conceded that she was a good teacher and would have received a favorable evaluation from him at the end of the year but for the single incident which led to her dismissal. Parducci initiated suit, asserting that her dismissal for assigning Welcome to the Monkey House violated her First Amendment right to academic freedom.

The first question answered by the court was whether the assigned reading was inappropriate for high-school juniors. The court found that while the story contained several vulgar terms and a reference to a rape, it was not obscene either under the standards of Roth v. U. S. or the stricter standards for minors set forth in Ginzberg v. New York. The second question was whether there was a substantial threat of disruption. The court noted that the principal testified that only three of the ninety students in the class objected to the assignment. There was no evidence that the assignment created a significant disruption in the educational processes of the school. The court concluded that Parducci's dismissal was an unwarranted invasion of her First Amendment right to academic freedom. It was ordered that Parducci be reinstated as a teacher for the duration of her contract, with the same rights and privileges which attached to her status prior to her illegal suspension. It was also ordered that she be paid her regular salary for both the period during which she was suspended and for the remaining period of her contract.

Mailloux V. Kiley 323 F. Supp 1387 (1971)

One year later, another case involving vulgar terms came before the courts. Roger Mailloux taught basic English to a class of about twenty-five students, boys and girls sixteen and seventeen years of age, all in their junior year at Lawrence (Massachusetts) High School. Mailloux assigned portions of a novel, The Thread That Runs So True, by Jesse Stuart. The novel describes experiences of the author as a young country school teacher in rural Kentucky. In the story, the teacher took over a one-room school in which the class had been seated with boys on one side, and girls on the other. The teacher intermingled the sexes for seating. Some parents complained that the new teacher was running a "courting school." During a discussion of the novel in Mailloux's class, some students said the complaint by the parents was ridiculous. Mailloux said that other things today are equally ridiculous; one example was taboo words. He wrote the word "goo" on the board and asked the class for a definition. No one was able to define it. Mailloux said that the word did not exist in English but in another culture it might be a taboo word. He then wrote "fuck" on the blackboard, and asked the class in general for a definition. A boy volunteered that the word meant "sexual intercourse." Mailloux never used the word orally, but explained, "we have two words, sexual intercourse, and this word on the board ... one ... is acceptable by society ... the other is not accepted. It is a taboo word." After a short discussion of taboos, Mailloux went on to other topics. At all times during the discussion, Mailloux pursued an educational goal. He did not attempt to probe the private feelings, attitudes, or experiences of his students. The next day, the parent of a girl in the class complained to the principal. Miss Horner, the head of the English department, was then asked to investigate the incident. Mailloux admitted the incident, and after a hearing, the school committee dismissed him on the charge of "conduct unbecoming a teacher." He sought relief.

The U. S. District Court found that: 1) the topic of taboo words had a high degree of relevance to the proper teaching of eleventh-grade English, 2) the word "fuck" is relevant to a discussion of taboo words, 3) students in an eleventh-grade class have a sophistication sufficient to treat the word from a serious educational viewpoint, 4) the class might be less disturbed by having the word written than if it had been spoken because most students had seen the word even if they had not used it, 5) Mailloux's calling upon the class for a volunteer to define the word was a reasonable teaching technique which avoided implicating anyone who did not wish to participate, and 6) the word "fuck" is in books in the school library. Then the court noted a disagreement among experts as to the appropriateness of the method Mailloux employed. The court also noted,

> Where, as here, a secondary school teacher chooses a teaching method that is not necessary for the proper instruction of his class, that is not shown to be regarded by the weight of opinion in his profession as permissible, that is not so transparently proper that a court can without expert testimony evaluate it as proper, but that is relevant to his subject and students and, in the opinion of experts of significant standing, serves a serious educational purpose, it is a heretofore undecided question whether the Constitution gives him any right to use the method or leaves the issue to the school authorities.

The court argued that, in this case, "the state may suspend or discharge a teacher for using the method" but only if the state proves that the teacher "was put on notice either by a regulation or otherwise that he should not use that method." In Mailloux, there was no regulation warning the teacher not to use the method. And, because of the uncertainty among the experts, it was not self-evident that a teacher should not have used the method.

The court concluded that Mailloux's discharge was a violation of due process. But the court made it clear that school authorities are free, when they realize that a teacher is using an improper teaching method, to suspend him until he ceases to use the method. This opinion seems to run counter to the findings in Keefe and Parducci. Without a clear judicial precedent from the high Court, the question of the faculty right to their own teaching methods remains unresolved.

Expression of Views

The AAUP's concept of academic freedom includes a teacher's freedom from censorship to express his own views as a citizen. On a few occasions, courts have had to consider certain "unpopular" statements and actions of teachers in determining what restraints might properly be placed on such expressions of teachers.

Sweezy v. New Hampshire 354 U. S. 234 (1957)

In 1951, the New Hampshire legislature passed a statute declaring "subversive organizations" unlawful and "subversive persons" ineligible for employment by the state government. In 1953, the legislature adopted a resolution authorizing the Attorney General to investigate violations of the act of 1951. Paul Sweezy, a visiting lecturer at the University of New Hampshire, was summoned to appear before the Attorney General on two separate occasions. On January 5, 1954, Sweezy testified about his previous associations. He denied that he had ever been a member of the Communist Party, or that he had ever been part of any effort to overthrow the government by force or violence. The questioning covered many subjects. During the course of the interrogation, Sweezy declined to answer several questions which he claimed were not pertinent to the subject under inquiry or which transgressed the limitations of the First Amendment. Specifically, he refused to disclose his knowledge of the Progressive Party of New Hampshire, or of persons with whom he was acquainted in that organization. The Attorney General again summoned Sweezy to testify on June 3, 1954. He inquired about Sweezy's prior contacts with Communists. Sweezy admitted that he styled himself a "classical Marxist" and a "socialist. " Again, at the second hearing, the Attorney General asked, and Sweezy refused to answer, questions concerning the Progressive Party and its predecessor, the Progressive Citizens of America.

The Attorney General also turned to an event which had not yet occurred at the time of the first hearing. On March 22, 1954, Sweezy delivered a lecture to a humanities class of one hundred students at the University of New Hampshire. This talk was given at the invitation of the faculty teaching that course. Sweezy refused to answer the following questions regarding his talk:

What was the subject of your lecture?

Didn't you tell the class at the University of New Hampshire on Monday, March 22, 1954, that Social-ism was inevitable in this country?

Did you advocate Marxism at that time?

Did you express the opinion, or did you make the statement at that time that Socialism was inevitable in America?

Did you in this last lecture on March 22 or in any of the former lectures espouse the theory of dialec-tical materialism?

Sweezy maintained that the questions were not pertinent to the matter under inquiry, and that they infringed upon his First Amendment rights. Following the hearings, Sweezy was called before the Superior Court of Merrimack County to answer the questions which the court had ruled were pertinent. Sweezy refused to answer for constitutional reasons. The court found him in contempt and sentenced him to jail until he cooperated.

The U.S. Supreme Court set aside (6-2) the verdict on the grounds that the resolution of the state legislature had not authorized the specific questions asked of Sweezy. The Court ruled that it was the legislature's responsibility to determine which facts and information are useful to its investigation. In this case, the New Hampshire legislature had delegated that task to the Attorney General. The Court then went on to make a point relevant to academic freedom and the expression of un-popular views. According to the Court, in the opinion written by Chief Justice Earl Warren, "to impose any straitjacket upon the intellectual leaders in our colleges and universities would imperil the future of our Nation." Warren continued,

Scholarship cannot flourish in an atmosphere of sus-picion and distrust. Teachers and students must al-ways remain free to inquire, to study, and to evalu-ate, and to gain new maturity and understanding; otherwise our civilization will stagnate and die....

In Sweezy, the Court took a strong stand in favor of academic freedom.

Pickering v. Board of Education 391 U.S. 563 (1968)

More than a decade later, the Court further strengthened the freedom of expression of teachers. Marvin Pickering, a teacher at Township High School District 205, Will County, Illinois, sent a letter to the editor of a local newspaper criticizing the way in which the Board of Education and the Superintendent of Schools had handled past proposals to raise funds for educational use. The letter also objected to the allocation of current revenues between the school's educational and athletic programs. Pickering's letter said in part:

> As I see it, the bond issue is a fight between the Board of Education that is trying to push tax-supported athletics down our throats with education, and a public that has mixed emotions about both of these items because they feel they are already paying enough taxes, and simply don't know whom to trust with any money. I must sign this letter as a citizen, taxpayer and voter, not as a teacher, since that freedom has been taken from the teachers by the administration. Do you really know what goes on behind those stone walls at the high school?

> Did you know that these letters had to have the approval of the superintendent before they could go in the paper? That's the kind of totalitarianism teachers live in at the high school, and your children go to school in.

The "Handbook for Teachers" specifically stated that material submitted to local newspapers should be checked with the principal and submitted in triplicate to the publicity coordinator. The Board held a hearing at which it was charged that Pickering made statements which damaged the professional reputations of Board members and of the school administration. The statements, it was argued, could be disruptive of faculty discipline, and could tend to foment controversy, conflict, and dissension among teachers, administrators, the Board of Education, and the residents of the district. According to the Board, Pickering's false statements included a claim that the Board had been spending $200,000 a year on athletics while neglecting the needs of teachers. This claim was incorrect in that the $200,000 per year figure included over $130,000 of non-recurring capital expenditures. Pickering had also claimed that the Board spent $50,000 yearly on transportation for athletics; the actual expenditures for athletics per year was $10,000. Pickering was dismissed because the Board determined that his letter was detrimental to the efficient operation and administration of the schools.

The U. S. Supreme Court ruled unanimously for Pickering, basing much of its thinking on the "actual malice" principle set forth in New York Times Company v. Sullivan. The
Court noted that the amounts spent on athletics, which Pickering reported erroneously, were matters of public record which
the Board could have refuted by publishing the accurate figures
itself in the same newspaper. They concluded that, in Pickering's case, "absent proof of false statements knowingly or
recklessly made by him, a teacher's exercise of his right to
speak on issues of public importance may not furnish the basis
for his dismissal. " Pickering's dismissal by the Board violated his constitutional right to free speech.

Rozman v. Elliott 335 F. Supp 1086 (1971)

The conflict between free speech and other societal aims
was an issue in Rozman v. Elliott. The competing interests
involved in this case were freedom of expression, assembly,
and petition on the one hand, and freedom to employ or not to
employ on the other. On May 4 and 5, 1970, Stephen Rozman,
an assistant professor without tenure in the Department of
Political Science at the University of Nebraska, was involved
in two demonstrations. One opposed President Nixon's decision
to invade Cambodia, and the other protested against the killing
and wounding of students at Kent State University. At the
height of the demonstrations, university administrators were
concerned with getting the students to leave the Military and
Naval Sciences Building voluntarily, and were reluctant to call
in police because such action might precipitate violence. At
this time, Rozman demanded that the University take a position expressing indignation with the Cambodian and Kent State
situations. Rozman was advised that the continued occupation
of the building was disruptive and he was directed to vacate
the building. He failed to do so and continued to remain with
the students until a voluntary evacuation took place on the
morning of May 5. After extensive investigation by administration and faculty committees, the Board of Regents unanimously adopted a resolution providing that Rozman's contract
would not be renewed. Rozman initiated court action.

The court noted that, by statute, the Board of Regents
had the responsibility for government of the University of
Nebraska. Thus, there was no question of the authority of
the Board of Regents to fail to reemploy Rozman so long as
he was afforded due process of law. The court decided that
due process was provided; the Board did not act arbitrarily

or capriciously, or for constitutionally impermissible reasons, and did afford Rozman a proper hearing. Concerning Rozman's claim that his free speech rights were violated, the court ruled that two areas of activity fell outside the scope of constitutionally-protected expression: when Rozman intruded into the responsibilities of the administrators who were negotiating an evacuation of the building, and when by his presence he contributed to a cancellation of a class and defied the administration's directive to leave the building. The court concluded "that a faculty member cannot assume, under the protective umbrella of the federal constitution, the role of or intrude into another's rightful role of conducting the workings of a university. " A faculty member's cooperativeness "was a matter of proper concern of the Board of Regents, who had to decide whether he was the kind of faculty member who should be employed by the university. "

Meinhold v. Taylor 414 U. S. 943 (1973)

In 1973, the courts further limited the right of faculty to express their views. Alvin Meinhold, a Nevada public school teacher with seven years of service, was discharged for "unprofessional conduct" because he privately stated to his own children that he did not believe in compulsory school attendance laws. Meinhold did not express his views in the classroom nor did he encourage his students to be truant. The Nevada Supreme Court ruled that "a teacher's right to teach cannot depend solely upon his conduct in the classroom" and upheld the firing.

The U. S. Supreme Court refused to hear the case and let stand Meinhold's dismissal for private comments made to his family. The Court thus supported the idea that a teacher's right to teach cannot depend solely upon conduct in the classroom. Justice William Douglas, who wanted the case reviewed, cited Pickering, which determined that teachers may not "constitutionally be compelled to relinquish the First Amendment rights they would otherwise enjoy as citizens. " Douglas concluded, "May Pickering publish his criticisms in the local newspaper with impunity while the petitioner must keep his views secret from his children lest they adopt them? "

City of Madison, Joint School District No. 8 v. Wisconsin Employment Commission 429 U. S. 167 (1976)

A somewhat remotely related case involved the question

of whether a teacher may speak in opposition to an agency
shop proposition at a public school board meeting. The Madison (Wisconsin) Board of Education and Madison Teachers
Inc. (MTI), a labor union, were negotiating a collective-
bargaining agreement during 1971. MTI submitted a number
of proposals. One called for the inclusion of a "fair-share"
clause, which would require all teachers, whether members
of MTI or not, to pay union dues to defray the costs of col-
lective bargaining. The negotiations became stalemated. At
a School Board meeting held on December 6, a portion of the
meeting was devoted to expression of opinion by the public.
The president of MTI took the floor and spoke on the subject
of the ongoing negotiations. He concluded his remarks by
presenting to the Board a petition signed by 1,300-1,400
teachers calling for the expeditious resolution of the negotiations. Next, a teacher named Holmquist stated that he represented "an informal committee of 72 teachers in 49 schools"
and that he desired to inform the Board of Education, as he
had already informed the union, of the results of a survey.
He then read a petition which had been circulated to the teachers in the district and stated that in the thirty-one schools
from which reports had been received, fifty-three per cent
of the teachers had signed the petition opposing "fair-share."
Later that evening, the Board met in executive session and
voted a proposal agreeing to all of the union's demands with
the exception of "fair-share." During a negotiating session the
following morning, MTI accepted the proposal and a contract
was signed on December 14. In January, 1972, MTI filed a
complaint with the Wisconsin Employment Relations Commission, claiming that the Board had committed a prohibited labor
practice by permitting Holmquist to speak at the December 6
meeting. MTI claimed that in so doing the Board had engaged
in negotiations with a member of the bargaining unit other than
the exclusive bargaining representative, thus violating Wisconsin law. The case reached the U.S. Supreme Court.

The Court, in a unanimous opinion, ruled that the circumstances did not present such a danger to labor-management
relations as to justify curtailing freedom of speech. Holmquist, it appeared, did not seek to bargain nor was he authorized by any group to bargain on their behalf. So, his brief
statement could not be considered as negotiation. The union
alone was authorized to negotiate with and enter into an agreement with the Board. The Court noted that the School Board
meeting at which Holmquist spoke was open to the public.
Holmquist spoke not merely as one of its employees but also
as a concerned citizen, seeking to express his views on an

important decision of his government. The Court noted that in Pickering it held that teachers may not be "compelled to relinquish the First Amendment rights they would otherwise enjoy as citizens to comment on matters of public interest in connection with the operation of the public school in which they work. " In this case, the right of a teacher to express his views was upheld.

Mt. Healthy City School District Board of Education v. Doyle 429 U. S. 274 (1977)

The Court decided another case involving expression of a teacher's views in 1977. Beginning in 1970, Fred Doyle, an untenured teacher in the Mt. Healthy, Ohio, school district, was involved in a series of incidents. In one case, he argued with another teacher until the incident ended with the other teacher slapping him. Doyle refused to accept an apology and insisted upon some punishment for the other teacher. On another occasion, Doyle argued with employees of the school cafeteria over the quantity of spaghetti which had been served him. At other times, he referred to students as "sons of bitches, " and made an obscene gesture to two girls who disobeyed him. In 1971, Doyle telephoned a Cincinnati radio station to report that the principal of his school had established a teacher dress and appearance code. The station quickly reported the adoption of the code as a news item. At the spring meeting of the Board of Education, Doyle's contract was not renewed. He requested the reasons for the decision and received a statement citing "a notable lack of tact in handling professional matters.... " All of the above specific instances were cited. Doyle initiated action, seeking reinstatement.

The U. S. Supreme Court held unanimously that Doyle's telephone call to the radio station was protected by the First Amendment. Because it had played a "substantial part" in the decision not to rehire Doyle, he was entitled to reinstatement with backpay. The Court noted that although constitutionally protected speech played a role in the decision not to rehire Doyle, that fact did not necessarily violate his constitutional rights. The District Court had erred when it failed to determine whether the Board of Education would have reached the same decision even in the absence of the protected telephone call. With such a determination, the decision not to rehire Doyle could have been upheld.

Contradictory court opinions leave the issue of expression of teacher views in a state of uncertainty.   Early Court decisions, Sweezy and Pickering, supported the right of teachers to express their personal views outside of the classroom. Rozman seemed to limit that principle somewhat by upholding the right of a university to dismiss a professor who participated in demonstrations to the point of interfering with administration efforts to run the university.   In Meinhold, the Court refused to hear a case involving a teacher's dismissal for comments made in the privacy of his own home.   Most recently, in City of Madison, Joint School District No. 8 and Mt. Healthy City School District Board of Education, the Court acknowledged the right of teachers to express their views under specific conditions.   Overall, though, the courts have left this issue in a somewhat unclear state.

Due Process

In 1972, the U. S. Supreme Court decided two cases which involved faculty claims of due process violation.   Both cases involved non-tenured members of a university faculty.

Board of Regents v. Roth 408 U. S. 564 (1972)

The amount of procedural protection afforded a Wisconsin State University teacher before separation corresponds to the level of job security.   As a matter of statutory law, a tenured teacher cannot be "discharged except for cause upon written charges. "   A non-tenured teacher is protected to some extent during his one-year term.   But there is no real protection for a non-tenured teacher who simply is not reemployed for the next year.   In 1968, David Roth accepted his first teaching job as assistant professor of political science at Wisconsin State University-Oshkosh.   He was hired for a fixed term of one academic year.   According to law, Roth was notified before February 1, 1969 that he would not be rehired for the 1969-70 academic year.   Roth was given no reason for the decision and no opportunity to challenge it at any type of hearing.   Roth brought action in court alleging that the decision not to hire infringed upon his rights.   First, he alleged that the real reason was to punish him for certain statements critical of the university administration, and that it therefore violated his right to freedom of speech.   Second, he alleged that the failure of university officials to give him notice of any reason for nonretention and an opportunity for

a hearing violated his right to procedural due process of law.
The District Court, and later the Court of Appeals, ordered
university officials to provide Roth with reasons and a hearing.

The U. S. Supreme Court considered only the issue of
whether Roth had a constitutional right to a statement of reasons and a hearing on the university's decision not to rehire
him for another year.   The majority decided (6-2) that the
terms of Roth's appointment secured absolutely no interest in
reemployment for the next year.   Roth had absolutely no
possible claim of entitlement to reemployment.   Justice Douglas filed a vigorous dissent in which he addressed himself to
the First Amendment issue.   Douglas feared an assault on
academic freedom if school authorities would be allowed to
discharge teachers because of their philosophical, political,
or ideological beliefs.   Roth had publicly criticized the administration for suspending an entire group of ninety-four
black students without determining individual guilt.   He also
criticized the administration as being authoritarian and autocratic.   He used his classroom to discuss what was being
done about the black incident.   Douglas concluded that without
a statement of the reasons for discharge and an opportunity
to rebut those reasons, Roth would be deprived of his constitutional rights if nonrenewal implicated the First Amendment.

Perry V. Sindermann 408 U. S. 593 (1972)

A companion case involved Robert Sindermann, who
between 1959 and 1969, was a teacher in the state college
system of Texas.   After teaching for two years at the University of Texas and four years at San Antonio Junior College,
he taught government and social science at Odessa Junior College.   He was employed at the college for four successive
years, under a series of one-year contracts.   During the
1968-69 academic year, however, controversy arose between
Sindermann and the college administration.   As President of
the Texas Junior College Teachers Association, Sindermann
left his teaching duties on several occasions to testify before
committees of the Texas legislature, and he became involved
in public disagreements with the policies of the college's
Board of Regents.   Specifically, he aligned himself with a
group advocating the elevation of the college to four-year
status, a change opposed by the Regents.   On one occasion,
a newspaper advertisement appeared over his name which was

highly critical of the Regents. In May, 1969, Sindermann's one-year employment contract terminated and the Board of Regents voted not to offer him a new contract for the next academic year. The Regents issued a press release setting forth allegations of insubordination. But they provided him no official statement of the reasons for the nonrenewal of his contract. In addition, they offered him no opportunity for a hearing. Sindermann brought action in court. He alleged primarily that the Regents' decision not to rehire him was based on his public criticism of the policies of the administration, and thus infringed his right to free speech. He also alleged that their failure to provide him an opportunity for a hearing violated procedural due process.

The U. S. Supreme Court affirmed, first of all, that Sindermann's lack of a tenure right to reemployment, taken alone, did not defeat his claim that the nonrenewal of his contract violated his constitutional rights. The Court noted that there was a genuine dispute in this case as to whether the college failed to renew the teaching contract on an impermissible basis; that is, as a reprisal against the exercise of free speech. The Court held that the college's granting of a summary judgement against Sindermann, without full exploration of the issues, was improper. The Court then referred to its Roth ruling, which affirmed that there was no right to a hearing before the nonrenewal of a nontenured teacher's contract, unless it could be shvwn "that the decision not to rehire him somehow deprived him of an interest in 'liberty' or that he had a 'property' interest in continued employment, despite the lack of tenure or a formal contract. " Sindermann alleged that this interest, though not secured by a formal contractual tenure provision, was secured by a no less binding understanding fostered by the college administration. Sindermann alleged that the college had a de facto tenure program, and that he had tenure under the program. He claimed that he legitimately relied upon an unusual provision that had been in the College's official faculty guide for many years:

> Teacher tenure: Odessa College has no tenure system. The administration of the college wishes the faculty member to feel that he has permanent tenure as long as his teaching services are satisfactory and as long as he displays a cooperative attitude toward his coworkers and his superiors, and as long as he is happy in his work.

Sindermann also claimed legitimate reliance upon guidelines

promulgated by the Coordinating Board of the Texas College and University System that provided that a person, like himself, who had been employed as a teacher in the state college and university system for seven years or more, has some form of job tenure. Sindermann claimed that a teacher with his length of service had no less a "property" interest in continued employment than a formally tenured teacher at other colleges. The Court acknowledged Sindermann's claim as a "legitimate claim of entitlement to job tenure. " The Court concluded (8-0) that "Proof of such a property interest would not, of course, entitle him to reinstatement. But such proof would obligate college officials to grant a hearing at his request, where he could be informed of the grounds for his nonretention and challenge their sufficiency. "

In this section, it has been clearly shown that non-tenured faculty have considerably less right to procedural safeguards than tenured members of the faculty. In Roth the Court ruled that a professor who was hired for a one-year term had no right to be informed of the reasons for nonre-tention, nor was he entitled to a hearing at which he could challenge those reasons. But in Sindermann the Court acknowledged the existence of an "informal" tenure system which entitled a professor, with considerable length of service, to specific safeguards when facing non-renewal.

Bibliography

Books

Bolmeier, Edward C. Landmark Supreme Court Decisions on Public School Issues. Charlottesville: The Michie Co., 1973.

Earle, Valerie, (ed.) On Academic Freedom. Washington, D. C. : American Enterprise Institute, 1971.

Hazard, William R. Education and the Law: Cases and Materials on Public Schools. New York: The Free Press, 1971.

Hook, Sidney. Academic Freedom and Academic Anarchy. New York: Cowles Book Company, 1970.

Joughin, Louis, (ed.) Academic Freedom and Tenure: A Handbook of The American Association of University

Professors. Madison: University of Wisconsin Press, 1969.

Kirp, David L. and Mark G. Yudof. Educational Policy and the Law: Cases and Materials. Berkeley: McCutchan Publishing Co., 1974.

Morris, Arval A. The Constitution and American Education. St. Paul: West Publishing Co., 1974.

Policy Documents and Reports. Washington, D. C.: The American Association of University Professors, 1977.

Articles

Aldrich, Ann and JoAnne V. Sommers. "Freedom of Expression in Secondary Schools," Cleveland State Law Review 19 (January, 1970), 165-76.

"Applying Freedman v. Maryland to Campus Speaker Bans," University of Pennsylvania Law Review 119 (January, 1971), 512-20.

Aspelund, Carl L. "Free Speech Rights of School Children," Loyola Law Review 16 (1969-70), 165-76.

Barrier, Mary L. "Restriction of the First Amendment in an Academic Environment," University of Kansas Law Review 22 (Summer, 1974), 597-605.

Berkman, Richard L. "Students in Court: Free Speech and the Functions of Schooling in America," Harvard Educational Review 40 (November, 1970), 567-95.

Chambers, M. M. "Speaker Bans and the Courts," Educational Forum 35 (May, 1971), 471-8.

Cutlip, James. "Symbolic Speech, High School Protest and the First Amendment," Journal of Family Law 9 (1969), 119-25.

Denno, Theodore F. "Mary Beth Tinker Takes the Constitution to School," Fordham Law Review 38 (October, 1969), 35-62.

Goldstein, Stephen R. "The Asserted Constitutional Right of Public School Teachers to Determine What They Teach," University of Pennsylvania Law Review 124 (January, 1976), 1293-357.

Graham, Edward M. "Freedom of Speech of the Public School Teacher," Cleveland State Law Review 19 (May, 1970), 382-92.

Mallies, Harry C. "Freedom of Expression in the Public Schools and the Law," Journal of Secondary Education 46 (March, 1971), 109-16.

McCoy, Joseph L. and Roger T. Clark. "Do College Students Have a Constitutionally Protected Right to Hear Outside Speakers?" Mississippi Law Journal 41 (Winter, 1969), 135-41.

Miller, Simon A. "Teacher's Freedom of Expression Outside the Classroom: An Analysis of the Application of Pickering and Tinker," Georgia Law Review 8 (Summer, 1974), 900-18.

Nahmod, Sheldon. "Black Armbands and Underground News-papers: Freedom of Speech in the Public Schools," Chicago Bar Record 51 (December, 1969), 144-53.

Shulman, Carol Harrnstadt. "Employment of Nontenured Faculty: Implications of Roth and Sindermann," Denver Law Journal 51 (1974), 215-33.

Sinowitz, B. E. "Court Rulings and Teacher's Right to Speak Out," Today's Education 62 (September-October, 1973), 50-60.

Cases

Abington School District v. Schempp; Murray v. Curlett 374 U.S. 203 (1963)

Adler v. Board of Education 342 U.S. 485 (1952)

Baggett v. Bullitt 377 U.S. 360 (1964)

Bartels v. Iowa; Bohning v. Ohio 262 U.S. 404 (1923)

Beilan v. Board of Public Education 357 U. S. 399 (1958)

Board of Regents v. Roth 408 U. S. 564 (1972)

Brooks v. Auburn University 296 F. Supp. 188 (1969)

City of Madison Joint School District No. 8 v. Wisconsin Employment Relations Commission 429 U. S. 167 (1976)

Cramp v. Board of Public Instruction of Orange County, Florida 368 U. S. 278 (1961)

Dickey v. Alabama State Board of Education 273 F. Supp. 613 (1967)

Dickson v. Sitterson 415 F. 2d. 228 (1969)

Duke v. State of Texas 327 F. Supp. 1218 (1971)

Eisner v. Stamford Board of Education 440 F. 2d. 803 (1971)

Engel v. Vitale 370 U. S. 421 (1962)

Epperson v. Arkansas 393 U. S. 97 (1968)

Fujishima v. Board of Education 460 F. 2d. 1355 (1972)

Goss v. Lopez 419 U. S. 565 (1975)

Guzick v. Drebus 431 F. 2d. 594 (1970)

Healy v. James 408 U. S. 169 (1972)

Keefe v. Geanakos 418 F. 2d. 359 (1969)

Keyishian v. Board of Regents 385 U. S. 589 (1967)

Mailloux v. Kiley 448 F. 2d. 1242 (1971)

Meinhold v. Taylor 414 U. S. 943 (1973)

Meyer v. Nebraska 262 U. S. 390 (1923)

Minersville School District v. Gobitis 310 U. S. 586 (1940)

Molpus v. Fortune 311 F. Supp. 240 (1970)

Mt. Healthy City School District Board of Education v. Doyle
429 U. S. 274 (1977)

Papish v. Board of Curators of the University of Missouri
410 U. S. 667 (1973)

Parducci v. Rutland 316 F. Supp. 352 (1970)

Perry v. Sindermann 408 U. S. 593 (1972)

Pickering v. Board of Education 391 U. S. 563 (1968)

Presidents Council, District 25 v. Community School Board
No. 25 409 U. S. 998 (1972)

Rozman v. Elliott 335 F. Supp. 1086 (1971)

Shelton v. Tucker; Carr v. Young 364 U. S. 479 (1960)

Slochower v. Board of Higher Education 350 U. S. 551 (1956)

Stacy v. Williams 306 F. Supp. 963 (1970)

Sweezy v. New Hampshire 354 U. S. 234 (1957)

Tinker v. Des Moines Independent Community School District
393 U. S. 503 (1969)

West Virginia State Board of Education v. Barnette 319 U. S.
624 (1943)

Whitehill v. Elkins 389 U. S. 54 (1967)

Wieman v. Updegraff 344 U. S. 183 (1952)

Wood v. Strickland 420 U. S. 308 (1975)

CHAPTER V

OBSCENITY

As late as the Civil War period, obscenity was a crime that was rarely prosecuted in America. In the early 1870s, Anthony Comstock, an ardent crusader for decency, organized the New York Society for the Suppression of Vice. Even though the Society obtained increased numbers of convictions, the condition of obscenity case law remained weak. Comstock campaigned relentlessly, and largely through his efforts, new federal obscenity legislation was secured in 1873. The law provided a maximum punishment of a $5,000 fine, or a five-year prison term, or both, for anybody who was caught sending obscene material through the mail. Comstock was also instrumental in implementing the new law. As a special agent of the Post Office Department, he received part of the fines collected in prosecuting the new obscenity law. Until his death in 1915, Comstock, and his friends at the Society, seized tons of obscene cards, letters, books, papers, pamphlets, or other written matters, and prosecutions for obscenity law violations became rather common. "Comstockery" signalled the beginning of obscenity censorship in America.

TESTS OF OBSCENITY

The problem of determining exactly what "obscenity" is has proven to be difficult for legislatures and courts. "Obscenity" has been defined and regulated according to different standards over the past century. The specific tests of obscenity are explicated in the following section.

Hicklin Rule

An 1868 English court case had an effect on the regulation of obscene materials in America for many years thereafter.

Regina v. Hicklin L. R. 3Q. B. 360, 370 (1868)

In Hicklin, Lord Chief Justice Cockburn ruled that an anti-Catholic pamphlet, The Confessional Unmasked, was obscene. Lord Cockburn established as the test for obscenity "whether the tendency of the matter charged as obscene is to deprave and corrupt those whose minds are open to such immoral influences and into whose hands a publication of this sort might fall." The "Hicklin rule" was accepted by courts in America and vigorously approved by Anthony Comstock.

Three characteristics of the Hicklin test should be noted. First, a work did not have to harm or offend an "average person." If a book could be assumed to have a bad effect on "those whose minds are open to such immoral influences," whether it be a child, an abnormal adult, or any member of the subclass of society, it could be seized. Printed material could be suppressed if it was potentially offensive to any particular subclass of the society. It did not have to apply to the average adult. Second, material could be judged obscene if any part of the work was obscene. The work was not evaluated in terms of its impact as a whole; rather, if any portion of the work was found to be obscene, the work was judged obscene in total. This characteristic gave rise to the practice of judging a literary work by examining passages taken out of context. Third, obscenity was judged on the basis of a work's intent. American judges speculated about the thoughts induced by the reading of printed material. Judges sought to ban any work which produced "thoughts of a most impure and libidinous character" without any concern that antisocial actions be correlated with the printed material.

In 1913, in United States v. Kennerley, Judge Learned Hand voiced a protest against the Hicklin rule. He questioned whether ultimately "men will regard that as obscene which is honestly relevant to the adequate expression of innocent ideas ... " and he suspected that "shame will long prevent us from adequate portrayal of some of the most serious and beautiful sides of human nature.... " But the Hicklin rule continued to have a leading impact on obscenity in America until the 1950s.

Roth Test

In 1957, the U. S. Supreme Court set forth a second test of obscenity. The "Roth test" was the predominant standard until 1973. During that period, obscenity tended to be defined and regulated by considerably relaxed standards.

Roth v. United States;
Alberts v. California 354 U. S. 476 (1957)

Businessman Samuel Roth published and sold books, photographs, and magazines in New York City. In order to solicit sales, he used circulars and other forms of printed advertising. He was arrested and subsequently convicted of mailing circulars in violation of the federal obscenity statute (18 U. S. C. § 1461). David Alberts conducted a mail-order business from Los Angeles. He was convicted of violating the California Penal Code by keeping for sale obscene and indecent books, and by composing and publishing an obscene advertisement of the books. The printed matter involved in the Roth and Alberts cases could hardly be considered literary classics. Roth's publications included such titles as Sexual Conduct of Men and Women, Wild Passion, and Wanton by Night, while Albert's works were such as The Love Affair of a Priest and a Nun, Male Homosexuals Tell Their Stories, and The Prostitute and Her Lover. When these cases reached the U. S. Supreme Court in 1957, a significant chapter in the history of obscenity law was written.

In the Roth and Alberts cases, the Court confronted the issue of whether obscenity is protected by the First Amendment. This was the first time that issue had been faced squarely by the Court. The justices concluded that obscenity was not constitutionally protected. Then, the Court examined the nature of obscenity and arrived at a definition. According to the "Roth test," obscenity involves "whether to the average person applying contemporary community standards, the dominant theme of the material taken as a whole appeals to prurient interest." This requirement for obscenity focuses on several elements. First, the Court noted differences between sex and obscenity. Obscene material must deal with sex, but must do so in a manner which appeals to prurient interest. The portrayal of sex, in and of itself, is insufficient cause to suppress material. Second, the test applies to the average person. The printed material must be capable of affecting somebody other than a particularly susceptible individual. It must be applicable to "normal" persons. Third, the material must violate "contemporary community standards." Yet it wasn't until 1964, in Jacobellis v. Ohio, that the meaning of "community" became clear. The term "community" was defined as national in scope. Accordingly, contemporary "community" standards, in effect meant, contemporary "national" standards. Fourth, the material must be considered as a whole. It is not judged merely by the effect of an isolated excerpt. Concern must be with the dominant theme of the piece.

The convictions of Roth and Alberts were upheld. The vote in Roth was 6-3, and in Alberts, 7-2. Justice John Harlan concurred in Alberts, but dissented in Roth. He perceived a difference in the state and federal power to regulate obscenity. Protecting morality was primarily the function of the states, which were free to experiment with various types of obscenity controls. In Alberts, the California statute was based on the idea that printed words can "deprave or corrupt" the reader and can incite to anti-social and immoral action. There was nothing in the due process clause which forbids California to prosecute on those grounds. Roth was convicted under a federal statute which made it criminal to sell any book which "tends to stir sexual impulses and lead to sexually impure thoughts." Harlan could not agree that such a book necessarily is "utterly without redeeming social importance." Harlan felt the federal government had no business to impose a blanket ban over the nation against the sale of a particular book. Federal obscenity laws could involve only hard-core pornography. Harlan continued to hold this position in several ensuing cases.

Justices William Douglas and Hugo Black dissented in both cases. They objected to a test which punished thoughts provoked, rather than anti-social behavior. They also felt that a test which rested on what is offensive to the community's standards was too loose, and allowed for community censorship that was unduly capricious. They concluded that the broad sweep of the First Amendment should be given full support. They had "the same confidence in the ability of our people to reject noxious literature" as they had "in their capacity to sort out the true from the false in theology, economics, politics, or any other field."

Attorney General v. The Book Named "Tropic of Cancer"
184 N. E. 2d 328 (1962)

In the years following Roth, several cases involved application of the Roth test. An early case involved Henry Miller's Tropic of Cancer, which was first published in the

United States by Grove Press in 1961. The book is an account of the sex experiences of an American who visited Paris in the hope of becoming a writer, and who, for the most part, lived the life of a down-and-outer, sponging on friends. The tale graphically describes sex episodes in minute detail. Of the 318 pages of the book, there are sex episodes on 85 pages, and all are described with precise physical detail and four-letter words.

The Attorney General of Massachusetts initiated proceedings against the book under state law which urged action against any obscene, indecent, or impure book which was being distributed in the state. The trial judge was "irresistibly" led to the conclusion that the book was obscene, indecent, and impure. The Supreme Judicial Court of Massachusetts disagreed; it concluded that the First Amendment protects material which has literary, artistic, newsworthy, or scientific value. If the appeal of the material, taken as a whole, to normal adults is not predominantly prurient, suppression cannot be allowed. It is irrelevant that some or even many people might think the book to be at many places filthy, repulsive, vulgar, and nauseating. Much of modern art, literature, and music is likely to seem ugly and thoroughly objectionable to persons who have different standards of taste. Professors of literary studies, including Harry T. Moore, Mark Schorer, and Morton Bloomfield testified that Miller's book had merit. According to the critics, Miller's description of the city of Paris and his depiction of a type of life in Paris in the thirties was impressive, and rose to great literary heights. A majority of the court concluded that the predominant effect of Tropic of Cancer was not prurient, and the book was judged not to be obscene.

Jacobellis v. Ohio 378 U.S. 184 (1964)

In 1964, the Court applied Roth in a case involving the medium of film. "Les Amants" (The Lovers) was a French film about a woman bored with her life and marriage. She abandons her husband and family for a young archaeologist with whom she falls in love. There is an explicit love scene in the film. The film was shown in approximately 100 of the larger cities in the United States, including Columbus and Toledo, Ohio. Nico Jacobellis, manager of a motion picture theatre in Cleveland Heights, Ohio, was convicted for showing the film. The objection was based almost entirely on the explicit scene. He was fined $2,500, and sentenced to prison if the fine was not paid. He appealed.

The case reached the U.S. Supreme Court. The majority felt (6-3) that applying local standards was unconstitutional. The meaning of "community standards," as established in Roth, referred to "national standards." According to the opinion of Justice William Brennan;

> We thus reaffirm the position taken in Roth to the effect that the constitutional status of an allegedly obscene work must be determined on the basis of a national standard. It is, after all, a national Constitution we are expounding.

After viewing the film, the Court concluded that it was not obscene in terms of the Roth test.

A Book Named "John Cleland's Memoirs of a Woman of Pleasure" v. Attorney General of Massachusetts 383 U.S. 413 (1966)

The Roth test was further explained in 1966. The Massachusetts Attorney General initiated action to have John Cleland's Memoirs of a Woman of Pleasure, also known as Fanny Hill, declared obscene. As law required, an order was published in a Boston daily newspaper, and a copy of the order was sent to G. P. Putnam's Sons, publisher and copyright holder of the work. Then, a trial judge decided that the book was obscene and not entitled to the protection of the First and Fourteenth Amendments. In the first ten pages of the book, Fanny Hill, a fifteen-year-old girl who came to London to seek household work, goes to an employment office where she meets the mistress of a bordello. Justice Tom Clark describes the rest of the book:

> The remaining 200 pages of the book details her initiation to various sexual experiences, from a lesbian encounter with a sister prostitute, to all sorts and types of sexual debauchery in bawdy houses and as the mistress of a variety of men. These scenes run the gamut of possible sexual experience such as lesbianism, female masturbation, homosexuality between young boys, the destruction of a maidenhead with consequent gory descriptions, the seduction of a young virgin boy, the flagellation of a male by female, and vice versa, followed by fervid sexual engagement, and other abhorrent acts, including over two dozen separate bizarre

descriptions of different sexual intercourse between
male and female characters. In one sequence four
girls in a bawdy house are required in the presence
of one another to relate the lurid details of their
loss of virginity and their glorification of it. This
is followed the same evening by 'publik trials' in
which each of the four girls engages in sexual intercourse with a different man while the others witness,
with Fanny giving a detailed description of the movement and reaction of each couple. In each of the
sexual scenes the exposed bodies of the participants
are described in minute and individual detail. There
is a most vivid and precise description of the response, condition, size, shape, and color of sexual
organs before, during, and after orgasms. There
are some short transitory passages between the
various sexual episodes, but for the most part they
only set the scene and identify the participants for
the next orgy, or make smutty reference and comparison to past episodes.

The Court applied the Roth test, noting that three elements
must be present: the dominant theme taken as a whole must
appeal to a prurient interest, the material must be patently
offensive in light of contemporary community standards, and
the material must be utterly without redeeming social
value.

The Court judged Memoirs (6-3) to be a novel with
literary merit. The book displays skill in characterization
and reveals a gift for comedy. The work plays a role in the
history of the English novel. Memoirs contains a moral --
namely, that sex with love is superior to sex in a brothel.
The book has some literary value. Each of the three criteria
must be applied independently; the social value of the book
can neither be weighed against nor canceled by its prurient
appeal or patent offensiveness. Thus, even though Memoirs
possesses only a modicum of social value, it cannot be judged
as obscene. The book was not obscene because it is not
"unqualifiably worthless."

Mishkin v. United States 383 U.S. 502 (1966)

In 1966, the Court also heard Mishkin v. U.S. Edward
Mishkin operated a bookstore near Times Square in New York
City. His publishing specialty was sadism and masochism.

He had instructed authors under his employ to depict extremes
in sexuality. His works included several portrayals of
scantily-clad women being whipped, tortured, and abused. He
produced and sold in excess of fifty different paperbacks, including such works as Dance with the Dominant Whip, Cult of
the Spankers, Swish Bottom, Mrs. Tyrant's Finishing School,
and Stud Broad. Mishkin was found guilty of violating the
New York Penal Law. He was sentenced to three years in
prison and fined $12,500. He appealed. Mishkin's defense
was based on the idea that the books did not appeal to the
prurient interest of an average person. Mishkin argued that
the average person would be disgusted and sickened by such
works.

The U.S. Supreme Court ruled (6-3) that when material
is designed for and primarily disseminated to a clearly defined
deviant sexual group, rather than the public at large, "the
prurient-appeal requirement of the Roth test is satisfied if the
dominant theme of the material taken as a whole appeals to
the prurient interest of the members of that group...." In
this case,

> No substantial claim is made that the books depicting
> sexually deviant practices are devoid of prurient ap-
> peal to sexually deviant groups. The evidence fully
> establishes that these books were specifically con-
> ceived and marketed for such groups. Appellant
> [Mishkin] instructed his authors and artists to pre-
> pare the books expressly to induce their purchase
> by persons who would probably be sexually stimu-
> lated by them.

The Court dismissed Mishkin's argument and upheld his conviction.

Redrup v. New York 386 U.S. 767, 771 (1967)

Three years later, in Redrup v. New York, a review
of three state cases, the Court wrote a short per curiam
opinion which explained differences in the thinking of Court
members over the preceding few years as to the appropriate
test and scope of obscenity regulation. The Court went on to
reverse (7-2) the obscenity convictions in the three state
cases, noting that no matter which judicial thinking was applied, the convictions could not stand. Thus began a six-year
policy of issuing summary reversals, without opinion, of any

conviction which at least five justices, each applying his own
standard, found to be under the protection of the First Amendment. From 1967 to 1973, the Court determined thirty-one
cases in this manner. These cases became known as the
"Redrup reversals" and marked a period of minimal regulation of obscenity.

Miller Test

The obscenity standard set up by the Earl Warren
Court was overturned on June 21, 1973, when Nixon appointees Lewis Powell, Harry Blackmun, William Rehnquist, and
Warren Burger were joined by Byron White to constitute a
five-man majority in Miller v. California.

Miller v. California 413 U.S. 15 (1973)

Marvin Miller distributed unsolicited, sexually-explicit
advertising brochures to unwilling recipients. The brochures
advertised four books entitled Intercourse, Man-Woman, Sex
Orgies Illustrated, and An Illustrated History of Pornography,
and a film entitled "Marital Intercourse." The brochures
contained some descriptive printed material, but they primarily consisted of pictures which explicitly depicted men and
women engaging in a variety of sexual activities, often with
genitals prominently displayed. A brochure arrived through
the mail to a restaurant in Newport Beach, California. The
manager of the restaurant opened the brochure, and complained to the police. Miller was eventually convicted. He
appealed.

In this case, the U.S. Supreme Court re-examined the
definition of obscenity, and established new guidelines. The
Court determined, first of all, that obscenity occurred when
"the average person applying contemporary community standards would find that the work, taken as a whole, appeals to
the prurient interests." In Miller, the Court redefined the
term "community." No longer were contemporary "community" standards to be considered as "national" in scope. It
was not realistic nor constitutionally sound to view the First
Amendment as requiring that people of one state accept conduct found tolerable in another state. People in different
states vary in their tastes and attitudes. For example, people in Maine or Mississippi may vary from people in Las
Vegas or New York City. According to the Court, "this

diversity is not to be strangled by the absolutism of imposed uniformity. '' Secondly, obscenity could be determined when ''the work depicts or describes, in a patently offensive way, sexual conduct specifically defined by the applicable state law. '' As examples of what might be regulated as ''patently offensive'' by state statute, the Court cited representations of normal or perverted, actual or simulated ultimate sexual acts, and descriptions of masturbation, excretory functions, and lewd exhibition of the genitals. A third guideline concerned whether ''the work, taken as a whole, lacks serious literary, artistic, political, or scientific value. '' The Court thereby rejected the ''utterly without redeeming social value'' element of the Roth test and substituted the words ''does not have serious literary, artistic, political or scientific value. '' Ensuing Court decisions elaborated on the meaning of the ''Miller test. ''

Paris Adult Theatre I v. Slaton 413 U.S. 49 (1973)

On the same day that the Court heard Miller, it decided a case which involved the commercial showing of two ''adult'' films. Paris Adult Theatres I and II were adult movie theatres in Atlanta, which advertised ''Atlanta's Finest Mature Feature Films. '' On the door of the theatre was a sign saying: ''Adult Theatre--You must be 21 and able to prove it. If viewing the nude body offends you, Please Do Not Enter. '' On December 28, 1970, Georgia filed complaints alleging that films exhibited by the theatres were obscene. The district attorney alleged that the films ''Magic Mirror'' and ''It All Comes Out in the End'' depicted sexual behavior which was hard-core pornography that left little to the imagination. A trial judge indicated that while the material was obscene, displaying the films in a commercial theatre surrounded by proper notice to the public of their nature, and by reasonable protection against exposure to minors, was constitutionally permissible. However, the Georgia Supreme Court reversed, holding that the films were hard-core pornography, and their exhibition was not protected by the First Amendment.

This decision was affirmed (5-4) by the U.S. Supreme Court. The Court stressed that they ''do not undertake to tell the States what they must do but rather to define the area in which they may chart their own course in dealing with obscene material. '' The Court reaffirmed that obscene material was not entitled to the protection of the First Amendment,

and categorically disapproved the notion that obscene films
acquire constitutional immunity from state regulation simply
by being exhibited for consenting adults. Instead, the Court
noted that there are legitimate state interests at stake in
stemming the tide of commercialized obscenity. The Court
concluded that states may legitimately regulate commerce in
obscene material and control its exhibition in public places.

Kaplan v. California 413 U. S. 115 (1973)

In another case, heard the same day as Miller, the
Court made it clear that a book with no pictures whatsoever
can constitute an example of "hard-core" pornography. Murray Kaplan, the proprietor of the Peek-A-Boo Bookstore in
Los Angeles, was convicted for selling to an undercover officer a copy of Suite 69, an unillustrated book with repetitive
descriptions of sexual conduct. During the trial, each juror
inspected the book. But the prosecution offered no expert
testimony that the book was "utterly without socially redeeming value," nor any evidence of "national standards." Kaplan
appealed the conviction.

When the case reached the U. S. Supreme Court, the
majority held (5-4) that "Suite 69 appeals to the prurient
interest in sex and is beyond the customary limits of candor
within the State of California." The state did not always have
to present "expert" evidence that a book lacked "redeeming
social value." In light of the nature of the book, there was
adequate evidence to sustain Kaplan's conviction. The book
was not protected by the First Amendment. Thus, the Court
supported state control; the "contemporary community standards" of California constituted an adequate test for obscenity
and "expert" evidence of obscenity was not required of the
prosecution. The Court also noted that the absence of pictorial description does not necessarily entitle a work to First
Amendment protection. Even though most "hard-core" pornography involves pictures, expression based on words alone
is not guaranteed constitutional protection.

Jenkins v. Georgia 418 U. S. 153 (1974)

In 1974, the Court heard two cases which provided an
opportunity to clarify and refine the standards established in
Miller. In the first case, a conviction for showing nudity in
films was overturned. Billy Jenkins managed a theatre which

showed the movie "Carnal Knowledge. " The film is basically
a story of two young males, roommates and lifelong friends,
who are constantly preoccupied with their sex lives. The
film stars Jack Nicholson, Art Garfunkel, Candice Bergen,
and Ann-Margaret. The film appeared on several "Top Ten
Films of 1971" lists and received many favorable reviews.
Ann-Margaret, in fact, was nominated for an Academy Award.
Jenkins was arrested and tried before a jury who viewed the
film and judged it to be obscene. He was convicted of distributing obscene material, fined $750, and sentenced to
twelve months' probation.

The U. S. Supreme Court's unanimous opinion, written
by Justice William Rehnquist, noted that the general subject
of the film "Carnal Knowledge" is sex. There is nudity and
scenes in which sexual acts are "understood" to be occurring.
Yet the camera does not focus on actors at sexually critical
moments, and "ultimate sexual behavior" is only intimated.
The Court emphasized that even though the film shows occa-
sional nudity, "nudity alone does not render material obscene
under Miller's standards. " The Court also stated that even
though questions of appeal to the prurient interest or of patent
offensiveness are "essentially questions of fact, " the Miller
test did not grant juries "unbridled discretion" in determining
what constitutes sexual conduct depicted in a patently offensive
way. The Court, after viewing the film, found nothing in the
movie to fall within the patently offensive standards established in Miller. It would be "wholly at odds" with Miller
to affirm this obscenity conviction, "even though a properly
charged jury unanimously agreed on a verdict of guilty. " The
film simply did not depict sexual conduct in a patently offensive way. Jenkins' conviction was overturned.

Hamling v. United States 418 U.S. 87 (1974)

Another 1974 case clarified the Miller test. William
Hamling and five other defendants were convicted for mailing
55,000 copies of an advertisement for The Illustrated Presidential Report of the Commission on Obscenity and Pornography. One side of the advertising brochure contained a
collage of photographs from the Illustrated Report portraying
heterosexual and homosexual intercourse, sodomy, and a variety of other sexual acts including fellatio, cunnilingus, masturbation, and lesbian love scenes. The pictures were material that had been shown to persons by the Commission as
part of the research basis for the Report. At Hamling's

trial, which took place prior to the Court's Miller opinion, the instructions to the jury regarding determination of obscenity and the admission of evidence were based on "national" standards. He was convicted. He appealed, contending that he had not been convicted under the appropriate test, which according to Hamling, should have been Miller.

The U. S. Supreme Court noted (5-4) that "national" standards were no longer permissible. The result of Miller should be "to permit a juror sitting in obscenity cases to draw on knowledge of the community or vicinage from which he comes in deciding what conclusion 'the average person, applying contemporary community standards' would reach in a given case." The Hamling case had been tried in the Southern District of California where, presumably, jurors from throughout the district were available to serve on the panel. The jurors would draw upon the standards of that "community." But, the Supreme Court noted, a District Court may admit evidence of standards existing in some other place if such evidence would enable jurors to better resolve the issues. Hamling's conviction was upheld because, in his case, no harm or prejudice resulting from the application of "national community standards" could be shown.

Ward v. State of Illinois 97 S. Ct. 2085 (1977)

In 1977, the Court continued to define the details of the Miller test. Wesley Ward was arrested for selling two publications, Bizarre World and Illustrated Case Histories, a Study of Sado-Masochism, to a police officer who purchased them in Ward's store. After being found guilty, Ward was sentenced to one day in jail, and fined $200. He appealed, challenging the constitutionality of the Illinois obscenity law "for failure to conform to the standards of Miller." Ward asserted that sado-masochistic materials may not be constitutionally proscribed because they were not expressly included in the examples of the kinds of sexually-explicit materials that the Court had cited in Miller to explicate its obscenity definition.

In Ward, the Court noted (5-4) that those specifics cited in Miller were offered merely as "examples"; they "were not intended to extend constitutional protection to the kind of flagellatory materials that were among those held obscene in Mishkin." Ward's conviction was affirmed.

Overall, the Miller test represents a strong anti-obscenity standard in comparison with the Roth test. But, in spite of the prominence of this standard in the courts, national public opinion tends to favor limitations on censorship, and upholds the right of consenting adults to decide for themselves what sexually-oriented materials they will tolerate. X-rated movies and "adult" printed materials abound throughout the country.

CENSORS

Supreme Court justices have generally agreed that obscenity is a type of communication that is not protected by the First Amendment. Through the years, several agencies and organizations have been quick to assume the role of censor and regulator of obscene materials. In this section, various censoring agents are examined in terms of their acceptability by the U.S. Supreme Court.

Customs Officials

Prior to 1930, customs officers barred the entry into the United States of such literary classics as Voltaire's Candide, Rousseau's Confessions, Boccaccio's Decameron, Casanova's Memoirs, Apuleius' Golden Ass, and Cummings' The Enormous Room. Even though some of these books had already been published in the United States, the customs officials seized and confiscated the books. In 1930, Congress amended the Tariff Act and authorized the Secretary of the Treasury to admit books of acknowledged scientific or literary value when imported for noncommercial purposes. In addition, the act provided that when a work was seized the federal district attorney was to institute judicial proceedings for the forfeiture of the book. Any interested party could demand a jury trial.

United States v. One Book Called "Ulysses"
72 F. 2d 705 (1934)

In 1933, an attempt was made to prevent the entry into the U.S. of a copy of James Joyce's Ulysses on the ground that the work was obscene, and therefore not importable. It was contended that the book was subject to seizure, forfeiture, and destruction. When the case reached the New York

District Court, Judge J. Woolsey analyzed the book. He
noted that Joyce, in writing Ulysses, experimented with a
unique literary genre. Joyce used lower middle-class characters living in Dublin, and not only described what they did
on a certain day in June, 1904, as they went about the city
performing their usual occupations, but also depicted what they
were thinking about at the same time. Joyce attempted to
demonstrate how the stream of consciousness with its constantly changing impressions carries not only what is the focus of each person's observation at the present time, but also
residue of recent and distant past impressions. Joyce showed
how each of these impressions affected the actions of the
characters he described. By telling fully what his characters
were thinking about, Joyce was misunderstood and was subjected to numerous attacks. In order to sincerely and honestly realize his purpose, Joyce had to use certain words
which were commonly considered obscene. Joyce was often
accused of being preoccupied with sex in the thoughts of his
characters. But the words were such as would be naturally
and habitually used by the types of characters Joyce described.
Woolsey concluded that in spite of its unusual frankness,
Ulysses was not obscene and could enter the United States.
Even though the book tended to excite "sexual impulses or
lustful thoughts" its net effect was a powerful commentary on
the inner lives of men and women. Judge Woolsey's analysis
was affirmed by the Circuit Court of Appeals. Ulysses,
therefore, was admitted into the United States.

Post Office Officials

The second-class mail privilege is a vital asset to a
periodical. With it, the publisher pays substantially lower
postal rates, thereby obtaining a competitive advantage. Congress has determined that periodical publications are entitled
to the second-class mail provision as long as they have a
legitimate list of subscribers and, among other requirements,
are "published for the dissemination of information of a public character, or devoted to literature, the sciences, arts,
or some special industry...." Congress, however, made obscene material non-mailable, and established criminal punish-
ments in order to enforce the law. Over the years, some
court cases have involved efforts at controlling obscenity by
restricting the use of the United States mails. An early case
reached the Supreme Court in 1946.

Hannegan v. Esquire, Inc. 327 U. S. 146 (1946)

Esquire, a monthly periodical known as the "Magazine for Men," was granted a second-class permit in 1933. Ten years later, a citation was issued by the Postmaster General to show cause why the permit should not be suspended or revoked. The specific issues of Esquire challenged by the Postmaster General were for the months of January through November, 1943. These issues contained columns on topics of current interest, short stories, sports features, articles by prominent newsmakers, a book review section, a theatrical department, a section on the lively arts, and pictorial features. These issues contained, for example, pictures of war action, photographs of game birds, and reproductions of famous paintings. None of these sections was questioned. But, according to the Postmaster General, some recurrent features gave the magazine a dominant theme. The features were jokes, cartoons, pictures, articles, and poems which emphasized mainly sex. After a hearing, the Postmaster General revoked the second-class permit. He did not find that Esquire contained obscene material, but rather that the magazine did not meet required conditions of the second-class privilege. He claimed that some "writings and pictures may be indecent, vulgar, and risque and still not be obscene in a technical sense." But, in order for a publisher to enjoy unique mail privileges, he was bound to do more than refrain from disseminating obscene material. He was obligated to contribute to the public good and the public welfare. It was on this ground that the Postmaster General revoked the second-class privilege.

In a unanimous opinion, the Supreme Court rescinded the order. The Court held that Congress did not intend "to clothe the Postmaster General with the power to supervise the tastes of the reading public of the country." If the Postmaster General was allowed wide powers in granting and withholding the mail privilege, he would have the power to individually "make or break" a publication, as well as the power to impose political, religious, economic, literary, and aesthetic standards on the American press.

Grove Press v. Christenberry 276 F. 2d 433 (1960)

In another case involving the mails, the New York Postmaster detained D. H. Lawrence's novel, Lady Chatterley's Lover. After a hearing, the book was held to be "obscene and non-mailable. " The Postmaster General argued that the work was "replete with descriptions in minute detail of sexual acts, " and that the "descriptions utilize filthy, offensive and degrading words and terms. " In his view, "any literary merit the book may have is far outweighed by the pornographic and smutty passages and words. " He concluded that the book, taken as a whole, was obscene and filthy.

The Second Circuit Court of Appeals noted that expert evaluations held Lady Chatterley's Lover as a distinguished novel, and D. H. Lawrence as one of the great writers of the era. The court cited the views of literary scholars Archibald MacLeish, Mark Schorer, Malcolm Cowley, Alfred Kazin, John Middleton Murry, and Harry T. Moore. Applying the Roth test, the court found that Lady Chatterley's Lover, considered as a whole, did not appeal predominantly to prurient interests. In the story, Constance Chatterley is frustrated over her aristocratic husband's being rendered impotent by a war wound which has paralyzed his left side. She is drawn to another man of lower class, becomes pregnant by him, seeks to divorce her husband, and leaves her class for a life with the other man. Yet this story is not the major thrust of the book. The work attacks three things Lawrence despised: industrialization of the English midlands, the British caste system, and inhibited sex relationships. Lawrence perceives these three factors as instruments of repression of natural man and he appeals for greater freedom. In Lady Chatterley's Lover, the heroine is taught naturalness in self-expression by her lover. The book contains increased intimacy between the two characters, as well as greater use of four-letter words, as Lawrence moves to the book's climax. Such vivid sex descriptions and the use of "natural" language showed how the characters achieved fulfillment and naturalness in their lives. The language was subordinate, but highly useful, to the development of Lawrence's central purpose. To the court, that was not prurient. The Post Office did not appeal the case.

Manual Enterprises v. Day 370 U.S. 478 (1962)

The Postmaster General was also denied censorship power by the Court in a 1962 case. Magazines entitled M A Nual, Trim, and Grecian Guild Pictorial consisted largely of photographs of nude or near-nude male models.

They also contained several advertisements for independent photographers who offered nudist photographs for sale. On March 25, 1960, the Alexandria, Virginia postmaster withheld delivery of 405 copies of these magazines pending a ruling by his superiors as to whether the magazines were mailable. Shortly, J. Edward Day, Postmaster General of the United States, announced that the magazines were obscene, and that they also contained information about where obscene matter could be obtained. The magazines were thus not mailable. The Postmaster noted that the magazines were not physical culture or body-building magazines, but were composed primarily for homosexuals and were read mainly by homosexuals. In his view, the magazines did not have any interest for sexually normal individuals.

The Supreme Court determined (6-1) that even though the material was patently offensive to some, and it did have prurient appeal to a small group of homosexuals, it was not patently offensive to that group. Even though the pictures in the magazine may be unpleasant and uncouth, they were not obscene. Concerning the advertising, the Court noted that if the Post Office were able to bar a magazine from the mails without proof of the publisher's knowledge (scienter) of the character of the magazine's advertisements, it could potentially restrict the public's access to constitutionally protected material. Under such conditions materials which might otherwise be entitled to constitutional protection might be denied a legitimate avenue of access to the public. The Court upheld the right of the magazine to use the mails.

Rowan v. U.S. Post Office Department 397 U.S. 728 (1970)

In previous cases, the courts were reluctant to allow the Postmaster General the power of censorship. In Rowan, the Court did approve the right of an individual to censor his or her own mail with the help of the Post Office. In the 1960s public concern grew over the use of mail facilities to distribute unsolicited lewd or salacious advertisements that receivers judged offensive. Complaints to the Postmaster General about such activity had reached nearly 250,000 annually when Congress passed the Postal Revenue and Federal Salary Act of 1967. Title III of the act is entitled "Prohibition of pandering advertisements in the mails." It provides a way in which a householder may be insulated from advertisements that offer for sale matter which, according to the recipient's sole discretion, seems erotically arousing or sexually provocative.   When an individual notifies the postmaster that advertisements have been received which appear to be obscene, the postmaster must order the sender to stop any future mailings of such materials to the individual. Also, the postmaster must order the sender to delete the name of the individual from all mailing lists under the sender's control.   Daniel Rowan initiated a court action after receiving several prohibitory notices from the postmaster.   He claimed the law violated his right of free speech.

The Supreme Court noted (8-0) that this case differed from previous cases involving Post Office control.   In this instance, the individual was allowed complete discretion in choosing whether or not he desired to receive further material from a specific sender.   The only determination left to the Postmaster General was whether or not the mailer had removed the individual's name from the mailing list.   The Court recognized that people are inescapably captive audiences for many purposes, but that an individual must be able to exercise control over unwanted mail.   The right of every person "to be let alone" must be measured against the right of others to communicate.   Here, the Court felt that the right to communicate must stop at the mailbox of an unreceptive individual.   The constitutionality of the federal law was upheld.

Blount v. Rizzi 400 U.S. 410 (1971)

Acting under the authority of the Postal Reorganization Act, Postmaster General Winton Blount withheld from the mails the magazines Mail Box and Book Bin on the ground that they were obscene.   The case reached the U.S. Supreme Court.

The Court declared (9-0) the law unconstitutional.   The law placed the burden of initiating judicial review on the owner of the withheld material, and not with the censor, where it must rest if it is to comply with the requirements of Freedman v. Maryland, a case that is described in detail in the next section of this chapter.   Regarding Post Office control overall, it can be concluded that the Court has been reluctant to place censorship control in the hands of an individual Post Office official.   Only when the receiving individual has had sole determination of the control, as in Rowan, has Post Office detention of obscene materials been approved.

Prior Restraint

The doctrine of prior restraint involves the censorship of obscene material prior to its appearance in print or exhibition at a theatre. This form of censorship is one of the most effective because it clearly prevents the obscenity from ever reaching the reading or viewing audience. The courts have consistently struck down censorship in the form of prior restraint. However, an exception to that pattern occurred in 1961.

Times Film Corporation v. Chicago 365 U.S. 43 (1961)

Times Film Corporation owned the exclusive right to publicly show the film "Don Juan" in Chicago. The corporation applied for a permit under a Chicago ordinance which required submission of all motion pictures for examination prior to their public exhibition. Times Film sent in the license fee, but refused to submit the film for pre-screening. A city official denied issuance of the permit because the corporation refused to submit the film for examination. The corporation brought suit, contending that the code was a prior restraint which violated the First and Fourteenth Amendments.

The Supreme Court agreed that the ordinance imposed a previous restraint. The issue, in this case, however, was whether constitutional protection included complete and absolute freedom to show, at least once, every kind of motion picture. In arriving at its decision, the Court cited Roth v. United States, which decided that obscenity is not constitutionally protected communication. The Court also cited Near v. Minnesota, in which Justice Charles Hughes noted that there may exist some "exceptional cases" regarding prior restraint; for example, "the primary requirements of decency may be enforced against obscene publications." In Times Film Corporation, even though there was no knowledge of the content of "Don Juan," Chicago was judged to have an obligation to protect its citizens against the dangers of obscenity in the public showing of films. Prior restraint was justified. The denial of the permit was affirmed by the Court (5-4).

Freedman v. Maryland 380 U.S. 51 (1965)

In 1965, the Court struck down a prior restraint ordinance. Ronald Freedman challenged the constitutionality of the Maryland motion picture censorship statute by showing the film "Revenge at Daybreak" at his Baltimore theatre, without first submitting the film to the State Board of Censors. The State admitted that the film was not objectionable, and would have received a license if properly submitted.

When the case reached the U. S. Supreme Court the justices established specific standards for censorship of films. First, the burden of proving that the film was unprotected expression must rest on the censoring agency. Thus, the censor, rather than the exhibitor, must have the burden of initiating judicial proceedings. Second, any restraint prior to judicial review can only be for a brief period to preserve the status quo. Third, there must be assurance of a prompt judicial review. In this case, the Maryland law did not meet these tests. First, after the censor disapproved the motion picture, the exhibitor had to assume the burden of starting judicial proceedings, and of persuading the courts that the film was protected communication. Second, after the Board acted against a film, showing was prohibited pending judicial review, however protracted. Under the statute, Freedman could have been convicted if he had shown the movie after unsuccessfully seeking a license, even though no court had ever ruled on the obscenity of the film. Third, the Maryland code provided no guarantee of prompt judicial determination. The Maryland law failed to provide adequate safeguards against undue inhibition of protected expression. The Supreme Court, in a unanimous opinion, overturned the law as an invalid previous restraint.

Southeastern Promotions v. Conrad 420 U.S. 546 (1975)

In 1975, the Court overturned a decision on the grounds of previous restraint. Southeastern Promotions applied for the use of the Tivoli, a city-leased theatre, in order to present the rock musical "Hair." The musical had played for three years on Broadway and had been performed in more than 140 cities in the United States. Directors of the Chattanooga Memorial Auditorium examined some outside opinions and even though none of them had seen the play or read the script, decided that an application to present the rock musical "Hair" should be rejected as not "in the best interest of the community." Sometime later, Southeastern sought an injunction permitting use of another auditorium. After a three-day hearing on the content of "Hair," the District Court concluded that conduct in the production--group nudity and simulated sex--constituted obscene behavior, not protected by the First Amendment.

The Supreme Court held (5-4) that refusing the use of facilities for this production was decided by personal judgment about the musical's content, and this constituted prior restraint. And that restraint was final. It was not merely a temporary bar while necessary judicial proceedings took place. Prior restraint can be acceptable only when "it takes place under procedural safeguards designed to obviate the dangers of a censorship system." In this case, the procedural safeguards established in Freedman were lacking. First, Southeastern Promotions, rather than the censor, bore the burden for obtaining judicial review and the burden of proof. Second, since effective review on the merits of the request was not obtained until more than five months later, the restraint altered the status quo. Southeastern was forced to forego the initial dates planned for the program and to seek to schedule the performance at a later date. Third, the system failed to provide a procedure for judicial determination. The Court concluded that any restraint must be implemented under a system that provides prompt judicial review with minimal restriction of First Amendment rights. In Southeastern Promotions, the Court reinforced the notion that prior restraint, as a form of regulating obscenity, can be employed only when the Freedman criteria are met.

State Boards and Commissions

States have established boards and commissions in order to censor obscenity. The courts have, as early as 1915, been asked to judge the constitutionality of such state systems of censorship.

Mutual Film Corporation v. Industrial Commission of Ohio
236 U.S. 230 (1915)

In 1913, Ohio enacted a code which established a board of film censors. Mutual Film Corporation, a business with a stock of 2,500 reels and an annual profit of $300,000, brought suit, arguing that the law abridged freedom of speech and press.

The Court, however, in a unanimous decision, held that motion pictures are "capable of evil," and are therefore in need of a censor.

> They [films] are mere representations of events, of
> ideas and sentiments published and known; vivid,
> useful, and entertaining, no doubt, but ... capable
> of evil, having power for it, the greater because of
> their attractiveness and manner of exhibition. It
> was this capability and power ... that induced the
> state of Ohio ... to require censorship before exhi-
> bition....

The Court regarded the code as within the power of government. The Court's opinion seriously questioned the inclusion
of film in the category of speech and press, because of film's
commercial nature. According to the Court, "the exhibition
of moving pictures is a business, pure and simple, originated
and conducted for profit, like other spectacles, not to be regarded, nor intended to be regarded ... as part of the press
of the country, or as organs of public opinion." The Court
observed that "there are some things which should not have
pictorial representation in public places and to all audiences."
In Mutual Film Corporation, the Court approved the censorship of motion pictures by a state board of censors.

Burstyn, Inc. v. Wilson 343 U.S. 495 (1952)

The notion that film was entitled to First Amendment
protection was established in the "Miracle" case of 1952.
"The Miracle" was a forty-minute, Italian-made film directed
by Roberto Rossellini. It tells the story of a poor, simple-
minded girl who while tending her goats on a mountainside
one day meets a bearded stranger. She thinks he is St.
Joseph, her favorite saint, and that he has come to take her
to heaven. While she pleads with him to transport her, the
stranger plies the girl with wine and apparently has intercourse with her, although this scene is only briefly and dis-
creetly implied. Later, the girl finds she is pregnant. Some
townspeople humor her, but others mock and hit her. Accompanied only by a goat, she gives birth within a church and
murmurs, "My son! My love! My flesh!" After obtaining
a license from the Motion Picture Division of the New York
State Education Department, the film was shown along with
two French films, Jean Renoir's "A Day in the Country" and
Marcel Pagnol's "Jofroi." All had English subtitles. The
trilogy was titled "Ways of Love," and opened on December
12, 1950, at the Paris Theatre on 58th Street in Manhattan.

A debate about the film began immediately. The film
was attacked as "a sacrilegious and blasphemous mockery of

Christian religious truth" by the National Legion of Decency,
a private Catholic organization for film censorship.   However,
the National Board of Review recommended the film as "especially worth seeing. " New York critics on the whole
praised "The Miracle, " and on December 27 they selected the
"Ways of Love" as the best foreign language film of 1950.
On Sunday, January 7, 1951, a statement by Francis Cardinal
Spellman, condemning the film and urging "all right thinking
citizens" to unite to strengthen censorship laws, was read at
all masses in St. Patrick's Cathedral.   Then, Allen Tate,
the prominent Catholic poet and critic wrote: "The picture
seems to me to be superior in acting and photography but
inferior dramatically. . . .   In the long run what Cardinal
Spellman will have succeeded in doing is insulating the intelligence and faith of American Catholics with the assumption
that a second-rate motion picture could in any way undermine
their morals or shake their faith. " In light of this controversy, the Chairman of the Board of Regents appointed a
Committee to review the action of the Motion Picture Division
in granting the license.   After viewing the picture, the committee declared it "sacrilegious. "   The Board of Regents
rescinded the license in February.   The case reached the
highest Court.

The issue facing the United States Supreme Court was
the constitutionality of the New York statute which permitted
banning motion pictures on the ground that they were sacrilegious.   In the "Miracle" case, the Court unanimously overturned the principle established in Mutual Film Corporation,
that movies were not entitled to the protection of the First
Amendment because of their commercial nature.   The Court
recognized that motion pictures are a significant medium for
the communication of ideas.   The importance of film as a
vehicle of public opinion is not diminished by the fact that
films are intended to entertain, as well as to inform.   Books,
newspapers, and magazines are published and sold for profit
and are safeguarded by the First Amendment.   Commercial-
ization should have no different impact where motion pictures
are concerned.

The Court did not, however, outlaw film censorship
if exercised within narrowly defined rules.   But the justices
did hold that the term "sacrilegious" as used in the New York
statute was vague.   Under such a criticism, the most careful
censor would find it virtually impossible to neglect favoring
one religion over another, and would be vulnerable to a tendency to ban the expression of unpopular sentiments sacred to
a religious minority.   However, the Court did not determine

whether a state may censor films under a clearly-drawn statute designed to prevent the showing of obscenity. Instead, they simply concluded (9-0) that a state may not bar a movie on the basis of a censor's conclusion that it is "sacrilegious. "

Kingsley International Pictures Corp. v. Regents of University of State of New York 360 U. S. 684 (1959)

In 1959, the Court overturned a New York statute which banned the showing of a motion picture that was "immoral. " As the distributor of the film, "Lady Chatterley's Lover, " Kingsley International Pictures submitted the film to the Motion Picture Division of the New York Education Department for a license. Finding three isolated scenes in the film "immoral, " the Division refused to issue a license unless the scenes were deleted. The distributor requested that the Regents reconsider, but they upheld the denial on an even broader ground, that the whole theme of this film, "the presentation of adultery as a desirable, acceptable and proper pattern of behavior, " was immoral. The case came before the U. S. Supreme Court.

The Court held (9-0) that the ban on this film violated the First Amendment guarantee of the freedom to advocate ideas. Such guarantees protect advocacy of the view that adultery may sometimes be proper. The guarantee was not restricted to the expression of ideas that are ordinary or shared by a majority. But the Court did not decide one of Kingsley's contentions, that is, that a state lacks the power to require films of any kind to be licensed prior to their showing.

Bantam Books v. Sullivan 372 U. S. 58 (1963)

In 1956, the Rhode Island Legislature created the Rhode Island Commission to Encourage Morality in Youth, with the task of educating the public concerning obscene printed material. The Commission also had the duty of recommending the prosecution of all violations. The Commission's practice was to notify a distributor that certain books or magazines had been reviewed and had been declared by a majority of the Commission's members to be objectionable for sale to persons under eighteen years of age.

Max Silverstein & Sons, the exclusive wholesale

distributor of certain paperbacks throughout Rhode Island, had received at least thirty-five notices. Among the paperbacks listed as objectionable were Peyton Place by Grace Metalious and The Bramble Bush by Charles Mergendahl. Many of the other 106 publications which, as of January, 1960, had been listed as objectionable, were issues of such magazines as Playboy, Rogue, and Frolic. The typical notice thanked Silverstein in advance for his cooperation, usually reminding him of the Commission's duty to suggest to the Attorney General prosecution of purveyors of obscenity. Silverstein stopped further circulation of copies of the blacklisted publications. He refused to fill pending requests for the publications and rejected new orders. He instructed his employees to pick up all unsold copies from retailers, and then promptly returned them to the publishers. A local police officer frequently visited Silverstein to check what action had been taken. Silverstein usually informed the officer that a certain number of the copies had been returned. Silverstein cooperated in order to avoid a court proceeding. Soon, four publishing companies, including Bantam Books, started a court action in order to have the law creating the Commission declared in violation of the Constitution.

The U. S. Supreme Court declared that though the Commission was limited to informal sanctions, the threat of invoking legal action showed that the Commission deliberately set about to achieve the suppression of publications deemed objectionable, and succeeded in that goal. The Court also noted that Silverstein's compliance with the notices was not voluntary. He simply could not disregard the public officer's threats to institute criminal proceedings against him if he did not comply. The Commission's notices were phrased virtually as orders and were understood to be such by Silverstein, especially when followed up by police visitations. These blacklists of printed materials were more than mere legal advice; "they plainly serve as instruments of regulation independent of the laws against obscenity." The Commission operated as an agency not to advise but to suppress, and was thus a form of prior restraint. The Court pinpointed another fault of this system. The Commission's operation was a form of regulation superimposed upon Rhode Island's criminal regulation of obscenity, which at the same time eliminated safeguards of the criminal process. Criminal sanctions may be invoked only after a determination of obscenity in a trial procedure. The Commission's system provided no safeguards whatever against the suppression of non-obscene, constitutionally protected, material. The Court invalidated (8-1) the Rhode Island system of informal censorship.

Supreme Court decisions involving state censorship boards and commissions do not lead to a firm conclusion. In 1915, in Mutual Film Corporation, the Court upheld an Ohio board of film censors on the ground that film has unique corruptive power. In 1963, in Bantam Books, the Court rejected a Rhode Island system of censorship. For the most part, however, as is evident in Burstyn and Kingsley International Pictures Corp., the Court has been somewhat reluctant, over the years, to take a firm stand on the acceptability of state censorship boards and commissions.

Local Officials

Local police and judicial officials can play a part in the regulation of obscenity, if proper safeguards are provided. In 1957, in Kingsley Books v. Brown, a New York criminal code which authorized the chief executive of a city to stop the sale of printed matter found after due trial to be obscene was upheld by the Supreme Court.

Kingsley Books, Inc. v. Brown 354 U. S. 436 (1957)

A New York statute authorized a legal officer of a city to act against the sale or distribution of any indecent written or printed material. In accordance with this law, on September 10, 1954, a complaint was filed against Kingsley Books, charging the company with displaying for sale paper-covered obscene books. Copies of fourteen different booklets, under the general title of Nights of Horror, were ordered surrendered to the sheriff for destruction. When the case came to trial, the judge decided that the booklets were obscene; they were "dirt for dirt's sake. " He ordered that further distribution be stopped, and that the books be destroyed. The judge, however, refused to enjoin the distribution of later issues because that would "impose an unreasonable prior restraint upon freedom of the press. "

The Supreme Court upheld (5-4) the constitutionality of the statute. It was a proper regulation of obscenity that placed a restraint upon printed matter after publication, and after a determination of obscenity. In this case, the New York law was upheld because it "is concerned solely with obscenity and ... it studiously withholds restraint upon matters not already published and not yet found to be offensive. " In addition, according to the law, Kingsley was given the right to a trial within one day after joinder of issues and decision within two days after conclusion of trial. Such a procedure, as practiced in New York, does not amount to prior censorship and does not violate freedom of speech and thought.

Marcus v. Search Warrants of Property 367 U. S. 717 (1961)

In Marcus, the Court overturned a procedure involving a search warrant giving police officers too broad discretion. The case began in October, 1957, when Police Lieutenant Coughlin of the Kansas City Police Department Vice Squad was conducting an investigation into the distribution of allegedly obscene magazines. He visited Kansas City News Distributors, which was managed by Homer Smay. He showed Smay a list of books, and Smay admitted that his company distributed all but one of the items on the list. The next day Coughlin purchased copies of the magazines. Then he filed a complaint in Circuit Court stating that Smay kept obscene publications for sale. No copy of any magazine was shown to the circuit judge. The judge issued a search warrant granting power for any peace officer in Missouri to seize obscene material anytime within ten days. The warrant was executed by Lieutenant Coughlin and other police officers on October 10. Distributors' stock of magazines ran into the hundreds of thousands, and probably closer to a million copies. The officers examined the publications in the stock on the main floor of the establishment, not confining themselves to Lieutenant Coughlin's list. They seized all magazines which in their judgment were obscene. After three hours, the examination was completed and the magazines seized were hauled away in a truck and put on the fifteenth floor of the courthouse. A similar procedure was followed at five other newsstands. Approximately 11,000 copies of 289 magazines and some books and photographs were seized.

The issue in this case was whether the use of the search warrant to suppress obscene publications abused protected expression. The U. S. Supreme Court believed (9-0) the safeguards in this instance failed to assure that non-obscene material was adequately protected. The Missouri warrants gave the broadest discretion to the officers; they specified no publications, and left to the individual judgment of the police officers the determination of any magazines which they believed to be obscene. In several instances, if not in all, police officers made decisions on the spot with little opportunity for reflection and deliberation. Officers were provided with no criteria which would enable informed discretion because there was no point in the operation before seizure which focused on the question of obscenity. Procedures which sweep so broadly, and with such lack of discrimination, are obviously improper.

A Quantity of Copies of Books v. Kansas 378 U. S. 205 (1964)

In 1964, the Court struck down a Kansas statute that allowed seizure of allegedly obscene books prior to determination of obscenity, and their destruction after such determination. The Attorney General obtained an order instructing a local sheriff to seize copies of certain paperback novels at P-K News Service in Junction City, Kansas. After a hearing, the sheriff was directed to destroy the 1,715 copies of 31 novels which had been seized.

The Supreme Court reversed (7-2) the decision. It held that the procedures were constitutionally inadequate because they did not safeguard against the suppression of non-obscene books. In this case, the Kansas statute failed to comply with the requirements set down in Kingsley Books. By not affording P-K an adversary hearing prior to seizure, the procedure leading to the seizure was constitutionally deficient. If seizure of books can precede determination of their obscenity, there is danger of abridgment of the right to unobstructed circulation of non-obscene books.

In the cases cited thus far in this section, all of which deal with print, the Court stressed that local officials violate the Constitution when they act upon a search warrant which contains a broad sweep, as well as when the procedure lacks a determination of obscenity prior to seizure.

Heller v. New York 413 U. S. 483 (1973)

In the cases cited above, the Court was concerned with printed material. In Heller v. New York the Court examined the procedure for obtaining a search warrant and for providing a hearing in cases regarding film. Saul Heller managed a commercial movie theatre in the Greenwich Village area of New York City. On July 29, 1969, the theatre showed "Blue Movie," a film depicting a nude couple engaged in ultimate sexual acts. Three police officers saw part of

the film, and on the basis of their observations an assistant
district attorney requested a judge to see the performance.
On July 31, the judge purchased a ticket and saw the entire
film.   There were about 100 persons in the audience.   At the
end of the showing, the judge signed a search warrant for the
seizure of the film and the arrest of the theatre manager.
At trial Heller was found guilty.   He appealed, claiming that
his rights had been violated in the specific procedure followed
by authorities in this case.

The U. S. Supreme Court decided (5-4) that there was
no necessity of holding an adversary hearing prior to the
seizure of one copy of a film for use as evidence in a criminal trial.   The Court noted, however, that a film cannot be
seized by police as evidence until a warrant is issued by a
judge who has viewed the film and judged it to be obscene.
Following seizure, an adversary hearing must be held to
determine if the movie is, in fact, obscene.   The theatre
owner must be given the opportunity to be represented at the
hearing.   The Court contrasted this procedure with that out-
lined in the A Quantity of Copies of Books and Marcus cases.
Those cases concerned the seizure of large quantities of
printed materials for the purpose of destroying them.   In such
instances, the Court has upheld the requirement of a previous
judicial determination of obscenity in an adversary hearing in
order to prevent the uninterrupted circulation of non-obscene
printed matter.   But seizing films to destroy them is a different matter than seizing a single copy of a film for the
purpose of using it as evidence in a criminal proceeding.   In
this case, the Court also decided that the theatre owner could
continue to show the film if he has a second copy.   And, if
there were no other copies available, the owner of the seized
film might make a copy so that it could be shown pending the
adversary proceeding.

Roaden v. Kentucky 413 U. S. 496 (1973)

In a case heard on the same day, the Court reaffirmed
the notion that seizure cannot occur without the issuance of
a warrant following determination of obscenity.   The events
of this case began in September, 1970, when the sheriff of
Pulaski County, Kentucky purchased a ticket to see the film
"Cindy and Donna," which was playing at a drive-in theatre.
After viewing the movie, he determined it was obscene, went
to the projection room, arrested theatre manager Harry
Roaden, and seized the film.   There was no warrant and no
prior determination of obscenity.   Roaden was convicted.

The U.S. Supreme Court decided (5-4) that the seizure of the film without a warrant was illegal; a warrant could have been easily obtained. The police procedure in this case functioned as a prior restraint much like the seizure of all the books in a particular bookstore.

It is clear, based on the cases examined in this section, that, in the event of seizing a film or book, some judicial activity must be a prerequisite to police action. And the adversary hearing on the issue of obscenity must be held promptly after seizure. Finally, a theatre owner can make a copy of his film and show the movie pending the adversary hearing.

Industry Regulation

In 1968, the Court struck down a city ordinance on the ground that it was unconstitutionally vague. The case is worth studying because it stimulated an effort by the film industry to regulate motion pictures.

Interstate Circuit, Inc. v. Dallas 390 U.S. 676 (1968)

A Dallas law authorized a motion picture classification board to classify films as "Suitable" or "Not Suitable" for persons under sixteen. Films had to be advertised as "not suitable for young persons" when so classified, and persons under sixteen were not admitted to such films unless accompanied by a guardian or spouse. Films were classified as "not suitable" when they described violence, sexual promiscuity, extra-marital activity, or abnormal sexual relations in a manner likely to incite delinquency or sexual promiscuity on the part of young persons. When the Board classified the film "Viva Maria" as "not suitable for young persons," Interstate Circuit, Inc. brought suit.

The U.S. Supreme Court ruled (8-1) that the standards were unconstitutionally vague. The term "sexual promiscuity" was not defined in the law. Depending upon a censor's moral judgment, this could involve activity from the obvious to any sexual contacts outside a marital relationship. In the film, the portrayal of "sexual promiscuity" was implicit rather than explicit; it was a result of inference by the viewer. The ordinance did not require the Board to give reasons for its action. The Court noted that the law's vagueness was not

excusable even if it was particularly designed to control expression with respect to children. Nor was it less objectionable because the regulation of expression was one of
classification, rather than direct suppression.

Shortly after this case, the motion picture industry
adopted a rating system. As of November 1, 1968, the Motion Picture Association of America (MPAA) Code rated films.
The initial system contained the following ratings:

G - suggested for General audiences
M - suggested for Mature audiences; parental discre-
   tion advised
R - Restricted, people under 16 not admitted unless
   accompanied by adult
X - persons under 16 not admitted

The system has experienced slight modification. The current
ratings include:

G - General audiences. Film contains no material
   most parents are likely to consider objectionable even for younger children.
PG - Parental guidance suggested. Some material
   might be unsuitable for children.
R - Restricted. Film contains adult-type material.
   Persons under 17 require accompanying parent
   or adult guardian.
X - This is patently an adult-type film. No one under
   18 admitted.

Community Standards

In Miller, the Court held that what constitutes appeals
to the prurient interest and what is patently offensive are in
fact to be measured by contemporary standards of the community. In 1977, the Court set forth a specific way in which
such standards might be determined.

Smith v. United States 431 U.S. 291 (1977)

Between February and October, 1974, Jerry Lee Smith
mailed various materials from Des Moines, Iowa to post
office box addresses in Mount Ayr and Guthrie Center, two
communities in southern Iowa. This was done at the written

request of postal inspectors using fictitious names. The mailings consisted of issues of Intrigue magazine, and films entitled "Lovelace" and "Terrorized Virgin, " depicting nude males and females engaged in fellatio, cunnilingus, masturbation, and sexual intercourse. Smith was indicted on seven counts of violating the federal obscenity law, which prohibits the mailing of obscene materials. He pleaded not guilty. At trial the judge instructed the jury that contemporary community standards were established by what is accepted in the community as a whole. The jurors were entitled to draw on their own knowledge of the views of the average person in the community. The jury found Smith guilty on all seven counts. He was sentenced to three months of imprisonment and three years' probation. He appealed on the grounds that the Iowa obscenity statute in effect at the time he was arrested, which proscribed only the dissemination of obscene materials to minors, set forth the applicable community standard, and that the prosecution had not proved that the materials at issue had offended that particular standard.

The U. S. Supreme Court had to decide whether a jury is entitled to rely on its own knowledge of community standards, or whether a state legislature may declare what the community standards shall be; and when such a declaration has been made, whether it is binding in a federal prosecution. The Court noted (5-4) the impossibility of a state legislature's defining contemporary community standards of appeal to prurient interest or patent offensiveness, largely because of that body's isolation from a particular community. The Court said there was room for state legislation regarding the obscenity issue, but "the question of the community standard to apply, when appeal to prurient interest and patent offensiveness are considered, is not one that can be defined legislatively. " The Court concluded that "though state legislatures are not completely foreclosed from setting substantive limitations for obscenity cases, they cannot declare what community standards shall be.... "

Based on Smith, the most accepted current censors seem to be the specific jurors who apply contemporary community standards in accordance with their own understanding of the tolerance of the average person in the community. In essence, the message of Smith is that the jury has "discretion to determine what appeals to prurient interest and what is patently offensive. "

SCOPE AND LIMITATIONS

The U. S. Supreme Court has rendered several decisions which clarify the scope of and place limitations on obscenity regulation. Some of those decisions are considered in the following section.

Scienter

Legal dictionaries define scienter as the degree of knowledge on the part of the accused that is necessary to make the individual legally responsible for the consequences of his action. In 1959, the Court considered the applicability of scienter to obscenity cases.

Smith v. People of the State of California
361 U. S. 147 (1959)

Eleazar Smith, the proprietor of a Los Angeles bookstore, was convicted and sentenced to jail under a city ordinance for possessing obscene material in his place of business. The offense consisted solely of the possession of a certain book found to be obscene. No element of scienter, that is, knowledge by Smith of the obscene character of the book, was considered. Thus, the ordinance imposed a "strict" or "absolute" criminal liability. He appealed.

The Court ruled (8-1) that the ordinance had an unconstitutional tendency because it dispensed with the element of scienter. Writing for the Court, Justice William Brennan pointed out that if a bookseller is liable while unaware of the obscene contents, he will restrict his volume of books to those he has inspected. Distribution of books which are both obscene and not obscene would be impeded. Thus, a law which ignores scienter "tends to impose a severe limitation on the public's access to constitutionally protected matter."

Pandering

Pandering involves exploiting the lusts of persons. In Ginzburg, the Court upheld an obscenity conviction based largely on the activity of pandering.

Ginzburg v. United States 383 U. S. 463 (1966)

Book-dealer Ralph Ginzburg sent three publications through the mail: Eros, a hard-cover magazine containing articles and photo-essays on the subjects of love, sex, and sexual relations; Liaison, a bi-weekly newsletter dedicated to "keeping sex an art and preventing it from becoming a science"; and The Housewife's Handbook on Selective Promiscuity, a short book which claimed to be a sexual autobiography detailing candidly the author's complete sexual experiences from age three to 36. The book contained her opinions on such subjects as sex education in schools, laws regulating private consensual adult practices, and the equality of women in sexual relationships. Ginsburg also sent through the mail advertising which explained how and where the publications might be obtained. In order to distribute these materials, Ginzburg sought mailing privileges from the postmasters of Intercourse and Blue Ball, Pennsylvania. These localities were selected because of the value their names had for selling the publications. The facilities were inadequate to handle the anticipated volume of mail, so the requests were denied. Mailing privileges were then obtained from Middlesex, New Jersey. Thereafter, several million circulars soliciting subscriptions for Eros and Liaison were mailed from that post office, and over 5,500 copies of the Handbook were mailed. The advertising boasted about the sexual candor of the publications. Inserted in each advertisement for Housewife's Handbook was a "GUARANTEE" which read, "Documentary Books, Inc. unconditionally guarantees full refund of the price of THE HOUSEWIFE'S HANDBOOK ON SELECTIVE PROMISCUITY if the book fails to reach you because of U. S. Post Office censorship interference." Similar slips appeared in the advertising for Eros and Liaison. This form of advertising eliminated any doubt as to what the purchaser was being asked to buy.

Ginzburg was tried upon twenty-eight counts of violating the federal obscenity statute. Each count alleged that a specific individual received by mail one of the three publications, or advertising telling how the publications might be obtained. The prosecution admitted that the materials in and of themselves might not be obscene under the Roth test. However, in the context of the advertising campaign, they had clearly become so. Commercial exploitation had made them obscene. A Pennsylvania judge convicted Ginzburg, fined him $28, and sentenced him to five years in prison.

The U. S. Supreme Court said (5-4) that the question of obscenity may include consideration of the setting in which the materials were presented as an aid in determining the issue of obscenity. In the Ginzburg case, the materials were sold as part of the sordid business of pandering, that is, "the business of purveying textual or graphic matter openly advertised to appeal to the erotic interest of their customers. " Deliberate representation of the publications as erotically stimulating leads the reader to accept them as prurient. On the basis of pandering, a majority of the Court upheld Ginzburg's conviction.

Minors

Two Court opinions identify the scope of obscenity regulations as they apply to youth. In the first case, Butler v. Michigan, a law was declared unconstitutional which tended to reduce the adult to the level of youth. In the second case, Ginsberg v. New York, the Court examined the constitutionality of an obscenity statute which outlawed the sale to minors of material defined to be obscene on the basis of its appeal to youth, regardless of whether or not it was obscene to adults.

Butler v. State of Michigan 352 U. S. 380 (1957)

The Michigan Penal Code made it a crime to make available for the general public a book which could incite youth to violent, depraved, or immoral acts. Alfred Butler was charged with selling to a Detroit policeman what the trial judge described as "a book containing obscene, immoral, lewd, lascivious language or descriptions, tending to incite minors to violent or depraved or immoral acts, manifestly tending to the corruption of the morals of youth. " Butler was found guilty and fined $100. He appealed.

The U. S. Supreme Court noted that the Michigan law prevented distribution of books to the general public because of the undesirable influence they may have upon minors. The adult population was reduced to reading only what was fit for children. According to the Court, the law was "not reasonably restricted to the evil with which it is said to deal. " The Court unanimously reversed Butler's conviction. The Butler decision is significant because it freed adult literature from obscenity tests that might be appropriate for childrens' literature.

Ginsberg v. New York 390 U. S. 629 (1968)

In Ginsberg, the Court upheld a statute which outlawed the sale to minors of material defined as specifically obscene for them. Sam Ginsberg and his wife operated "Sam's Stationary and Luncheonette" on Long Island. The couple operated a lunch counter and, among other things, they sold magazines. In October, 1965, Ginsberg was arrested for personally selling two "girlie" magazines to a sixteen-year-old boy without attempting to ascertain the age of the boy. A court judge determined that the magazines contained pictures which portrayed female nudity. He judged that the pictures represented nudity in a manner which predominantly appeals to the prurient interest of minors, is patently offensive to prevailing standards in the adult community, and is utterly without redeeming social importance to minors. Ginsberg was tried and found guilty.

The U. S. Supreme Court recognized (6-3) the constitutionality of the state statute which regulated the sale of pornography to children through special standards, broader than those embodied in legislation aimed at regulating the dissemination of such matter to adults. The Court emphasized that parents have primary authority in their household for the rearing of their children. Nowhere in the New York statute was there any prohibition against parents, who so desire, purchasing the magazines for their children. The Court also recognized the independent interest of the state in the well-being of its youth. The state has an interest in protecting the "welfare of children" and seeing that they are "safeguarded from abuses." The Court upheld the statute and Ginsberg's conviction.

Privacy

Several Court decisions have clarified the relationship between obscenity and privacy. In 1969, an important decision was handed down by the Court.

Stanley v. Georgia 394 U. S. 557 (1969)

Robert Stanley was suspected of being involved in bookmaking activities. Under the authority of a search warrant, government agents entered Stanley's home and located very little evidence of bookmaking activity, but while

searching a desk drawer in an upstairs bedroom, they found
three reels of eight-millimeter film. Using a projector and
screen found in the living room, they viewed the films which
showed "successive orgies by nude men and women engaging
in repeated acts of seduction, sodomy, and intercourse. " A
state officer concluded that the films were obscene, and
seized them. Stanley was charged with possession of obscene
material, and placed under arrest. He was tried, convicted,
and sentenced to one year in jail.

Before the U. S. Supreme Court, Stanley argued that
the Georgia law violated the Constitution because it punished
mere private possession of obscene material. Stanley asserted the right to read and view what he pleased. He claimed
the right to satisfy his intellectual and emotional needs in
the privacy of his own home. He asserted a right to freedom
from state inquiry into the contents of his library. To counter, Georgia argued that Stanley did not have such rights;
there are certain materials that an individual may not read,
or even possess. The Court unanimously supported Stanley,
ruling "that a State has no business telling a man, sitting
alone in his own home, what books he may read or what
films he may watch. "

United States v. Thirty-seven (37) Photographs
402 U. S. 363 (1971)

In the following years, several cases limited the scope
of the Stanley principle. On October 24, 1969, Milton Luros
returned to the United States from Europe. He brought with
him in his luggage 37 photographs which customs agents
seized as obscene. The photographs were intended to be used
in a hard cover edition of The Kama Sutra of Vatsyayana,
a book candidly depicting several sexual positions. At a
hearing, it was decided that the statute was unconstitutional,
and the photographs were ordered returned to Luros. The
case went to the U. S. Supreme Court.

In terms of the Stanley case, the Court ruled (6-3)
that Luros' situation did not involve the privacy of his own
home. Instead, it concerned the seizure of obscene materials
possessed at a port of entry. The emphasis in Stanley was
on the freedom of thought in the privacy of one's home. A
port of entry was not Luros' home. Luros' right to be let
alone neither prevents the search of his luggage, nor the
seizure of obscene, unprotected materials discovered to be

in his possession during such a search.   The Court reversed
the findings of the hearings.

United States v. Reidel 402 U. S. 351 (1971)

At the same time, the Court heard United States v.
Reidel.   Federal obscenity law forbids the knowing use of the
mails for the delivery of obscene matter.   In 1970, Norman
Reidel was convicted for having mailed a copy of an illustrated booklet entitled "The True Facts about Imported Pornography. "   The booklet had been mailed to a postal inspector, who had answered a newspaper advertisement which read:
"IMPORTED PRONOGRAPHY--Learn the true facts before
sending money abroad.   Send $1. 00 for our fully illustrated
booklet.   You must be 21 years of age and so state.   Normax
Press, P. O. Box 989, Fontana, California, 92335. "   Reidel
appealed.   The case reached the U. S. Supreme Court.

This case involved the issue of the distribution of
obscene materials to willing recipients who acknowledge being
adults.   The Stanley principle was not applicable.   Reidel was
distributing obscenity through the mails, and had no complaint
about unwanted governmental intrusion into the privacy of his
home.   Reidel made no claims about governmental violations
of his private thoughts; instead, he stood squarely on a
claimed First Amendment right to do business in obscenity,
and use the mails in the process.   The Court noted that obscenity and its dissemination is outside the protection of the
First Amendment.   The Court ruled (7-2) that the Stanley
principle was not relevant; it did not sanction the use of the
channels of commerce to disseminate obscene matter, nor
did it sanction the Postal Service to be a party to such
activity.

United States v. Orito 413 U. S. 139 (1973)

In U. S. v. Orito, the Court acknowledged that Congress possesses the power to prevent obscene material from
entering the stream of commerce.   George Orito was convicted for knowingly transporting on Trans World Airlines,
from San Francisco to Milwaukee, 83 films which were
"lewd, lascivious, and filthy materials. "   The District Court
accepted Orito's argument that the Stanley case had established the right to possess obscene material in the privacy
of the home, and that there existed a correlative right to
receive, transport, and distribute such material.

The U. S. Supreme Court, however, ruled (5-4) that the District Court had erred in overturning Orito's conviction on "privacy" grounds. The zone of privacy established by Stanley does not extend beyond the home. Congress could regulate interstate commerce in obscene materials "based as that regulation is on the legislatively determined risk of ultimate exposure to juveniles or to the public and the harm that exposure could cause. " The case was remanded.

United States v. 12 200-ft. Reels of Super 8mm Film
413 U. S. 123 (1973)

In a similar case, movie films, photographs, color slides, and other printed and graphic matter which were being carried from Mexico to the United States, were seized by customs officers at the Los Angeles Airport as being obscene. The importer was convicted. He appealed. The District Court overturned the conviction by accepting the argument that Stanley, by acknowledging "the right to possess obscene material in the privacy of the home creates a right to acquire it or import it from another country. "

The U. S. Supreme Court held (5-4) that the focus in Stanley was on freedom of thought and mind in the privacy of the home, and a port of entry is not a traveler's home. The Court would not approve the importation for private use of obscene material.

In this case, as in Orito, Reidel, and Thirty Seven (37) Photographs, the Court severely restricted the "privacy" ruling in Stanley. The Court firmly upheld governmental power to regulate interstate transportation, delivery through the mails, or importation from abroad of obscene materials for personal possession or use.

Passerby Visibility

During the 1970s the Court, on at least two occasions, examined the question of passerby visibility. Specifically, the Court was presented situations in which passersby were exposed to offensive, if not obscene, films at an outdoor theatre.

Rabe v. Washington 405 U. S. 313 (1972)

William Rabe, a Richland, Washington drive-in theatre

operator, was convicted for exhibiting an X-rated picture on
a screen visible to passersby and nearby residents.   The film
"Carmen Baby" is a loose adaptation of Bizet's opera "Carmen. "   The picture contains sexually frank scenes but por-
trays no ultimate sexual acts.   A police officer twice viewed
the film from outside the theatre fence and arrested Rabe
under a statute which made it a crime to knowingly display
an obscene motion picture.

The Supreme Court reversed (9-0) the conviction on a
technicality.   The Court noted that in order to avoid a charge
of vagueness, a law must give fair notice that certain conduct
is proscribed.   The Washington law did not mention that the
location of the exhibition of a film was an "element of the
offense somehow modifying the word obscene. "   The Court
held that the showing at a drive-in theatre of a motion picture
cannot be criminally punished unless the law gives a fair
notice that the location of the showing is a vital element.

Erznoznik v. City of Jacksonville 422 U.S. 205 (1975)

The same issue arose in 1975.   The case involved a
Jacksonville code which prohibited displaying nudity in a film
shown by a drive-in movie theatre with a screen visible from
a public place or street.   Richard Erznoznik was convicted
of violating the ordinance by showing "Class of '74, " a movie
in which female buttocks and bare breasts were shown.   He
appealed.

The Supreme Court determined (6-3) that the Jacksonville code was overbroad.   It discriminated among movies
solely on the basis of content.   The effect of the ordinance
was to deter drive-in theatres from showing films containing
any nudity, even if the film was innocent or educational.
Such movies are entitled to First Amendment protection and
should be free from special controls directed at the content.
The ordinance was not directed specifically against sexually-
explicit nudity.   A law which restricted films which were
legally obscene could be valid.   In addition, the ordinance
was an unlawful method of traffic regulation because it singled
out movies containing nudity from all other films which might
distract a passing motorist.   The deterrent effect was significant since theatre owners, in order to avoid prosecution,
"must either restrict their movie offerings or construct adequate protective fencing which may be extremely expensive or
even physically impracticable. "   A law restricting films at

all drive-ins having passerby visibility could be valid. The
Court concluded "that the limited privacy interest of persons
on the public streets cannot justify this censorship of otherwise protected speech on the basis of its content. "

Zoning Restrictions

In many bigger cities throughout America, obscene
activity is located in a particular section of town. Law
enforcement agencies tend to ignore this few-block area where
the dealers in pornography traffic, as long as there are no
major citizen complaints or any extremely gross pornographic
activity. Adult bookstores and adult theatres are located in
"erogenous zones" within the central city because such areas
are less than desirable for other commercial activity but
convenient for the customers of places featuring pornography.

Young v. American Mini Theatres 427 U. S. 50 (1976)

In a recent case, the Court considered whether a city
could restrict the geographic location of motion-picture
theatres that exhibit non-obscene but sexually-oriented films.
In 1972, Detroit amended an "Anti-Skid Row Ordinance" by
providing that, unless a special waiver was granted, no adult
theatre may be located within 1, 000 feet of any two other
"regulated uses" (a term identifying ten establishments such
as adult book stores, bars, cabarets, pool halls, hotels), or
within 500 feet of a residential area. An "adult" theatre
was defined as one presenting "material depicting ... specified
sexual activities or specified anatomical areas. " American
Mini Theatres brought suit, seeking a declaration that the
ordinance was unconstitutional.

The U. S. Supreme Court supported (5-4) the ordinance.
In the opinion of Justice John Stevens, a "municipality may
control the location of theatres as well as the location of other
commercial establishments, either by confining them to certain specified commercial zones or by requiring that they be
dispersed throughout the city. " The Court went on to acknowledge that the content of films may be the basis for
zoning restrictions. Such regulation did not violate First
Amendment protection. In Young, the Court supported the
right of a city to specify locational requirements for adult
theatres. It was the city's business to decide whether to
"require adult theaters to be separated rather than concen-
trated in the same areas. "

In <u>Young</u>, the Court actually supported the regulation of protected speech which is sexually-oriented but not necessarily obscene. The policy differs markedly from the Court's recent policy of requiring that a film be declared obscene in a judicial proceeding, or that a film be in violation of statutory provisions for determining obscenity. In <u>Young</u>, the Court departed from its traditional principles of First Amendment protection. The message that seems clear in <u>Young</u>, as well as in other recent Court decisions, is that the Burger Court will continue to broaden the scope of obscenity regulation in America.

Bibliography

Books

Lewis, Felice Flanery. <u>Literature, Obscenity, & Law.</u>
    Carbondale: Southern Illinois University Press, 1976.

Schauer, Frederick F. <u>The Law of Obscenity.</u> Washington,
    D. C. : Bureau of National Affairs, 1976.

Sharp, Donald B. , ed. <u>Commentaries on Obscenity.</u>
    Metuchen, New Jersey: The Scarecrow Press, 1970.

Sunderland, Lane V. <u>Obscenity: The Court, the Congress
    and the President's Commission.</u> Washington, D. C. :
    American Enterprise Institute for Public Policy Research,
    1974.

Widmer, Eleanor, ed. <u>Literary Censorship in the '70s.</u>
    Belmont: Wadsworth Publishing, 1970.

Articles

"Community Standards, Class Actions, and Obscenity Under
    Miller v. California, " <u>Harvard Law Review</u> 88 (July,
    1975), 1838-74.

Friedman, Leon. "The Ginzburg Decision and the Law, "
    <u>The American Scholar</u> 36 (Winter, 1966-67), 71-91.

Gard, Stephen W. "Obscenity and the Right to be Let Alone:
    The Balancing of Constitutional Rights, " <u>Indiana Law
    Review</u> 6 (1973), 490-508.

Himes, Scott M. "Zoning, Adult Movie Theatres and the First Amendment: An Approach to Young v. American Mini Theatres, Inc. , " Hofstra Law Review 5 (Winter, 1977), 379-411.

Krislov, Samuel. "From Ginzburg to Ginsberg: The Unhurried Children's Hour in Obscenity Litigation, " Supreme Court Review (1968), 153-97.

Magrath, C. Peter. "The Obscenity Cases: Grapes of Roth, " Supreme Court Review (1966), 7-77.

Michaud, Leonard J. "Zoning: Content Classification for Adult Movie Theatres, " Loyola Law Review 22 (Fall, 1976), 1079-86.

Miller, Beverly G. "Miller v. California: A Cold Shower for the First Amendment, " St. John's Law Review 48 (March, 1974), 568-610.

Phillips, James M. , Jr. Southeastern Promotions, Ltd. v. Conrad: A Contemporary Concept of the Public Forum, " North Carolina Law Review 54 (February, 1976), 439-49.

Ragsdale, J. Donald. "Last Tango in Paris et al. v. The Supreme Court: The Current State of Obscenity Law, " Quarterly Journal of Speech 61 (October, 1975), 279-89.

Schauer, Frederick F. "Reflections on 'Contemporary Community Standards': The Perception of an Irrelevant Concept in the Law of Obscenity, " North Carolina Law Review 56 (January, 1978), 1-28.

Stuart, Shelley R. "Young v. American Mini Theatres, Inc. : A Limit on First Amendment Protection, " New England Law Review 12 (Fall, 1976), 391-418.

Cases

Attorney General v. The Book Named "Tropic of Cancer" 184 N. E. 2d. 328 (1962)

Bantam Books v. Sullivan 372 U. S. 58 (1963)

Blount v. Rizzi 400 U. S. 410 (1971)

A Book Named "John Cleland's Memoirs of a Woman of
  Pleasure" v. Attorney General of Massachusetts 383 U. S.
  413 (1966)

Burstyn, Inc. v. Wilson 343 U. S. 495 (1952)

Butler v. Michigan 352 U. S. 380 (1957)

Erznoznik v. City of Jacksonville 422 U. S. 205 (1975)

Freedman v. Maryland 380 U. S. 51 (1965)

Ginsberg v. New York 390 U. S. 629 (1968)

Ginzburg v. United States 383 U. S. 463 (1966)

Grove Press v. Christenberry 276 F. 2d. 433 (1960)

Hamling v. United States 418 U. S. 87 (1974)

Hannegan v. Esquire, Inc. 327 U. S. 146 (1946)

Heller v. New York 413 U. S. 483 (1973)

Interstate Circuit, Inc. v. Dallas 390 U. S. 676 (1968)

Jacobellis v. Ohio 378 U. S. 184 (1964)

Jenkins v. Georgia 418 U. S. 153 (1974)

Kaplan v. California 413 U. S. 115 (1973)

Kingsley Books, Inc. v. Brown 354 U. S. 436 (1957)

Kingsley International Pictures Corp. v. Regents of University of State of New York 360 U. S. 684 (1959)

Manual Enterprises v. Day 370 U. S. 478 (1962)

Marcus v. Search Warrants of Property 367 U. S. 717 (1961)

Miller v. California 413 U. S. 15 (1973)

Mishkin v. United States 383 U. S. 502 (1966)

Mutual Film Corporation v. Industrial Commission of Ohio
  236 U. S. 230 (1915)

Near v. Minnesota 283 U. S. 697 (1931)

Paris Adult Theatre I v. Slaton 413 U. S. 49 (1973)

A Quantity of Copies of Books v. Kansas 378 U. S. 205 (1964)

Rabe v. Washington 405 U. S. 313 (1972)

Redrup v. New York 386 U. S. 767, 771 (1967)

Regina v. Hicklin L. R. 3Q. B. 360, 370 (1868)

Roaden v. Kentucky 413 U. S. 496 (1973)

Roth v. United States; Alberts v. California 354 U. S. 476
   (1957)

Rowan v. U. S. Post Office Department 397 U. S. 728 (1970)

Smith v. People of the State of California 361 U. S. 147 (1959)

Smith v. United States 431 U. S. 291 (1977)

Southeastern Promotions v. Conrad 420 U. S. 546 (1975)

Stanley v. Georgia 394 U. S. 557 (1969)

Times Film Corporation v. Chicago 354 U. S. 43 (1961)

United States v. Kennerley 209 F. 119 (S. D. N. Y. , 1913)

United States v. One Book Called "Ulysses" 72 F. 2d. 705
   (1934)

United States v. Orito 413 U. S. 139 (1973)

United States v. Reidel 402 U. S. 351 (1971)

United States v. Thirty-Seven (37) Photographs 402 U. S. 363
   (1971)

United States v. 12 200-ft. Reels of Super 8mm Film 413
   U. S. 123 (1973)

Ward v. State of Illinois 97 S. Ct. 2085 (1977)

Young v. American Mini Theatres 427 U. S. 50 (1976)

CHAPTER VI

SILENCE

The Constitution explicitly guarantees the right to speak. Does it also guarantee the right not to speak? Does it guarantee the right not to be spoken to? The U. S. Supreme Court has, on several occasions, answered these questions in the affirmative. However, while the right to silence is constitutionally protected, it is not absolute. Under certain conditions, an individual may be required to speak, or be spoken to, against his or her will. In other situations, he or she enjoys a constitutional right to remain silent.

FREEDOM NOT TO COMMUNICATE

Several cases have reached the courts which involved claims of a constitutionally protected right to refuse to communicate. Some individuals refused to sign religious and loyalty oaths. Others declined to answer questions before governmental investigative committees. Persons accused of crime invoked the privilege against self-incrimination. Writers and publishers argued for the right to remain anonymous. These cases are analyzed in the following section.

Oaths

Throughout American history, states have required that a person pledge a specific oath as a condition of public employment. Some oaths were religious in nature; others concerned loyalty to the state and nation. In the past two decades, court cases developed when individuals refused to pledge a specific oath. In these cases, the courts had to determine the constitutionality of such oaths.

Torcaso v. Watkins 367 U. S. 488 (1961)

In 1961, the U. S. Supreme Court overturned a

religious oath. The Governor of Maryland appointed Roy Torcaso to the office of Notary Public but the commission was denied when Torcaso refused to profess a belief in God. He brought action, charging that Maryland's requirement that state officers declare a belief in God violated the Constitution.

The Court agreed (9-0). The Court ruled that government cannot "impose requirements which aid all religious as against non-believers. " Government cannot "aid those religions based on a belief in the existence of God as against those religions founded on different beliefs. " The Maryland religious oath, as a test for public office, violated Torcaso's freedom of belief and religion. In this case, the Court upheld Torcaso's right not to communicate.

Elfbrandt v. Russell 384 U.S. 11 (1966)

The Court has also judged the constitutionality of state loyalty oaths. A 1966 case involved an Arizona act which required an oath from state employees to support the constitutions of the United States and Arizona. Any public servant who took such an oath and "knowingly" held membership in the Communist Party or other organization seeking to overthrow the government was not only subject to dismissal from office, but to prosecution for perjury as well. Barbara Elfbrandt, a teacher and a Quaker, decided she could not, in good conscience, take the oath. She did not know what it meant and could not get a hearing at which the precise meaning could be explained. She sought declaratory relief.

The U.S. Supreme Court found (5-4) the statute unconstitutional. According to Justice William Douglas, any person who joins an organization but does not participate in its unlawful activities poses no threat. Laws which are not restricted in scope to persons who join with the "intent" to further illegal action presume that the member shares the unlawful purposes of the organization. Such laws rest on the assumption of "guilt by association" which the Court has consistently rejected. The Arizona law was declared unconstitutional because of its overbreadth.

Connell v. Higginbotham 403 U.S. 207 (1971)

A similar case, heard five years later, involved a Florida loyalty oath. On January 16, 1969, Stella Connell

applied for a teaching position with the Orange County schools.
She was hired as a substitute fourth-grade teacher at Callahan
Elementary School.   Two months later, she was dismissed
from her teaching position for refusing to sign the loyalty
oath required of all Florida public employees.   She initiated
court action.   The loyalty oath in question involved five
clauses.   The District Court declared three clauses unconstitutional: 1) "I am not a member of the Communist Party";
2) "I have not and will not lend my aid, support, advice,
counsel or influence to the Communist Party"; and 3) "I am
not a member of any organization or party which believes in
or teaches, directly or indirectly, the overthrow of the Government of the United States or of Florida by force or violence. "

The Supreme Court heard an appeal regarding the re-
maining clauses.   The Court held (9-0) that the provision,
"I will support the Constitution of the United States and of the
State of Florida," required no more of Florida public employees than was required of any state or federal officer.
That clause was clearly constitutional.   However, the clause,
"I do not believe in the overthrow of the government of the
United States or of the State of Florida by force or violence,"
was held (8-1) to be unconstitutional because it provided summary dismissal from public employment.   The provision
violated due process.

Cole v. Richardson 405 U. S. 676 (1972)

In 1972, the Court upheld a Massachusetts loyalty oath.
Soon after she was hired as a research sociologist by the
Boston State Hospital, Lucretia Richardson was asked to take
an oath required of all public employees in Massachusetts.
Mrs. Richardson refused to take the oath because she believed
that it violated the Constitution.   Mrs. Richardson was informed that she could not continue as an employee of Boston
State Hospital unless she took the oath.   She again refused,
and was dismissed as an employee.   Mrs. Richardson filed
a complaint.   The District Court declared the law unconstitutional because of ambiguity.

When the case reached the U. S. Supreme Court, the
constitutionality of the Massachusetts oath was upheld.   The
oath was in two parts.   The first required a person to
"uphold and defend" the Constitution of the United States and
of the Commonwealth.   The Court unanimously agreed that

this pledge was generally indistinguishable from oaths the Court had recently approved. The second part required a person "to oppose the overthrow of the governments" of the United States or of the Commonwealth "by force, violence or by any illegal or unconstitutional method. " The Court determined (4-3) that the aim of this clause was clear. It required a commitment not to use illegal and constitutionally unprotected force to change the constitutional system. The second clause did not expand the obligation of the first; it did not require that specific action be taken in any specific situation. Even though the second clause might be redundant, that was no ground to strike it down. The Court concluded that "even though any word may be rendered vague and ambiguous by dissection with a semantic scalpel, it was not deemed warranted in this case. "

Cases discussed in this section, as well as others examined in the chapter on academic freedom, provide a thorough examination of the Court's treatment of oaths. In Torcaso, the Court struck down an oath which favored individuals who professed a belief in the existence of God. The oath violated freedom of belief and religion. In Elfbrandt, the Court overturned a loyalty oath which assumed guilt by association. In Connell, the Court struck down a provision which provided summary dismissal from public employment without a hearing. In Cramp, Baggett, Keyishian, and Whitehill, the Court rejected loyalty oaths of teacher-fitness that were ambiguous or overly broad. In Cole, however, the Court upheld a loyalty oath which was judged to be clear, and therefore constitutionally valid.

Investigative Committees

Several cases have reached the courts in which persons refused to answer the questions of governmental investigating committees on the ground that such answers might tend toward self-incrimination. The U. S. Supreme Court, in some cases, had to determine the scope of the protection afforded by the Fifth Amendment. In others, the Court had to decide whether an individual has a right to silence under the First Amendment. Both types of claims are considered in this section. Most of these cases involve hearings before the House Un-American Activities Committee. HUAC, which was established in 1938, directed a major portion of its energy to the investigation of Communist activities. During the years 1948 to 1952, HUAC stepped up its efforts to curb Communist endeavors.

Emspak v. United States 349 U. S. 190 (1955)

In December, 1949, Julius Emspak appeared before the committee, which was investigating possible Communist affiliation of certain members of the United Electrical, Radio & Machine Workers of America. Emspak, a member of the union and editor of UE News, the union publication, was asked 239 questions. Most dealt with the structure of the union, duties of its officers, and scope of its membership. Some questions concerned Emspak's alleged membership and activity in the Communist Party. Emspak answered many of them, but declined to answer 68 of the 239 questions, basing his refusal on "primarily the 1st Amendment, supplemented by the 5th. " In November, 1950, Emspak was indicted on grounds that his reference to "primarily the 1st Amendment, supplemented by the 5th" was insufficient to invoke Fifth Amendment privilege against self-incrimination. He was fined $500 and sentenced to six months in jail. He appealed.

The U. S. Supreme Court decided (6-3) that witnesses before congressional committees were not required to plead the Fifth Amendment privilege through any ritualistic formula; all that is necessary is an expression that may reasonably be expected to be understood as an attempt to invoke the privilege. In a companion case, Quinn v. United States, the Court arrived at the same conclusion. A witness who based his refusal to answer on "the First and Fifth Amendments" and "the First Amendment to the Constitution, supplemented by the Fifth Amendment, " had sufficiently invoked the privilege against self-incrimination.

Watkins v. United States 354 U. S. 178 (1957)

On April 29, 1954, John Watkins was subpoenaed as a witness before the House Committee on Un-American Activities. Watkins' name had been mentioned by two witnesses who testified before the committee at previous hearings. In 1952, Donald Spencer admitted having been a Communist from 1943 to 1946, and then claimed that he had been recruited into the Communist Party with the endorsement of Watkins. Spencer also said that Watkins had attended meetings at which only card-carrying members were admitted. In 1954, Walter Rumsey testified that he had been recruited into the Communist Party by Watkins. Rumsey added that he had paid Party dues to Watkins, who had assumed the name Sam Brown. Rumsey told the committee that he left the Party in 1944.

Watkins responded to those allegations claiming that he was not now nor had he ever been a card-carrying member of the Communist Party.   He denied the claims of both Spencer and Rumsey.   He admitted that he had, between 1942 and 1947, cooperated with the Communist Party and participated in Communist activities to a degree that might lead some people to believe he was a member.

Apparently satisfied with Watkin's answers on these points, the counsel for HUAC discussed another aspect of Rumsey's testimony.   Rumsey had identified a group of persons whom he had known as members of the Communist Party, and this list of names was read to Watkins.   Watkins stated that he did not know several of the people.   He also refused to answer questions that he believed were outside the proper scope of the committee's activities.   He said he would answer questions about himself, and about persons whom he believed to still be members of the Communist Party.   He would not, however, answer questions about persons who may have belonged to the Communist Party in the past but who had since terminated their membership.   He did not believe that HUAC had any right to expose persons publicly because of their past activities.   Charges were brought against Watkins.   He was found guilty of contempt, fined $100, and placed on probation.

Watkin's conviction was set aside.   The U.S. Supreme Court reaffirmed (6-1) that in congressional inquiries a witness cannot be compelled to testify against himself, be subjected to unreasonable search and seizure, or be denied First Amendment freedoms.   The Court was especially concerned about the summoning of a witness and compelling him to testify, against his will, about past beliefs and associations that are "judged by current standards rather than those contemporary with the matters exposed. "   There is "no congressional power to expose for the sake of exposure. "   The Court also noted that the committee did not state the subject under inquiry, and did not show the pertinence of the questions to the investigation.   Because Watkins was not given a fair opportunity to decide whether he was rightfully entitled to refuse to answer, his conviction necessarily violated due process.

Barenblatt v. United States 360 U.S. 109 (1959)

In Barenblatt v. United States, the Court upheld a

conviction, finding HUAC's questions obviously pertinent to the investigation. In June 1954, Lloyd Barenblatt appeared as a witness before the committee. He began his testimony by indicating that he had been a graduate student at the University of Michigan from 1947 to 1950, and an instructor in psychology at Vassar College from 1950 to 1954. Barenblatt objected generally to the right of the committee to inquire into his "political" and "religious" beliefs, or any "other personal and private affairs" or "associational activities." Barenblatt then refused to answer the following questions: 1) "Are you now a member of the Communist Party?"; 2) "Have you ever been a member of the Communist Party?"; 3) "Now, you have stated that you know Francis Crowley. Did you know Francis Crowley as a member of the Communist Party?"; 4) "Were you ever a member of the Haldane Club of the Communist Party while at the University of Michigan?"; and 5) "Were you a member while a student of the University of Michigan Council of Arts, Sciences or Professions?" Barenblatt did not invoke the Fifth Amendment, but rather objected to answering on the grounds stated earlier. He was cited for contempt. Upon conviction, a sentence of six months' imprisonment and a fine of $250 was imposed.

The U.S. Supreme Court upheld (5-4) the contempt conviction in this case. First, the Court determined that it was within the committee's authority to compel testimony. Second, unlike Watkins, the questions asked by the committee were judged to be pertinent to the subject matter of HUAC's investigation. Third, the action of the committee did not violate the First Amendment. The Court contrasted the protections of the First and Fifth Amendments, noting that "the protections of the First Amendment, unlike a proper claim of the privilege against self-incrimination under the Fifth Amendment, do not afford a witness the right to resist inquiry in all circumstances." In Barenblatt, the balance between individual and governmental interests was struck in favor of the government.

Ullmann v. United States 350 U.S. 422 (1956)

In 1956, the Court considered the specifics of the right to silence as protected by the Fifth Amendment. The case involved a challenge to the constitutionality of the congressional immunity legislation. In 1954, William Ullmann appeared before a federal grand jury in New York which was

investigating behavior thought to be dangerous to the national
security. When he was questioned about membership in the
Communist Party, Ullmann invoked the Fifth Amendment
privilege against self-incrimination. Ullmann was ordered to
testify under application of the Immunity Act of 1954. The
act provided that when national security was endangered, a
witness could be required to testify before a grand jury or
court but the witness would not be prosecuted (except for
perjury or contempt committed under testimony) because of
the compelled testimony, if he had claimed the privilege
against self-incrimination. Ullmann refused to testify, and
was ultimately convicted of contempt. He appealed on the
grounds that the act violated the Constitution.

The Court ruled (7-2) that the immunity provided by
the act was sufficiently broad to displace the protection afforded by the privilege against self-incrimination. Justices
Douglas and Black dissented on the ground that the right of
silence created by the Fifth Amendment was beyond the reach
of Congress. The guarantee against self-incrimination was
not only a protection against conviction and prosecution, but
a safeguard of conscience, human dignity, and freedom of
expression as well. The accused should be protected from
testimony which might expose him to disgrace as well as
that which could lead to criminal conviction. The majority,
however, upheld the ruling against Ullmann.

Uphaus v. Wyman 360 U.S. 72 (1959)

New Hampshire Attorney General Louis Wyman headed
a statewide committee which was investigating subversive
activities. Willard Uphaus, Executive Director of World
Fellowship, Inc. , a voluntary corporation maintaining a summer camp in New Hampshire, testified about his own activities, but refused to produce certain corporate records for
the years 1954 and 1955. The information sought consisted
of a list of the names of all the camp's nonprofessional employees for those two summer seasons, the correspondence
Uphaus had written to and about those persons who were
speakers at the camp, and the names of all persons who
attended the camp during those years. When Uphaus refused
to comply with the committee, he was judged in contempt and
committed to jail until he complied with the court order.

The Supreme Court examined two issues: the validity
of the contempt order for refusal to produce the list of

guests, and the claim that the "indefinite sentence" imposed upon Uphaus constituted such cruel and unusual punishment as to deny due process. The Court upheld (5-4) the conviction. The justices compared this case with Sweezy v. New Hampshire, noting that the academic and political freedoms were not present here in the same degree since World Fellowship was not a university or a political party. The Court noted that the Attorney General was commissioned to determine if there were any subversive people in New Hampshire. The obvious starting point of such an inquiry was to learn what persons were in the state. Any requests for lists of persons related directly to the purpose of the probe. The inquiries were "pertinent." The committee's demand for the lists was legitimate and the contempt judgment for refusing to produce them was valid. Examining the second issue, the Court argued that if Uphaus obeyed the order of the courts, he would be freed from jail. If, however, he chose to disobey, the Court found no objection to the "traditional remedy of contempt to secure compliance."

The cases cited in this section focus on the right of silence enjoyed by persons called before an investigative committee. In Emspak and Quinn, the Court determined that a person was not required to use a ritualistic formula to invoke the Fifth Amendment. An expression that could be understood as an attempt to invoke the privilege was sufficient. Several cases point to the conclusion that the Court is unwilling to allow an absolute privilege of silence under either the First or the Fifth Amendments. In Watkins, Barenblatt, and Uphaus, the Court noted that a witness may be required to testify about personal matters and associational activities when the questions have obvious pertinence to the purpose of the investigation. In Ullmann, the Court decided that a witness may be compelled to testify if immunity provided to the witness sufficiently substitutes for the protection afforded by the privilege against self-incrimination.

Criminal Suspects

In the mid-1960s the Court set forth some specific guidelines for the treatment of persons suspected of a crime. Two cases concerning the suspect's right to silence are particularly noteworthy.

Escobedo v. State of Illinois 378 U. S. 478 (1964)

In January, 1960, Danny Escobedo was arrested and

taken to police headquarters as a suspect in the fatal shooting
of his brother-in-law. Escobedo asked to consult with his
lawyer, and even though the lawyer was present at the police
station, they were not allowed to consult. While handcuffed
and standing, Escobedo was questioned for four hours.
Finally, Escobedo confessed. The confession was instru-
mental in his conviction. The case was appealed.

The U. S. Supreme Court determined (5-4) that the
confession was illegally obtained, and therefore inadmissible.
The Court also held:

> that no system of criminal justice can, or should,
> survive if it comes to depend for its continued
> effectiveness on the citizens' abdication through
> unawareness of their constitutional rights. No
> system worth preserving should have to fear that
> if an accused is permitted to consult with a lawyer,
> he will become aware of, and exercise, these
> rights. If the exercise of constitutional rights will
> thwart the effectiveness of a system of law enforce-
> ment, then there is something very wrong with that
> system.

The Court concluded that when a suspect has requested and
been denied an opportunity to consult with his lawyer, and the
police have not effectively warned him of his absolute constitutional right to remain silent, the accused has been denied
rights in violation of the Sixth Amendment. A statement
elicited by the police during such interrogation may not be
used against him at a criminal trial. The case was remanded.

Miranda v. State of Arizona; Vignera v. State of New York;
Westover v. United States; State of California v. Stewart
384 U. S. 436 (1966)

In 1966, the Court grouped four cases together, each
of which concerned statements obtained from suspects during
incommunicado interrogation in a police-dominated atmosphere, without full advisement of constitutional rights. In
Miranda v. Arizona, the police arrested the suspect and
took him to an interrogation room and secured a confession.
In Vignera v. New York, the suspect made oral admissions
to the police after interrogation in the afternoon, and then
signed an incriminating statement when questioned by an

assistant district attorney later that evening. In Westover v. United States, the suspect was handed over to the Federal Bureau of Investigation by local authorities after they had detained and interrogated him for a lengthy period. After two additional hours of questioning, the federal officers obtained signed statements from the suspect. In California v. Stewart, the local police held the suspect for five days in the station and interrogated him on nine occasions before they secured his inculpatory statement. Miranda, as well as the other suspects, was not given a full and effective warning of his rights at the outset of the interrogation process. In all of these instances, the suspect was convicted largely because of the confession. All appealed.

The U. S. Supreme Court noted (5-4) that confessions are a proper element in law enforcement. Any statement given freely and voluntarily without any compelling influences is admissible in evidence. However, when an individual is taken into custody and deprived of his rights by the authorities in any significant way, the privilege against self-incrimination is jeopardized. Procedural safeguards must be established to protect the privilege. The suspect must be warned that he has the right to remain silent, that anything he says can be used against him in court, that he has the right to consult with an attorney, and that if he cannot afford an attorney, one will be appointed for him. Unless such warnings are provided for the suspect, no evidence obtained as a result of interrogation can be used against him. In Miranda, as in Escobedo, the Court acknowledged that a suspect has a right not to communicate.

Anonymous Publication

A Los Angeles ordinance provided that no person could distribute any handbill which did not have printed on its face the names and addresses of the persons who had written and distributed the handbill. In 1960, this ordinance was challenged in the courts.

Talley v. California 362 U. S. 60 (1960)

Michael D. Talley distributed leaflets which urged readers to help an organization, the National Consumers Mobilization, boycott certain businessmen who carried products of manufacturers who failed to offer equal employment

opportunities to minority groups.   There also appeared a
blank, which, when signed, enabled the signer to enroll as a
member of the National Consumers Mobilization.   Each handbill had the following printed on its face:

> National Consumers Mobilization,
> Box 6533
> Los Angeles 55, Calif.
> PLeasant 9-1576

Talley was arrested and tried for violating the Los Angeles
ordinance.   The court held that the information printed on
the handbills failed to meet the requirements of the city
ordinance.   Talley was fined $10.   He appealed.

The U. S. Supreme Court agreed (6-3) that the law
violated Talley's right to free speech and press.   The requirement to include the information on the leaflet restricted
freedom to distribute information.   In the majority opinion,
Justice Hugo Black noted that throughout history, persecuted
groups have been able to criticize their oppressors either by
anonymous means, or not at all.   Colonial patriots frequently
concealed authorship in order to avoid prosecutions by
English-controlled courts.   The letters of Junius and the
Federalist Papers were published under fictitious names.
According to the Court, anonymity must be protected because
it had "sometimes been assumed for the most constructive
of purposes. "   Talley's conviction was overturned.

FREEDOM NOT TO BE SPOKEN TO

The Supreme Court has, in some instances, affirmed
the freedom not to be spoken to.   Sound amplification and
forced listening are two important issues with which the
Court has dealt.

Sound Amplification

People everywhere are concerned about maintaining
peace and quiet in their neighborhoods.   To protect this
interest, cities have passed ordinances which regulate the
use of sound amplification equipment.

Saia v. People of State of New York 334 U. S. 558 (1948)

Samuel Saia, a minister of the Jehovah's Witnesses,

obtained permission from the Chief of Police of Lockport,
New York to use sound equipment, mounted atop his car, to
amplify lectures on religious subjects. The lectures were
given in a public park on designated Sundays. When the
permit expired, he applied for another one but was refused
because complaints had been made. Saia nevertheless used
his equipment without a permit. He was tried and convicted
for violating a city ordinance prohibiting the use of sound
amplification devices except with permission of the Chief of
Police. Saia appealed.

The U. S. Supreme Court held (5-4) the ordinance
unconstitutional on its face because it established a previous
restraint on the right of free speech. The ordinance contained flaws. There were no standards established to guide
the Police Chief in granting permission. The statute did not
regulate the hours of use of loud speakers. It did not specify
the volume of sound (measured in decibels) allowed. The
Court noted that "any abuses which loud-speakers create can
be controlled by narrowly drawn statutes." The majority
opinion, written by Justice William Douglas, expressed fears
about the power of censorship inherent in the Lockport
ordinance. Douglas noted that, in Saia's case, a permit was
denied because some persons found the sound annoying. In
a future case, a permit may be denied because some people
find the ideas annoying. According to Douglas, "annoyance
at ideas can be cloaked in annoyance at sound." The Lockport ordinance was overturned.

Kovacs v. Cooper 336 U. S. 77 (1949)

A year later, the Court did an about-face and supported a Trenton, New Jersey ordinance. The code forbade
the use, on city streets, of any mobile sound devices which
send out loud and raucous noises. Charles Kovacs was accused of violating this ordinance. At trial, a policeman
testified that while patrolling his beat he heard a sound truck
broadcasting music. Upon investigating, he located the truck
on a public street near the municipal building. As he approached the truck, the music ceased and a man's voice could
be heard emanating from the truck. Kovacs admitted that
he operated the sound apparatus for the music. He also
admitted to speaking into the amplifier in order to comment
upon a labor dispute then occurring in Trenton. After being
convicted, Kovacs appealed.

The U.S. Supreme Court determined (5-4) that sound amplification in public places was subject to reasonable regulation. The Court noted that "city streets are recognized as a normal place for the exchange of ideas by speech or paper. But this does not mean the freedom is beyond all control." The Court expressed concern that "such distractions would be dangerous to traffic" and that "in the residential thoroughfares the quiet and tranquility so desirable for city dwellers would likewise be at the mercy of advocates of particular religious, social or political persuaders." The Trenton ordinance did not restrict the "communication of ideas or discussion of issues by the human voice, by newspapers, by pamphlets, by dodgers." The minority pointed out that ordinances could be written which protected a community from unreasonable use of public speaking devices without absolutely denying the use of a particular avenue of communication. An ordinance could restrict the volume of sound or the hours during which amplification was permitted, without infringing upon free speech. The majority, however, ruled that the Trenton code, which forbade talking on the streets through a loud-speaker in a loud and raucous tone, at any time, was a justifiable ordinance which did not violate First Amendment freedoms. Under the conditions specified in the Trenton ordinance, a person had a right not to be spoken to.

Forced Listening

In 1952, the Court decided a related case. This time the issue centered around whether a public transportation company could broadcast a radio program over loud-speakers on its vehicles.

Public Utilities Commission of District of Columbia v. Pollak
343 U.S. 451 (1952)

In March, 1948, Capital Transit Company, a privately-owned transportation system which operated in the District of Columbia, initiated "music-as-you-ride" radio programs which were played through loud-speakers in streetcars and buses. The programs, which were received from radio station WWDC-FM, consisted of a few commercial announcements on behalf of Capital Transit, and ninety per cent of musical selections. A poll of passengers showed that ninety-two per cent favored the programs. The entire procedure was subject to regulation by the Public Utilities Commission

of the District of Columbia, which at a hearing concluded that
the installation of radio equipment in the vehicles was not
inconsistent with the "public convenience, comfort, and
safety...." Franklin Pollak and Guy Martin initiated action
in the courts on the ground that the radio programs interfered
with their freedom of conversation by making it necessary
for them to compete against the programs in order to be
heard.

The U. S. Supreme Court decided (7-1) that the radio
programs did not violate either the First or the Fifth Amendments. Pollak and Martin contended that the First Amendment guarantees a right to listen only to those points of view
the listener wishes to hear. The Court found no issue of
this kind present in Pollak because there was no claim that
the radio programs had "been used for objectionable propaganda." The Court also found that the radio program did not
violate a person's right to privacy. It would be incorrect to
assume that the Fifth Amendment provides for each passenger
on a public vehicle a right to privacy substantially equal to
that which he is entitled to at home. No matter how complete the right to privacy is at home, it is limited by the
rights of others when a person travels in a method of public
conveyance. Under the conditions present in Pollak, a person
did not enjoy the right not to be spoken to.

In this chapter, cases have been presented in which
the U. S. Supreme Court analyzed whether an individual has
the freedom not to communicate and the freedom not to be
spoken to. Consideration of those cases leads to the general
conclusion that, under certain conditions and in specific
situations, a person does indeed enjoy a right to silence.

Bibliography

Articles

Bragg, Morgan Stevenson. "State Loyalty Oaths: A Constitutional Resurrection," University of Florida Law
Review 24 (Spring, 1972), 555-63.

Gordon, Robert T. , Jr. "Loyalty Oaths--Oath to Oppose
Overthrow of Government Does Not Violate First and
Fourteenth Amendments: No Administrative Hearing
Required When Oath Constitutional," Mississippi Law
Journal 43 (1972), 543-8.

Haiman, Franklyn S. "Speech v. Privacy: Is There a Right Not to Be Spoken To?" Northwestern University Law Review 67 (May-June, 1972), 153-99.

Nozette, Mark D. "Loyalty Oaths--Vagueness Standard Relaxed for 'Affirmative' Oaths," Cornell Law Review 58 (January, 1973), 383-98.

Cases

Barenblatt v. United States 360 U.S. 109 (1959)

Cole v. Richardson 405 U.S. 676 (1972)

Connell v. Higginbotham 403 U.S. 207 (1971)

Elfbrandt v. Russell 384 U.S. 11 (1966)

Emspak v. United States 349 U.S. 190 (1955)

Escobedo v. State of Illinois 378 U.S. 478 (1964)

Kovacs v. Cooper 336 U.S. 77 (1949)

Miranda v. State of Arizona; Vignera v. State of New York; Westover v. United States; State of California v. Stewart 384 U.S. 436 (1966)

Public Utilities Commission of District of Columbia v. Pollak 343 U.S. 451 (1952)

Quinn v. United States 349 U.S. 155 (1955)

Saia v. People of State of New York 334 U.S. 558 (1948)

Talley v. California 362 U.S. 60 (1960)

Torcaso v. Watkins 367 U.S. 488 (1961)

Ullmann v. United States 350 U.S. 422 (1956)

Uphaus v. Wyman 360 U.S. 72 (1959)

Watkins v. United States 354 U.S. 178 (1957)

CHAPTER VII

INTRUSION

The need to protect American citizens against unwarranted intrusions and uninvited encroachments certainly occupied the minds of the framers of our government. Their
concern was embodied within the Bill of Rights. The Third
Amendment protects against the illegal quartering of soldiers
within a person's house. The Fourth Amendment provides
for the security of individuals "in their persons, houses,
papers, and effects, against unreasonable searches and seizures. " The First Amendment guarantees the freedom of
persons to associate with individuals of their own choosing.
Though freedom from unwarranted intrusions is constitutionally protected, the nature and scope of such protection has
been clarified periodically by the courts.

SOLICITATION AND DISTRIBUTION

The courts have had to balance the freedom of solicitors and distributors against the right of citizens to be free
from uninvited intrusions at the front door of their homes,
or on the main streets of their cities. In such cases, the
peace and quiet of both the neighborhood and the community
have been at stake.

Door-to-door

In the past few decades, the U. S. Supreme Court has
evaluated the constitutionality of various city ordinances which
regulated door-to-door solicitation and distribution.

Lovell v. City of Griffin 303 U. S. 444 (1938)

An ordinance for the city of Griffin, Georgia prohibited

distributing any kind of literature without first obtaining written permission from the City Manager. Alma Lovell was convicted of violating the law and was sentenced to fifty days in prison in default of paying a fine of $50. Lovell had distributed, without the required permission, a religious pamphlet called The Golden Age, which set forth the gospel of the "Kingdom of Jehovah." Lovell did not apply for a permit because she regarded herself as sent "by Jehovah to do His work" and that such an application would have been "an act of disobedience to His commandment." The case was appealed.

In a unanimous opinion, the U. S. Supreme Court decided (8-0) that the ordinance was unconstitutional. The ordinance prohibited the distribution of "circulars, handbooks, advertising, or literature of any kind." It embraced "literature" in the widest sense. It was not restricted to "literature" that was obscene or offensive to public morals, or that advocated unlawful conduct. Instead, the ordinance prevented the distribution of literature of any kind, at any place, and in any manner without a permit. The statute was too broad.

Martin v. City of Struthers 319 U.S. 141 (1943)

In 1943, the Court considered the general issue of whether a person may distribute literature to residences. Struthers, Ohio is an industrial community and many of the residents work in the iron and steel industry. The inhabitants frequently work on swing shifts and sleep days. Casual bell-ringers could seriously interfere with their hours of sleep. Thelma Martin distributed literature door-to-door in Struthers on behalf of the Jehovah's Witnesses. She was convicted of violating a city ordinance which prohibited distribution of literature at a residence and was fined $10. She appealed.

The U. S. Supreme Court sided (6-3) with Martin. According to the Court, the ordinance was invalid because it conflicted with the freedoms of speech and press. A city does not have the power to prevent a person from going from residence to residence, ringing the doorbell for the purpose of distributing a leaflet announcing a religious meeting. Even though it is an inconvenience to be called to one's door to receive a leaflet, this is a small price to pay for the protection of free speech and press. An occupant could,

however, post a notice on the door indicating his desire not
to be disturbed by uninvited solicitors or distributors. The
ordinance was overturned because it "in effect, makes a person a criminal trespasser if he enters the property of another
for an innocent purpose without an explicit command from the
owners to stay away." A notice to stay away is necessary
to stop intrusions by "harmless" distributors.

Murdock v. Commonwealth of Pennsylvania 319 U. S. 105 (1943)

On the same day that the Court handed down the Martin
opinion, it decided a related case. The city of Jeannette,
Pennsylvania had an ordinance which prohibited persons from
soliciting without first obtaining a license and paying a tax.
Robert Murdock, a member of Jehovah's Witnesses, went
door-to-door in Jeannette, distributing literature and soliciting
people to buy various religious books and pamphlets. He had
not obtained a license. He was convicted and fined for violating the ordinance.

The Court noted that preaching the gospel through distribution of religious literature and through interpersonal
contact are accepted methods of evangelism which deserve the
same constitutional protection as more orthodox methods.
The Court then faced the single issue at stake in this case--
the constitutionality of the Jeanette ordinance which required
religious colporteurs to pay a license tax as a condition for
the pursuit of their activities. The Court concluded (5-4)
that the ordinance was unconstitutional because it restrained
in advance the freedoms "of press and religion and inevitably
tends to suppress their exercise." The tax did not acquire
validity simply because it was "nondiscriminatory" and treated
all peddlers, hucksters, solicitors, and distributors alike.
The majority of justices held that freedoms of press, speech,
and religion "are in a preferred position."

Breard v. City of Alexandria 341 U. S. 622 (1951)

In 1951 the Court placed limitations on door-to-door
solicitation. Jack H. Breard, a regional representative of
Keystone Readers Service Company, was in charge of a crew
of solicitors who went door-to-door in various cities soliciting
subscriptions for several nationally-known magazines, including the Saturday Evening Post, Today's Woman, Esquire,

American Home, Newsweek, Country Gentleman, Holiday, Ladies' Home Journal, Cosmopolitan, Pic, and True. Keystone then mailed the magazine from its home office in Pennsylvania to any new subscribers. Breard was arrested while soliciting in Alexandria, Louisiana, for violating a local ordinance which required obtaining prior consent of the owners of the residences solicited. Breard was found guilty and sentenced to pay a $25 fine or spend thirty days in jail. He appealed.

The U. S. Supreme Court compared the facts in Breard with those in Martin and concluded that door-to-door solicitation for commercial purposes could be prohibited by municipal ordinance. The Court decided that "subscriptions may be made by anyone interested in receiving the magazines without the annoyances of house-to-house canvassing ... those communities that have found these methods of sale obnoxious may control them by ordinance. " The Court decided (6-3) that door-to-door solicitation for a commercial purpose could be prohibited by municipal ordinance.

Hynes v. Borough of Oradell 425 U. S. 610 (1976)

In 1976, the Court examined the constitutionality of an ordinance which required certain solicitors to register with the police department for identification purposes. An Oradell, New Jersey ordinance required, for identification purposes, that advance written notice be given to the local police department by any individual desiring to solicit door-to-door for a recognized charitable or political cause. New Jersey state assemblyman Edward Hynes wished to campaign for reelection by canvassing door-to-door and speaking with voters. He brought suit, claiming that the ordinance unconstitutionally restricted that activity.

The U. S. Supreme Court held the ordinance unconstitutional because of vagueness. The ordinance lacked specific instructions as to what must be set forth in the required notice, what the police would consider sufficient identification, and what standards would be used by those who apply the ordinance. There was also no clue as to what qualified as a "recognized charity" or a "political cause. " The judgment of the lower court was reversed (7-1) and the case remanded.

Overall, the Court has been protective of the free speech and press rights of solicitors and distributors. In

Lovell, the Court overturned an overly-broad statute that prohibited the distribution of literature "of any kind. " In Martin, the Court decided that a city ordinance cannot prevent an individual from distributing religious announcements door-to-door. In Murdock, an ordinance was held invalid because, by levying a license tax against solicitors, a city tended to suppress the exercise of First Amendment freedoms. In Hynes, an ordinance was held unconstitutional because of vagueness. The Court has, however, placed some limitations on soliciting. According to Martin, a person can prevent intrusions by uninvited solicitors by posting a notice to stay away. And, in Breard, the Court concluded that commercial solicitation could be prohibited by municipal ordinance.

Community-wide

The focus in the cases considered thus far has been on door-to-door solicitation. A 1946 case posed the question of whether a state can make it a criminal act for a person to distribute religious literature on the premises of a company-owned town, contrary to the wishes of the town's management.

Marsh v. State of Alabama 326 U. S. 501 (1946)

Chickasaw, a suburb of Mobile, Alabama, was owned by the Gulf Shipbuilding Corporation. Otherwise, the town very closely resembled any other town. The property contained buildings, streets, sewers and a sewage disposal plant, and an acre in which places of business were situated. Businessmen rented the store buildings and the United States used one of the places as a post office from which carriers delivered mail to the residents of the area. A policeman patrolled the town. The residents used the business section as their regular shopping center. To do so, they made use of a company-owned paved street and sidewalk located alongside the store fronts in order to enter and leave the businesses and the post office. Company-owned roads at each end of the business section joined a four-lane public highway. There was nothing to stop highway traffic from coming into the business section and upon arrival a person could make free use of the facilities located there. The town and its shopping district were accessible to and freely used by the general public. There was nothing to differentiate this town from any other town and shopping center except that the title

to the property belonged to a private corporation. Grace
Marsh, a Jehovah's Witness, walked along the sidewalk and
stood near the post office and began to distribute religious
leaflets. The corporation had posted in the stores a notice
which declared the area as private property and prohibited
any distribution or solicitation without written permission.
Marsh was told that she could not distribute the literature
without a permit and that no permit would be issued. When
she was asked to leave, she refused. She was arrested and
charged with violating the 1940 Alabama law which made it
a crime to remain on private premises after having been
warned not to do so. She was convicted.

The U. S. Supreme Court reversed (5-3) and noted that
the many people who live in company-owned towns must make
decisions which affect the welfare of the community and the
nation. They must be informed and in order to have access
to proper information, distribution of literature must be un-
censored. The Court saw no more reason for depriving those
people of the freedom of speech and press than for curtailing
those freedoms with respect to any other citizen. The Court
concluded that when the rights of owners of property are
balanced against the free press and religion freedoms of the
people, "the latter occupy a preferred position."

Organization for a Better Austin v. Keefe
402 U.S. 415 (1971)

In 1971, the Court again confronted the issue of a
community-wide ban on distribution. Organization for a
Better Austin, a racially integrated community organization
in the Austin neighborhood of Chicago, was formed in order
to "stabilize" the racial ratio in the area. For several years
the boundary of the black segregated area of Chicago had
moved progressively west toward Austin. OBA, in its efforts
to "stabilize" the area, had opposed and protested such real
estate tactics as "blockbusting" and "panic peddling." OBA
contended that Jerome Keefe, a real estate broker, engaged
in activities which aroused the fear in white residents that
blacks were moving into the area, and then by exploiting their
reactions, was able to secure listings and sell homes to
blacks. According to OBA, Keefe had promoted sales in this
manner since 1961 by using flyers, phone calls, and personal
visits to Austin residents without concern for whether the
persons had indicated any desire to sell their homes. Community meetings were held with Keefe to attempt to convince

him to alter his practices, but he contended that it was his
right to solicit real estate business as he saw fit.

During September and October, 1967, members of OBA
distributed leaflets throughout Westchester, the Chicago suburb
in which Keefe resided, which criticized Keefe's real estate
activities. Leaflets were distributed in shopping centers,
passed out to some parishioners attending Keefe's church, and
left at the doors of his neighbors. The distribution of the
leaflets was conducted in a peaceful and orderly manner on
all occasions; there was no disruption of traffic. Keefe initiated action and the lower courts issued an injunction which
prohibited OBA from passing out leaflets anywhere in Westchester. The court ruled that OBA activities intruded upon
Keefe's right to privacy. The court viewed OBA activities
as coercive and intimidating rather than informative.

The U.S. Supreme Court cited Near v. Minnesota in
ruling (8-1) that the injunction, by imposing previous restraint, constituted an impermissible restraint on First
Amendment freedoms. The injunction did not serve to redress alleged wrongs, but to suppress distribution of literature "of any kind" on the basis of previous publications. The
injunction was vacated.

In Organization for a Better Austin, as in Marsh, the
Court upheld the free speech and press rights of solicitors
and distributors. In Organization for a Better Austin, the
Court vacated a lower court injunction that imposed a
community-wide ban on distributing leaflets. In Marsh, the
Court rejected a community-wide ban against soliciting and
distributing within a company-owned town. It can be concluded that the Court has generally supported the free speech
and press rights of solicitors and distributors in those cases
involving both door-to-door and community-wide intrusions.

SEARCH AND SURVEILLANCE

In recent years, there has been a notable increase in
uninvited snooping into the personal lives and property of
American citizens. Such action constitutes another form of
intrusion.

Criminal Suspects

The courts have consistently tried to maintain the

guaranteed rights of the accused.   An important area concerns
the acceptable techniques and the permissible extent of police
searches and seizures.   One of the first important cases to
deal with this issue was decided in 1950.

United States v. Rabinowitz 339 U. S. 56 (1950)

A printer possessed a machine which could illegally
forge valuable "overprints" on stamps.   He subsequently
identified Albert J. Rabinowitz as one of the customers to
whom he had delivered large numbers of stamps bearing the
forged overprints.   A few days later, a postal employee went
to Rabinowitz's store and purchased four of the questionable
stamps.   They were sent to an expert, who subsequently
determined that the overprints were forgeries.   A warrant was
then issued for Rabinowitz's arrest.   Officers, accompanied
by two stamp experts, went to Rabinowitz's store, arrested
him, and over his objection, searched the office for about
an hour-and-a-half.   They seized 573 stamps on which forged
overprints had been found, along with some other stamps
which were subsequently returned to Rabinowitz.   Rabinowitz
was charged with knowingly selling four forged stamps with
intent to defraud, and with concealing in his possession the
573 forged stamps.   At trial, motions to suppress the evidence pertaining to the 573 stamps were denied.   Offering
no evidence, Rabinowitz was convicted.   The Court of Appeals
reversed on the grounds that because the officers had time to
procure a search warrant and had failed to do so, the search
was illegal and the evidence should have been excluded.

The U. S. Supreme Court determined (5-3) that there
was a permissible area of search beyond the person proper.
In this case, the premises under the control of the person
arrested were subject to search without a search warrant.
Such a search was not "unreasonable. "   The Court concluded
that "the relevant test is not whether it is reasonable to procure
a search warrant, but whether the search was 'reasonable'. "

Chimel v. California 395 U. S. 752 (1969)

In 1969 the Court heard a similar case.   Police officers went to the home of Ted Chimel with a warrant for his
arrest on suspicion of the burglary of a coin shop.   They
were allowed in the house by his wife and waited there until
he returned from work.   After serving the arrest warrant,
the policemen conducted an extensive search of the house

which turned up several coins. These items were admitted into evidence at Chimel's trial over his objection. He was convicted.

On appeal, the U. S. Supreme Court noted (7-2) that when an arrest is made, it is reasonable for the arresting officer to search the person arrested in order to remove any weapons that the person might use in an attempt to escape. Otherwise, the policeman's safety might be in danger. There is justification to search the person arrested or the area within the immediate vicinity. There is, however, no justification for routinely searching any room other than that in which an arrest occurs. Such searches may be made only with a search warrant. The decision in Chimel, in effect, negated Rabinowitz. Rabinowitz had granted police officers the power to engage in searches not justified by probable cause because the officers arrested suspects at home rather than somewhere else. In Chimel, the search went beyond the suspect's person and the area nearby. According to the Court, there was no justification, without a search warrant, for extending the search beyond that area.

Mapp v. Ohio 367 U. S. 643 (1961)

In 1961 the Court further clarified the law of search and seizure by resolving the issue of admissibility of evidence obtained by a search. Dollree Mapp and her fifteen-year-old daughter by a former marriage lived on the top floor of a two-family dwelling. In May, 1957, three Cleveland police officers arrived at the Mapp residence and were informed that a suspect in a recent bombing was hiding out in there. The officers knocked on the door and demanded entrance, but Mapp refused to admit them without a search warrant. About three hours later, when additional officers arrived, the police again sought entry. When Mapp did not come immediately to the door, the policemen forcibly opened the door and entered. Mrs. Mapp demanded to see the search warrant. A piece of paper, which an officer claimed to be the warrant, was shown to Mrs. Mapp. When she grabbed the "warrant," a struggle ensued and she was eventually handcuffed because she had been "belligerent." Officers then conducted a wide-spread search throughout the house and eventually located some allegedly pornographic pamphlets and photographs. Mrs. Mapp was arrested and convicted of knowingly possessing obscene materials. At the trial, however, no search warrant was produced by the prosecution, and the failure to provide such an important procedural artifact was never explained.

When the case arrived at the U. S. Supreme Court, Ohio argued that even if the search was conducted in an unreasonable manner, the evidence could still be used at trial. The Court cited Wolf v. Colorado, in which it was held that even though the state violated the Constitution by procuring evidence by an unreasonable search and seizure, the courts of the state may nonetheless admit the evidence; it is a matter for the state to decide. In Mapp, the Court overturned Wolf. The justices declared (6-3) that the exclusionary rule is an essential part of both the Fourth and Fourteenth Amendments. Evidence obtained by an invalid search and seizure was inadmissible in both state and federal courts.

Ker v. California 374 U. S. 23 (1963)

Two years later, the Court upheld a search in which police officers entered the suspect's apartment without either a search or an arrest warrant. Los Angeles police had observed a conversation taking place between a known narcotics peddler, Roland Murphy, and a man sitting in a parked automobile. Police followed the man as he drove away but lost contact with him. By checking the license number of the car with the Department of Motor Vehicles, the police learned the name and address of the car's owner: George Douglas Ker, 4801 Slauson. At various times over the preceding year, police officers had received information that Ker was selling marijuana from his apartment and that he was possibly obtaining it from Murphy. Officers proceeded immediately to the address and found the automobile which they had been following. They went to the office of the building manager and obtained from him a pass key to Ker's apartment, unlocked and opened the door, and found Ker and his wife, Diane, sitting in the apartment. A package of marijuana was on the top of the kitchen sink.

A divided Supreme Court held (5-4) that, in this case, there was probable cause for the arrests. The entry into the apartment was for the purpose of the arrests and the search was incident to these arrests. The arrests and the search were lawful. The evidence was admissible in court.

Aguilar v. Texas 378 U. S. 108 (1964)

The Court went one step further the next year by setting standards for the issuance of a search warrant. Two policemen applied to a Houston Justice of the Peace for a search warrant because they had "received reliable information from a credible person and [did] believe" that drugs were

kept at Nick Aguilar's home. The police informed Aguilar
that they had a warrant. After hearing some noise inside,
the officers forced their way into the house and seized Aguilar
as he was attempting to dispose of a packet of narcotics. At
his trial, the judge overruled Aguilar's objection to the introduction of evidence obtained by the warrant. Aguilar was
convicted of illegal possession of heroin and sentenced to
twenty years in the penitentiary.

The U. S. Supreme Court concluded (6-3) that the
search warrant should not have been issued because the officers had not provided a sufficient basis for a finding of probable cause. The officers' affidavit in support of their application for a warrant contained no "affirmative allegation" that
the unidentified source "spoke with personal knowledge." For
all that appeared, the officers merely suspected that there
were narcotics in Aguilar's possession. The magistrate accepted "without question" the informant's "suspicion," "belief,"
or "mere conclusion." The Court insisted that the magistrate
must perform a "neutral and detached" function and not operate merely as a rubber stamp for the police.

Coolidge v. New Hampshire 403 U. S. 443 (1971)

A 1971 case dealt with the same issue. During their
investigation of the murder of a fourteen-year-old girl, the
police obtained evidence that implicated Edward Coolidge in
the crime. Witnesses placed Coolidge at the site where the
girl's body was found on the night she disappeared. Also,
Coolidge's wife gave police weapons he owned, one of which
was used to kill the girl. This evidence was brought before
the attorney general of New Hampshire. Acting in his capacity as a justice of the peace, he issued arrest and search
warrants. The police arrested Coolidge at his home and had
his 1951 Pontiac searched. Coolidge was convicted. He
appealed, contending that the search warrant was invalid since
it had been issued by a person with a direct and substantial
interest in the outcome of the case, instead of by a "neutral
and detached magistrate."

The Supreme Court agreed, noting (5-4) that, here, determination of probable cause was made by the Attorney
General--the enforcement agent leading the investigation and the
chief prosecutor. It concluded: "When the right of privacy must
reasonably yield to the right of search is ... to be decided by a
judicial officer, not by a policeman or Government Enforcement
agent." In Coolidge, as in Aguilar, the Court determined that a
warrant had been issued without meeting the standards established for the issuance of search warrants.

Terry v. Ohio 392 U.S. 1 (1968)

In 1968, the Court confronted the question of whether the police may "stop and frisk" suspicious persons. Detective Martin McFadden was patrolling in downtown Cleveland when his attention was attracted to two men, one of whom was John Terry. McFadden noticed that their behavior "didn't look right." The men were focusing their attention on a particular store in such a way that McFadden believed they were "casing" it. He approached the men, identified himself as a police officer, and asked for their names. The answers were mumbled. Because he suspected the men might have a gun, McFadden grabbed Terry and patted down the outside of his clothing. He felt a pistol in Terry's left breast pocket but could not remove it by reaching inside the coat. So, he took off Terry's coat and confiscated the gun. Terry was convicted for carrying a concealed weapon and sentenced to one to three years' imprisonment. At trial, Terry's request to suppress the evidence on grounds that McFadden's behavior constituted an unreasonable search and seizure was denied.

When the case reached the U.S. Supreme Court, the justices admitted that even a limited search of the outer clothing constituted a severe intrusion upon cherished personal security. They concluded (8-1), however, that where a police officer observes unusual behavior which suggests that criminal activity may be imminent and the persons involved may be armed and dangerous, and after proper identification and reasonable inquiry by the police officer, a carefully limited search of the outer clothing may be conducted. Any weapons so seized could be introduced in evidence.

Sibron v. New York; Peters v. New York 392 U.S. 40 (1968)

In 1968 the Terry doctrine was applied to companion cases which involved the conviction of two men on the basis of evidence obtained by police frisking. Nelson Sibron was convicted of the unlawful possession of heroin. While patrolling his beat, police officer Anthony Martin observed Sibron talking to people whom Martin knew from past experience to be narcotics addicts. Martin did not overhear any of these conversations and did not see anything pass between Sibron and the others. Martin then approached Sibron and said, "You know what I am after." Sibron mumbled something and reached into his pocket. At that instant, Martin thrust his hand into the same pocket, finding several envelopes which contained heroin.

When the case reached the U. S. Supreme Court, the justices determined that the heroin was inadmissible as evidence against Sibron. There was no probable cause to arrest Sibron for any crime. Martin merely saw Sibron talking to some known narcotics addicts. He did not know the content of these conversations. Also, Martin had no reasonable grounds to believe that Sibron was armed and dangerous. Martin's statement to Sibron made it clear that he sought narcotics, not a weapon, in Sibron's pocket. The Court concluded (8-1) that "the inference that persons who talk to narcotics addicts are engaged in the criminal traffic in narcotics is simply not the sort of reasonable inference required to support an intrusion by the police upon an individual's personal security. "

The companion case involved what the Court felt were sufficient grounds for arrest. New York City Police Officer Samuel Lasky was at home when he heard a noise at his door. When he looked through the peephole he saw two men tiptoeing toward the stairway. Lasky had lived in the apartment for twelve years and did not recognize the men. He suspected burglary. When Lasky opened his door, the men began to run. Lasky gave chase and apprehended Herbert Peters, who explained that he was visiting his girl friend. Peters refused to tell Lasky her name because she was a married woman. Lasky frisked Peters for weapons and discovered a hard object in his pocket which did not feel like a gun, but could have been a knife. Lasky removed the object, which turned out to be Peter's burglary tools. Peters was convicted for possessing the tools.

The Court ruled (9-0) the search reasonable. The officer heard strange noises and observed the men tiptoeing in the hallway and fleeing down the stairs. The Court felt that there were sufficient grounds for an arrest. In Terry, the Court approved a limited search of outer clothing for concealed objects. This principle was denied in Sibron, but observed in Peters.

United States v. Ramsey 431 U. S. 606 (1977)

The courts have recognized an exception to the search

warrant requirement of "probable cause. " Federal regulations
allow certain officials to search persons or property at the
point of entrance to the country. Such officials need only
"reasonable cause to suspect" the importation of contraband
to inspect incoming international mail. The regulations,
however, prohibit the reading of any correspondence without
a search warrant. In accord with the regulations, George
Kallnischkies, a customs inspector, opened some bulky,
letter-sized airmail envelopes from Thailand, a source of
narcotics. The envelopes contained heroin. Charles Ramsey
and James Kelly were subsequently convicted of narcotics
offenses and sentenced to imprisonment for a term of ten to
thirty years. The Court of Appeals reversed, holding that
the Constitution requires that "before international letter mail
is opened, a showing of probable cause be made to and a
warrant secured from a neutral magistrate. "

The U. S. Supreme Court reversed (6-3), noting the
law which explicitly states that,

> Any of the officers or persons authorized to board
> or search vessels may ... search any trunk or
> envelope, wherever found, in which he may have a
> reasonable cause to suspect there is merchandise
> which was imported contrary to law....

The Court argued that, under the circumstances, the customs
inspector had reasonable cause to suspect that there was
contraband in the envelopes, and therefore the search was
authorized by the law. The majority opinion, written by
Justice William Rehnquist, went on to note that such a search
"does not impermissibly chill the exercise of free speech
under the First Amendment, and any 'chill' that might exist
under such circumstances is not only 'minimal' but is also
wholly subjective. "

United States v. Martinez-Fuerte; Sifuentes v. United States
428 U. S. 543 (1976)

The Ramsey decision demonstrated the priority of the
national interest in border searches. In two cases consolidated on appeal, the Court ruled that border searches at
permanent checkpoint locations removed from the physical
border did not abridge the Fourth Amendment. Vehicles
driven by both Amado Martinez-Fuerte and Rodolfo Sifuentes
were routinely stopped by the Border Patrol at a permanent

checkpoint located on a major highway for brief questioning. Martinez-Fuerte and Sifuentes were subsequently convicted of smuggling illegal aliens found in the automobiles.

The Supreme Court upheld (7-2) the convictions. Even though the Fourth Amendment "imposes limits on search and seizure power in order to prevent arbitrary and oppressive interference by enforcement officials with privacy and personal security of individuals," the stops were not illegal. Indeed, the Court argued, the public interest must be weighed against the Fourth Amendment interest of the individual. Under the circumstances, the public interest in regulating border traffic far outweighed the individual's right to privacy. There was no need to base such stops on "reasonable suspicion." The Court noted that privacy in the automobile is not afforded the same protection as privacy in one's residence.

Olmstead v. United States 277 U.S. 438 (1928)

In the past century the Court has had to deal with the complexities of an increasingly technological society. Electronic surveillance, in particular, has led to new sophistication in police techniques. The Court has responded accordingly. In 1928 the Court heard Olmstead v. United States. Roy Olmstead managed a business which dealt in the illegal, large-scale transportation and sale of liquor. Overall, more than fifty persons were employed in the operation as executives, salesmen, deliverymen, bookkeepers; an attorney was also retained. Two ships transported the liquor to British Columbia, where smaller vessels were used to transport the items to the state of Washington. A ranch located in suburban Seattle was used as an underground cache. In a bad month, sales for the operation amounted to $176,000; the aggregate for a year amounted to at least two million dollars. The information which led to the discovery of this operation was based upon telephone communications intercepted by federal prohibition officers. The wiretaps did not trespass upon Olmstead's property as they were connected in the basement of an office building and in the streets near the telephone lines of Olmstead's residence. At trial, Olmstead argued that the wiretapped evidence should not be admitted on the grounds that the wiretapping was an unreasonable search and seizure under the Fourth Amendment, and that admission of the conversations compelled him to testify against himself, violating the Fifth Amendment. Olmstead was convicted for violating the National Prohibition Act. He appealed.

The U. S. Supreme Court held (5-4) that wiretapping
did not constitute search and seizure, and that information
obtained by wiretapping could not be excluded at the trial.

> The language of the [Fourth] Amendment cannot be
> extended and expanded to include telephone wires,
> reaching to the whole world from the defendant's
> house or office. The intervening wires are not part
> of his house or office, any more than are the high-
> ways along which they are stretched ... where ad-
> mission of evidence in criminal prosecution does
> not violate the Constitution, courts have no discre-
> tion to exclude it on ground that it was secured by
> unethical means.

The dissenting justices, however, maintained that such wiretapping clearly invaded privacy. In his opinion, Justice Louis
Brandeis warned of the dangers inherent in wiretapping.

> The evil incident to invasion of the privacy of the
> telephone is far greater than that involved in tam-
> pering with the mails. Whenever a telephone line
> is tapped, the privacy of the persons at both ends
> of the line is invaded, and all conversations between
> them upon any subject, and although proper, con-
> fidential, and privileged, may be overheard. More-
> over, the tapping of one man's telephone line in-
> volved the tapping of the telephone of every other
> person whom he may call, or who may call him.
> As a means of espionage, writs of assistance and
> general warrants are but puny instruments of tyr-
> anny and oppression when compared with wire-
> tapping.

Nardone v. United States 302 U. S. 379 (1937)

In 1934, Congress passed the Federal Communications
Act, section 605 of which provided that "no person not being
authorized by the sender shall intercept any communication
and divulge or publish the existence, contents, substance,
purport, effect, or meaning of such intercepted communication
to any person. " Frank Nardone and some associates were
tried and convicted of smuggling alcohol, largely because
federal agents turned states evidence by testifying to the
substance of long distance calls the defendants made. Section
605, however, provided that "no person" shall "divulge or

publish" the substance of such calls to "any person." Olmstead had been convicted at a time when the Radio Act of 1927
was in effect. That act did not specify that wiretaps were
illegal. The language of the Communications Act was
unequivocal--"no person" could make and divulge wiretaps.

The U. S. Supreme Court held (7-2) that wiretap evidence was inadmissible at a trial in any federal court. However, this decision did not stop wiretapping by federal agents.
They interpreted the ruling to apply only to surveillance that
intercepted communications and afterward divulged the contents
of those communications. In their view, the decision did not
apply to wiretapping which remained secret.

Schwartz v. Texas 344 U. S. 199 (1953)

In 1953 the Court decided whether Section 605 applied
to the state. Thomas Schwartz, a pawnbroker, conspired
with two men to rob places which Schwartz designated, and
to bring the booty to him. The three would divide the pro-
ceeds. The two men then robbed a Dallas woman of her
valuable jewels and brought the loot to Schwartz. Friction
developed when Schwartz delayed settlement with the robbers.
Eventually, Schwartz tipped off the police where they could
locate one of the men, who was subsequently jailed. The man
then agreed to telephone Schwartz and enable police officers
to record the conversation. This evidence was used to convict Schwartz as an accomplice to robbery.

The U. S. Supreme Court held (8-1) that the rule of
inadmissibility of wiretapped evidence did not apply to state
courts. The Court said that "although the intercepted calls
would be inadmissible in a federal court, it does not follow
that such evidence is inadmissible in a state court." Furthermore, "evidence obtained by a state officer by means
which would constitute an unlawful search and seizure under
the Fourth Amendment ... is nonetheless admissible in a
state court ... while such evidence, if obtained by a federal
officer, would be clearly inadmissible in a federal court."
The Schwartz decision left the wiretapping issue in a contradictory condition. Wiretapped evidence was not admissible
in federal courts, but was admissible in state courts.

Lee v. Florida 392 U. S. 378 (1968)

In 1968 the Court, in effect, overruled Schwartz. For

more than a week, police used recording equipment to monitor telephone calls to and from Clyde Lee. He was ultimately convicted in a Florida court for violating state lottery laws.

On appeal, the Supreme Court decided (6-3) that the use of wiretap information by the court was unlawful.

> There clearly is a federal statute, applicable in Florida and every other State, that made illegal the conduct of the Orlando authorities in this case. And that statute, we hold today, also made the recording of the petitioners' telephone conversations inadmissible as evidence in the Florida court.

Evidence obtained through wiretapping was now inadmissible in both state and federal courts.

Berger v. New York 388 U.S. 41 (1967)

In the wiretap decisions covered thus far, the Court did not prohibit wiretapping per se or rule on forms of electronic surveillance as they concern the right to privacy. The Court simply applied section 605 of the Federal Communications Act to the admission of wiretap information in the courts. In 1967, the Court ruled that wiretapping and eavesdropping are searches and seizures under the Fourth Amendment. A New York statute authorized judges to permit wiretaps and buggings "upon oath or affirmation ... that there is reasonable ground to believe that evidence of a crime" may be obtained. Police officers who applied for warrants were required to describe the particular person to be overheard and the purpose of the eavesdrop. Ralph Berger was convicted of conspiring to bribe the chairman of the New York liquor authority on evidence obtained by a recording device. Berger claimed that the New York statute was unconstitutional because it did not require a description of the particular conversations to be seized and a showing of probable cause.

In the majority view of the U.S. Supreme Court, the New York statute was unconstitutionally broad. The Fourth Amendment required that a warrant could only be issued upon probable cause supported by oath or affirmation and upon a description of the place to be searched and the persons or objects to be seized. New York's statute lacked both of these requirements. The Fourth Amendment requires "particularity, " but "by its very nature eavesdropping involves an intrusion on privacy that is broad in scope. " The Court concluded (6-3) that the Fourth Amendment does not absolutely prohibit such searches and seizures "but it does prescribe a constitutional standard that must be met before official invasion is permissible. " In his concurring opinion, Justice William Douglas observed that electronic surveillance "is a violation of the Fourth and Fifth Amendments no matter with what nicety and precision a warrant may be drawn. " In fact, "it is the greatest of all invasions of privacy. "

Katz v. United States 389 U. S. 347 (1967)

In another 1967 case the Court specified conditions for the issuance of warrants. Charles Katz telephoned information on bets and wagers from a telephone booth in Los Angeles to locations in Boston and Miami. FBI agents used an electronic listening device attached to the outside of the booth to record the conversations. They were used at Katz's trial and he was convicted. He appealed.

The U. S. Supreme Court decided (7-1) that by electronically listening to and recording Katz's words while he was using the telephone booth, the government violated Katz's privacy. This constituted a search and seizure subject to the requirements of the Fourth Amendment. The Court then decided that the search, in this case, did not comply with constitutional standards. Police officers were not required, prior to the search, to present their estimate of probable cause to a neutral magistrate. They were not required to observe precise limitations in their search. Nor were they directed to notify the magistrate in detail of all that had been seized. The Court ruled, in effect, that even though the officers had acted voluntarily with restraint in this case, those restraints must necessarily be imposed by a judicial officer. They were not. In both Berger and Katz, the Court demanded that electronic surveillance follow the constitutional standards governing the usual types of searches and seizures.

Throughout the past fifty years, the Court has refined and reformulated the law concerning permissible searches and seizures. For many years, the Rabinowitz standard allowed enforcement officials to make "reasonable" searches. The relevant question was not whether a valid search warrant was obtained, but only if the search itself was reasonable. The

Court was willing to grant a wide spectrum of discretion to enforcement officers. In Chimel, however, the Court concluded that police do not have authority to search routinely beyond the suspect's person. While conceding that policemen have the right to search for and remove weapons from a potentially dangerous suspect, the Court significantly narrowed the definition of "reasonable" search.

The issue of admissibility of evidence obtained by a search also came before the Court. Whereas Rabinowitz allowed evidence from questionable searches to be admitted, Mapp clearly demonstrated that evidence obtained without a search warrant would be excluded from trial in both state and federal courts. The subsequent Ker, Aguilar, and Coolidge cases clarified "probable cause" and provided precise standards for the issuance of search warrants. Not only did a search warrant have to be procured, but the warrant had to be issued on a comparatively rigorous demonstration of probable cause.

The Court has noted some instances where enforcement officials retain discretion. In Terry, the Court ruled that a limited search of the outer clothing, though an intrusion upon personal security, could be a "reasonable" search under the Fourth Amendment. Sibron and Peters clarified the limits of the Terry doctrine. These cases demonstrated that officers have discretion to conduct searches of outer clothing only if they have reasonable grounds to believe their actions are warranted. In Ramsey, the Court noted that officers retain authority to search incoming international mail. Martinez-Fuerte and Sifuentes pointed to the compelling state interest in regulating the traffic of people and property over national borders. The Court also noted that automobiles are not afforded the same protection as private dwellings.

In Nardone, wiretap evidence became inadmissible in federal courts. Only nine years before, in Olmstead, the Court noted that wiretapping not only was permitted, but that such activity did not even constitute a search or seizure as defined by the Fourth Amendment. Nardone, however, did not restrict all instances of wiretapping. In Schwartz, the Court noted that although wiretap evidence was inadmissible in federal courts, such a rule did not apply to state proceedings. In Lee, the Court ruled that wiretap evidence was inadmissible in both federal and state courts. The Berger and Katz decisions relegated electronic surveillance to the realm of searches and seizures. Undoubtedly, the great

strides made in surveillance technology during the past few
decades demanded some response by the Court. Overall, the
Court has tended to restrict the use of electronic devices
while defending the procedural safeguards of the accused.

Private Citizens

In recent years, American citizens have had to face
several types of surveillance. Supermarkets and department
stores have installed one-way mirrors and closed-circuit
television sets in an effort to curb shoplifting. Business
executives tape conversations with customers, employees,
and associates. Consumers seeking credit cards have dossiers prepared which contain information of the widest variety.
Job applicants receive a thorough examination of their back-
ground, including a detailed investigation of their private
lives. During the late 1960s and early 1970s, political activists, civil rights leaders, and liberal government political
figures were the focus of widespread spying by the FBI, CIA,
and branches of the military. In most cases, the content of
such dossiers was kept secret, even from the people investigated. A 1971 case illustrates the nature and scope of governmental "snooping" that became prevalent.

Laird v. Tatum 408 U.S. 1 (1972)

In 1967 the U.S. Army was called upon to assist local
authorities in quelling civil disorders in Detroit, Michigan.
To enhance its efforts, the Army developed a data-gathering
system to enable more efficient direction of Army personnel.
The system consisted of the collection of information about
public activities that were thought to have some potential for
civil disorder. The information was then stored in a compu-
ter data bank at Army Intelligence headquarters at Fort
Holabird, Maryland. Arlo Tatum, executive director of the
Central Committee for Conscientious Objectors, and twelve
other individuals who felt they were targets of Army surveillance sued on the grounds that the Army was conducting unlawful surveillance of lawful civilian political activity.

The U.S. Supreme Court heard the case. The issue
was whether a person had his First Amendment rights
"chilled" by the mere existence of governmental investigative
and data-gathering activity. Tatum argued that the "chilling"
effect resulted from the potential abuse of power by the

military and the potential later misuse of gathered data. In
his minority opinion, William Douglas called army surveillance of civilians a "gross repudiation of our traditions."
The Court's majority opinion, however, prepared by Chief
Justice Warren Burger, held (5-4) that "allegations of a subjective 'chill' are not an adequate substitute for a claim of
specific present objective harm or a threat of specific future
harm." Army surveillance could be challenged in court, but
only if individuals could demonstrate "actual or threatened
injury." This Tatum had failed to demonstrate.

Privacy Act of 1974 (PL 93-579)

During the 1960s both houses of Congress investigated
the information-gathering techniques utilized by the federal
government. Hearings were conducted regarding the use of
wiretapping and lie-detector devices, maintenance of data-
banks, and accessibility to information gathered through
criminal justice and military surveillance. The investigation
revealed a growing intrusion into personal privacy because of
increasing governmental acquisition of large amounts of personal information about citizens. At the culmination of its
inquiry, Congress passed the Privacy Act of 1974.

The purpose of the act is to provide safeguards by
which persons may be aware of the particular personal data
that are collected by the federal government about them, and
by which they may specify how those data are used. To
carry out this purpose, the act requires that: 1) agencies
publicly report the existence of all record-systems maintained
about individuals, 2) data contained in all record-systems
must be accurate, complete, relevant, and current, 3) individuals can inspect and correct errors in files about themselves, 4) data gathered for one purpose cannot be used for
another without the person's permission, and 5) agencies must
keep an accurate account of the disclosure of records. Any
officer or employee of an agency who wilfully violates the act
is guilty of a misdemeanor and subject to a fine of not more
than $5,000. Under the act, a person may sue an agency
for refusing to release data, for denying an appeal to amend
a record, and for failure to act upon an appeal within thirty
days.

The Privacy Act has limitations. Certain record-
systems may be exempted from disclosure. Among these are
files maintained by the CIA, law enforcement agencies,

national defense and foreign policy organizations, and the armed forces. In addition, the act applies only to records held by federal agencies; it does not apply to state and local governments, or to private organizations. Nonetheless, the Privacy Act of 1974 affords the citizen some control over the collection and distribution of personal information at a time of extensive intrusion into the personal lives of private citizens by both governmental and non-governmental organizations.

HARASSMENT

Harassment is a form of governmental intrusion that tends to have a limiting, exhausting, or irritating effect on the behavior of citizens. In this section, consideration is given to harassment of a citizen's travel rights, sexual mores, reputation, and appearance.

Travel

In a few cases, the U.S. Supreme Court has considered the constitutionality of governmental restrictions on travel.

Kent v. Dulles 357 U.S. 116 (1958)

Rockwell Kent wanted to attend a meeting of an organization, the World Council of Peace, to be held in Helsinki, Finland. He also wanted to visit England. His application for a passport was denied by Secretary of State John Foster Dulles on the grounds that Kent was a Communist. He sought declaratory relief.

The U.S. Supreme Court decided (5-4) that freedom of movement was a part of the American heritage.

> Freedom of movement across frontiers in either direction, and inside the country, may be as close to the heart of the individual as the choice of what he eats, or wears, or reads. Freedom of movement is basic in our scheme of values.

The right to travel is part of the freedom which the citizen cannot be denied without violating due process of law under the Fifth Amendment. The Secretary of State was not

entrusted with power to grant or withhold that right. The
Secretary's decision was reversed.

Aptheker v. Secretary of State 378 U. S. 500 (1964)

In 1964 the Court established a link between the right
to travel and First Amendment freedoms. Herbert Aptheker,
editor of Political Affairs, the theoretical organ of the Communist Party in the United States, held a valid passport. On
January 22, 1962, Aptheker was notified that his passport was
revoked because use of it would violate section six of the
Subversive Activities Control Act of 1950. The act provided
that a member of a registered Communist organization could
not apply for or use a passport. Aptheker admitted that he
was a member of the Communist Party and that revocation
of the passport was proper if section six was valid. He
argued, however, that section six was unconstitutional and
that it deprived Aptheker of his right to travel.

The majority opinion, written by Arthur Goldberg,
noted (6-3) that section six was unconstitutional because its
sweep was too broad and too indiscriminate. The law excluded such relevant considerations as the person's "knowledge, activity, commitment, and purposes in and places for
travel. " Goldberg also noted that "freedom of travel is a
constitutional liberty closely related to rights of free speech
and association. " And, in a concurring opinion, Hugo Black
found section six unconstitutional because it denied Aptheker
"the freedom of speech, press, and association which the
First Amendment guarantees. "

Zemel v. Rusk 381 U. S. 1 (1965)

In 1965 the Court upheld a restriction on travel. Until
1961, no passport was required to travel anywhere in the
Western Hemisphere. In that year, the United States severed
diplomatic relations with Cuba. Shortly thereafter, the State
Department eliminated Cuba from the list of areas for which
passports were not required and declared all outstanding
passports invalid for travel to Cuba unless endorsed by the
Secretary of State. In 1964, Louis Zemel, possessor of a
valid passport, requested permission to travel to Cuba. He
claimed that he wanted to make the trip "to satisfy my curi-
osity about the state of affairs in Cuba and to make me a
better informed citizen. " His request was denied and he
appealed.

The Court, in an opinion written by Chief Justice Earl Warren, decided (6-3) that the Secretary of State's restriction on travel, in this case, was constitutionally sound. Warren contrasted this case with earlier decisions. The issue in Kent and Aptheker had been whether a person could be refused a passport because of political beliefs or associations. In the case of Zemel, however, Secretary Dean Rusk refused to validate the passport not because of any characteristic peculiar to Zemel, but "because of foreign policy considerations affecting all citizens." Zemel's right to travel was denied because the Court upheld Executive authority to impose area restrictions on travel. Zemel also claimed that the restriction violated the First Amendment because it caused a decreased data flow. Warren agreed that the denial of travel to Cuba "renders less than wholly free the flow of information concerning that country," but concluded that "the right to speak and publish does not carry with it the unrestrained right to gather information." The Secretary's denial of Zemel's right to travel was upheld.

Kleindienst v. Mandel 408 U. S. 753 (1972)

Unlike the three previous cases which involved the right of an American to travel abroad, a 1972 case considered the right of a foreign journalist to enter the United States. Ernest Mandel, Belgian journalist and Marxist theorist, was invited to attend academic meetings in the United States. Mandel was denied permission to enter the country under a provision of the Immigration and Nationality Act of 1952, which refuses entry to anyone who advocates "the economic, international and governmental doctrines of world communism." The Attorney General could waive ineligibility but Attorney General Richard Kleindienst declined to do so on the ground that on a 1968 trip to the United States, Mandel had spoken at more universities than his visa application indicated. Thus, he had engaged in behavior not stated in his visa application.

The U. S. Supreme Court acknowledged (6-3) that Congress has absolute power to grant or deny entry to aliens. When the Attorney General, for a valid reason, refused to approve Mandel's entry, the judiciary should not set the determination aside. The freedom to travel, which exists for United States citizens wishing to travel abroad, does not apply similarly for foreigners wishing to enter the United States.

Sexual Mores

The Court has made decisions regarding the individual's ual's freedom from intrusion into his or her sexual conduct. One of the earliest cases involved counseling married couples about birth control.

Griswold v. Connecticut 381 U.S. 479 (1965)

During November, 1961, Estelle Griswold, Executive Director of the Planned Parenthood League of Connecticut, and Dr. Buxton, Professor at Yale Medical School and Medical Director for the Planned Parenthood League Center in New Haven, gave advice and supplies to married persons concerning the methods of preventing conception. They examined the wife and prescribed the best contraceptive device for her use. A fee was usually charged, but some couples were counseled free. Griswold and Buxton were arrested for violating a Connecticut statute which forbad any person from counseling others regarding the use of contraceptives. They were found guilty and fined $100 each. They appealed.

The U.S. Supreme Court affirmed (7-2) that the First Amendment protects not only the right to speak and print, but also the right to distribute, to receive, to read, to teach, and to associate, as well as the freedom of thought and inquiry. The Court also stressed that "the First Amendment has a penumbra where privacy is protected from governmental intrusion." The Connecticut law, by restricting the use, rather than the manufacture or sale, of contraceptives, was an unnecessarily broad intrusion upon the zone of privacy protected by several constitutional guarantees. The law intruded upon the privacy surrounding the marriage relationship.

Eisenstadt v. Baird 405 U.S. 438 (1972)

In 1972 the Court struck down a state law prohibiting access of contraceptives to unmarried persons. Massachusetts prohibited giving anyone other than a married person contraceptive medicines or devices, and even the distribution of such articles to married persons was allowed only through a registered pharmacist, or by a licensed physician. William Baird was convicted for exhibiting contraceptive materials while lecturing to students at Boston University, and for giving a package of Emko vaginal foam to a young woman at the close of his remarks. The Massachusetts Supreme Court overturned his conviction for showing the contraceptives on the ground that it violated freedom of speech, but upheld his conviction for distributing the foam.

When the case reached the U.S. Supreme Court, the justices concluded (6-1) that "whatever the rights of the individual to access to contraceptives may be, the rights must be the same to the unmarried and the married alike." The Court cited Griswold, where the right of privacy was protected in a married relationship. The Court noted that a married couple is not an independent entity with one mind and heart, but an association of two persons each with their own intellectual and emotional makeup. Accordingly, "if the right of privacy means anything, it is the right of the individual, married or single, to be free from unwarranted governmental intrusion into matters so fundamentally affecting a person as the decision whether to bear or beget a child." The Court concluded that the Massachusetts law violated the equal protection clause.

Roe v. Wade 410 U.S. 113 (1973)

During the 1970s a heated debate ensued between religious groups dedicated to protecting life and environmental organizations determined to control population growth. The issue reached the U.S. Supreme Court. A Texas abortion law, similar to those of most states, prohibited anyone from destroying a fetus except on "medical advice for the purpose of saving the life of the mother." Jane Roe, a pseudonym for an unmarried, pregnant woman, brought suit against Henry Wade, the District Attorney of Dallas County. She claimed that the Texas law intruded upon her privacy by denying to a pregnant woman the right to choose to terminate her pregnancy. Roe claimed that she had an absolute right to such a choice; the state could not intervene. Texas, however, argued that the power to protect prenatal life from and after conception constitutes a compelling state interest.

The Court did not agree fully with either viewpoint and concluded (7-2) that "the right of personal privacy includes the abortion decision, but that this right is not unqualified and must be considered against important state interests in regulation." The Court acknowledged that, at some point, "the woman's privacy is no longer sole and any right of privacy she possesses must be measured accordingly."

The "compelling" point was at approximately the end of the first trimester. From that point, a state may regulate abortion as it relates to maternal health. For the period of pregnancy preceding this "compelling" point, a physician may determine that the patient's pregnancy should be terminated. Such an abortion may occur free of interference by the state. In Roe, the Court declared the Texas code too broad because it failed to distinguish between abortions performed early and those performed later in pregnancy, and because it allowed abortion only in cases of saving the mother's life.

Doe v. Bolton 410 U.S. 179 (1973)

On the same day that the Court decided Roe, it handed down a decision involving the validity of Georgia's abortion statute. The law prohibited abortion, except in the cases of danger to the woman's life, likelihood of a serious birth-defective fetus, or pregnancy resulting from rape. Mary Doe was eight weeks pregnant when she applied for a therapeutic abortion. She had already placed two of her three children in a foster home because of her indigency. Her husband had abandoned her and she had been a mental patient at a state hospital. She had been advised that an abortion would be less dangerous to her health than if she gave birth to a child that she could not care for or support. Her application was denied by the Abortion Committee of Grady Memorial Hospital in Atlanta.

The Court reaffirmed its position in Roe, noting that a pregnant woman did not possess an absolute constitutional right to an abortion on demand. The Court did, however, overturn (7-2) the Georgia law because specific portions of the statute violated the Fourteenth Amendment. The faulty provisions required that abortions be conducted in hospitals, that abortions be approved by a hospital abortion committee, that two other physicians confirm the finding of the pregnant woman's doctor, and that abortions be available only to Georgia residents.

Planned Parenthood of Central Missouri v. Danforth, Attorney General of Missouri 428 U.S. 52 (1976)

In June, 1974, slightly more than a year after Roe and Doe had been decided, Missouri enacted an abortion law. Three days after the act became effective, Planned

Parenthood, a family-planning organization maintaining facilities in Columbia, Missouri, and two licensed physicians brought suit challenging the constitutionality of various provisions of the statute. The case reached the U. S. Supreme Court.

A divided Court upheld (5-4) certain of the provisions, but overturned others. The following provisions were declared constitutional: 1) "Viability" is defined as the point at which a fetus is "potentially able to live outside the mother's womb, albeit with artificial aid," and is presumably capable of "meaningful life outside the mother's womb." It is not necessary that a specified number of weeks in pregnancy be fixed by statute as the point of viability; such determination is essentially the responsibility of the attending physician. 2) Before submitting to an abortion during the first twelve weeks of pregnancy, a woman must consent in writing, and certify that her consent is informed and freely given. 3) Records must be kept by physicians and health facilities performing abortions. These materials could be useful to a state's interest in protecting the health of its female citizens, and might also be of considerable medical value.

The Court declared the following provisions unconstitutional: 1) A state cannot require written consent of the spouse of a woman seeking abortion during the first twelve weeks; it cannot delegate to a spouse power which the state itself is absolutely forbidden from exercising during the first trimester of pregnancy. Furthermore, the woman physically bears the child and is more directly and immediately affected by pregnancy. 2) A state cannot require written consent of the parent of an unmarried woman under 18; the abortion decision must be left to the medical judgment of the pregnant woman's attending physician. 3) Prohibiting, after the first twelve weeks of pregnancy, the abortion procedure of saline amniocentesis as "deleterious to maternal health" is an arbitrary regulation designed to prevent a vast majority of abortions after the first twelve weeks. The provision would force pregnancy terminations by methods more dangerous to the woman's health. 4) A state cannot require the physician to exercise professional care to preserve the fetus' life and health, whatever the stage of pregnancy, under penalty of manslaughter and liability for damages.

In the 1973 cases of Roe and Doe, the Court emphatically rejected the notion that the woman's right to abortion is absolute. Instead, the right "must be considered against important state interests in regulation. In 1976, in Planned Parenthood of Central Missouri, the Court specified some areas where state regulation is allowed and others where it is considered an intrusion into the woman's constitutionally protected privacy.

Lovisi v. Slayton 363 F. Supp. 620 (1973)

In 1973 a United States District Court heard a challenge against the constitutionality of a state sodomy law. The Lovisis, a married couple, were convicted of sodomy by a Virginia court. Mrs. Lovisi was also found guilty of sodomy with Earl Dunn, whom the Lovisis met through an advertisement in Swingers Life magazine. Photographs were taken of the threesome in the Lovisis' bedroom. It was unknown whether they were taken by Mrs. Lovisi's two daughters, aged 11 and 13, or whether they were taken by a timing device attached to the camera. At any rate, one of the girls took a picture to school and a teacher confiscated it. A conference was held at the school at which Mrs. Lovisi, the girls, school officials, local welfare authorities, and the police were present. At that conference, the girls claimed that there were other photographs at home. Police officers obtained a search warrant and subsequently "uncovered several hundred photographs, four hundred rolls of film, over a thousand paperback books and numerous magazines, all of which were of an obscene nature." Among the pictures seized were those depicting the Lovisis and Dunn engaged in the acts for which they were convicted. The Lovisis appealed, alleging that enforcement of the Virginia sodomy law against consensual acts by adults intruded upon their constitutional right of privacy.

The court concluded that the right to privacy inherent in the Constitution might extend to heterosexual relations involving oral-genital contact between consenting adults; however, the Lovisis voluntarily relinquished any right to privacy that would normally apply to their acts. The court based its finding "on the fact that the Lovisis took photographs of their sexual acts and then allowed these photographs to fall into their children's hands." In order for their sexual acts to be constitutionally protected, the Lovisis had responsibility for ensuring that the seclusion surrounding their acts was preserved. Yet the photos taken by the Lovisis were kept at home in such a way that the daughters had access to them. Furthermore, the snapshots were freely available throughout

the house to whomever lived there. The Lovisis failed to
meet their burden to preserve the seclusion of their sexual
acts. They thereby relinquished any right to privacy in the
performance of the acts, and they were lawfully prosecuted
under the Virginia statute.

Doe v. Commonwealth's Attorney for City of Richmond
425 U. S. 901 (1976)

In a 1976 case the Court upheld the Virginia sodomy
law. Two adult males challenged the constitutionality of the
statute, as it applied to consensual homosexual relations in
private. Contrasting this case with Griswold v. Connecticut
and Poe v. Ullman, the District Court's majority opinion
noted that while the intimacy of husband and wife is necessarily an essential and accepted feature of the institution of
marriage which the state has fostered and protected, it is a
different matter for a state to punish persons who establish
intimacies which the law has always forbidden. Behavior
such as adultery, homosexuality, fornication, and incest are
not necessarily immune from criminal inquiry, even if privately practiced. A dissenting opinion cited Eisenstadt v.
Baird to argue that "the legal viability of a marital-nonmarital
distinction in private sexual acts, if not eliminated, was at
the very least seriously impaired. " In Eisenstadt, the Court
had declined to restrict the right of privacy in sexual matters
to married couples. In the present case, however, the U. S.
Supreme Court unanimously affirmed the District Court's
majority opinion.

Since 1965, the courts have decided several cases
involving governmental intrusion into sexual privacy. In
Griswold, the Court overturned a law which prohibited the
advising of persons concerning the use of contraceptives;
such a law intruded upon the privacy of the marriage relationship. Eisenstadt extended the same freedom to unmarried
persons. In the Roe and Doe abortion cases, the Court noted
that a pregnant woman did not possess an absolute constitutional right to an abortion on demand; the right had to be
balanced against state interests. Then, in Planned Parenthood
of Central Missouri, the Court examined the specific nature
of some of those state interests. The courts also heard two
challenges to the Virginia sodomy statute. In Lovisi, a
District Court ruled that a married couple voluntarily relinquished any right to privacy by allowing photographs of their
sexual acts to be seen by others. In the other case,

Commonwealth's Attorney for City of Richmond, the Court
upheld the law in the face of a challenge concerning homosexual acts performed in private.

Reputation

A few cases reached the U.S. Supreme Court which
involved the claim that real or potential abuse to a person's
reputation was experienced as a result of illegal intrusions.
In 1971 the Court heard a case concerning this issue.

Wisconsin v. Constantineau 400 U.S. 433 (1971)

A Wisconsin statute provided for "posting," without
notice or hearing, the name of any person who "by excessive
drinking" becomes "dangerous to the peace" of the community.
Acting in accordance with the statute, the police chief of
Hartford posted a notice in all local liquor stores forbidding
the sale of liquor to Norma Constantineau for one year. She
initiated suit, claiming damages and asking for injunctive
relief.

The Court noted (6-3) that when an individual's "good
name, reputation, honor, or integrity is at stake" because
of governmental action, "notice and an opportunity to be heard
are essential." Constantineau's reputation was surely at
stake. While the posted sign was merely the mark of illness
to some, others viewed it as a stigma. The label was degrading. And, under the Wisconsin law, she was not afforded
a chance to defend herself. The law violated procedural due
process. In Constantineau, however, the Court did not rule
the "posting" invalid, only the process open to a "posted"
person.

Paul, Chief of Police, Louisville v. Davis 424 U.S. 693 (1976)

In 1976 a similar case reached the Court. In 1972,
two Kentucky police chiefs agreed to alert local merchants of
possible shoplifters who might be operating during the Christmas season. In early December they distributed to approximately 800 Louisville merchants a "flyer" which was titled
"Active Shoplifters." On page two appeared photographs and
the name of Edward Charles Davis, III. He was included in

the flyer because he had been arrested for shoplifting in 1971.
Shortly after circulation of the flyer, the charge against Davis,
who had pleaded not guilty, was dismissed.   Davis brought
action, seeking redress for the alleged violation of his constitutional rights.   He asserted that the "active shoplifter"
designation inhibited him from entering business establishments out of fear of being suspected of shoplifting and possibly apprehended.   Also, the degrading label seriously impaired
his future employment opportunities.

The Court acknowledged that there are zones of privacy
protected from governmental intrusion.   However, Davis
incorrectly claimed that the State intruded upon his privacy
by publicizing a record of an official act such as an arrest.
According to the opinion written by Justice William Rehnquist,
the Court held (6-3) that reputation alone does not implicate
any "liberty" or "property" interests sufficient to invoke the
procedural protection of the due process clause, and something more than simple defamation by a state official must
be involved to establish a claim.   The police chief's action
in distributing the flyer neither deprived Davis of any "liberty"
or "property" rights protected by the due process clause; nor
did it intrude upon his right to privacy.   The Court minority
argued that a person's good name and reputation fell within
the term "liberty."   Procedural protections should be provided before intruding upon an individual's reputation by
branding him as a criminal.   In Davis, however, the Court
discredited the thrust of Constantineau and excluded reputation
from constitutionally protected process.

Doe v. McMillan 412 U. S. 306 (1973)

A related case, heard by the Court in 1973, involved
the immunity rights of Congress under the speech and debate
clause.   In December, 1970, a congressional subcommittee
filed with the Speaker of the House a report (which was subsequently ordered by the House to be printed as a public
document) of its duly-authorized investigation into the plight
of the District of Columbia public school system.   About 45
pages of illustrative material were included in the 450-page
report "to give a realistic view of a disturbed school and the
lack of administrative attempts to rectify the multitudinous
problems there," to show the level of reading ability of
seventh graders who were given a fifth-grade history test, and
to illustrate suspension and disciplinary problems.   On these
pages of the report were reproduced "absence sheets, lists

of absentees, copies of test papers, and documents relating
to disciplinary problems of certain specially-named students. "
The plaintiffs in this case were parents and children who
brought suit, under pseudonyms, alleging that disclosure and
dissemination of the information contained in the committee
report had violated their right to privacy, hurt their reputations and future careers, and injured their physical and mental health.   The suit for damages and injunctive relief was
brought against John McMillan, the chairman of the House
Committee on the District of Columbia.   The courts dismissed
the suit, finding that the defendant's conduct was absolutely
privileged because of protections emanating from the speech
and debate clause and the official immunity doctrine.   The
case reached the U. S. Supreme Court.

The Court acknowledged that, even if the Court felt
that the inclusion of the names of individual children was
unnecessary in the report, congressmen and their aides are
immune from liability for their actions within the "legislative
sphere, " even though their conduct, if performed in other
than legislative contexts, would in itself be unconstitutional.
In this case, the Court decided (5-4) that the immunities of
the speech and debate clause are limited and that they were
applied too broadly in the lower courts.   The Court ruled
that: 1) Members of Congress and their committee aides
and employees are absolutely immune under the clause for
preparation of the committee report for distribution within the
halls of Congress.   2) The clause does not afford absolute
immunity from private suit to persons who, with congressional authorization, publicly distribute materials that infringe
on the privacy rights of individuals.   Members of Congress
might be held liable if they were responsible for public
dissemination of such a report.   3) The Public Printer or
the Superintendent of Documents might likewise be liable for
such distribution.   The Court concluded that the business of
Congress is to legislate; congressmen and aides are absolutely immune when they are legislating.   But when they act
outside the sphere of legitimate activity, they enjoy no special immunity from local laws protecting the good name or
the reputation of the ordinary citizen.   The case was remanded for appropriate further proceedings.

Appearance

A final area of harassment involves intrusion into an
individual's appearance.   The Court heard a relevant case
in 1976.

Kelley v. Johnson 425 U. S. 238 (1976)

Police officers in Suffolk County, New York were obligated to comply with grooming regulations which limited the length and appearance of hair, limited length and shape of sideburns, regulated size and configuration of mustaches, prohibited beards, wigs, and hair pieces. Edward Johnson, President of the Patrolman's Benevolent Association, brought suit against Eugene Kelley, Commissioner of the Police Department. Johnson claimed that the grooming standards violated his First Amendment freedom of expression and his right to "liberty ... without due process of law" as protected by the Fourteenth Amendment.

The Supreme Court opinion, written by Justice William Rehnquist, noted (6-2) that even though state employment may not be conditioned on the relinquishment of First Amendment rights, a state has wider latitude in imposing regulations on its employees than it does in restricting other citizens. Law enforcement authorities prefer similarity in the appearance of police officers. This practice makes police personnel obviously recognizable to the public and also tends to instill an "esprit de corps" within the police force. The Court concluded that hair grooming regulations were not irrationally enacted and therefore did not deprive policemen of their "liberty" interest under the Constitution. The regulations were upheld.

Kelley, as well as other cases cited in this section, indicates that freedom from governmental harassment is not absolute. Under certain conditions, the government can validly intrude into the areas of individual travel, sexual mores, reputation, and appearance.

Bibliography

Books

Dionisopoulos, P. Allan and Craig R. Ducat. The Right to Privacy: Essays and Cases. St. Paul: West Publishing Company, 1976.

Dixon, Robert G. , Jr. , et al. The Right to Privacy: A Symposium on the Implications of Griswold v. Connecticut. New York: DaCapo Press, 1971.

Articles

Belair, Robert R. "Less Government Secrecy and More Personal Privacy? Experience with the Freedom of Information and Privacy Acts," The Civil Liberties Review 4 (May-June, 1977), 10-8.

Caplis, Kevin J. "Electronic Surveillance and the Fourth Amendment: Warrant Required for Wiretapping of Domestic Subversives," De Paul Law Review 22 (Winter, 1972), 430-50.

"Electronic Surveillance and the Supreme Court: A Move Back?" De Paul Law Review 21 (Spring, 1972), 806-21.

James, Raymond C. "The Right to Travel Abroad," Fordham Law Review 42 (May, 1974), 838-51.

Mims, Stephen S. "Eisenstadt v. Baird: Massachusetts Statute Prohibiting Distribution of Contraceptives to Unmarried Persons Held Unconstitutional," Southwestern Law Journal 6 (October, 1972), 775-80.

Cases

Aguilar v. Texas 378 U. S. 108 (1964)

Aptheker v. Secretary of State 378 U. S. 500 (1964)

Berger v. New York 388 U. S. 41 (1967)

Breard v. City of Alexandria 341 U. S. 622 (1951)

Chimel v. California 395 U. S. 752 (1969)

Coolidge v. New Hampshire 403 U. S. 443 (1971)

Doe v. Bolton 410 U. S. 179 (1973)

Doe v. Commonwealth's Attorney For City of Richmond 403 F. Supp. 1199; 425 U. S. 901 (1976)

Doe v. McMillan 412 U. S. 306 (1973)

Eisenstadt v. Baird 415 U. S. 438 (1972)

Griswold v. Connecticut 381 U. S. 479 (1965)

Hynes v. Borough of Oradell 425 U. S. 610 (1976)

Katz v. Illinois 389 U. S. 347 (1967)

Kelley v. Johnson 425 U. S. 238 (1976)

Kent v. Dulles 357 U. S. 116 (1958)

Ker v. California 374 U. S. 23 (1963)

Kleindienst v. Mandel 408 U. S. 753 (1972)

Laird v. Tatum 408 U. S. 1 (1972)

Lee v. Florida 392 U. S. 378 (1968)

Lovell v. City of Griffin 303 U. S. 444 (1938)

Lovisi v. Slayton 363 F. Supp. 620 (1973)

Mapp v. Ohio 367 U. S. 643 (1961)

Marsh v. State of Alabama 326 U. S. 501 (1946)

Martin v. City of Struthers 319 U. S. 141 (1943)

Murdock v. Commonwealth of Pennsylvania 319 U. S. 105 (1943)

Nardone v. United States 302 U. S. 379 (1937)

Olmstead v. United States 277 U. S. 438 (1928)

Organization for a Better Austin v. Keefe 402 U. S. 415 (1971)

Paul, Chief of Police, Louisville v. Davis 424 U. S. 693 (1976)

Planned Parenthood of Central Missouri v. Danforth, Attorney General of Missouri 428 U. S. 52 (1976)

Poe v. Ullman 367 U. S. 497 (1961)

Roe v. Wade 410 U. S. 113 (1973)

Schwartz v. Texas 344 U. S. 199 (1953)

CHAPTER VIII

CONCLUSION

The development of freedom of expression in America has been a relatively arduous and complicated process. The extent to which different forms of expression have been permitted has varied appreciably through the years. In general, the Supreme Court has moved to broaden the scope of expression that is constitutionally protected. This movement, however, has been erratic. There are forms of expression, both written and verbal, symbolic and non-symbolic, which have been absolutely protected from both state and national interference. Conversely, there are other forms of expression that have never enjoyed constitutional protection. There is, in addition, a significant shadow area in which many questions remain unanswered. Depending upon the circumstances of a case and the relative weights of the competing claims involved, the Court has contradicted earlier decisions. Probably the most accurate observation that can be made about the Court's decisions is that the constitutional freedoms of speech, press, assembly, petition, and silence, though vigorously protected through the years, are not absolute.

Dissent

Dissent against perceived inadequacies of government actions has long been acknowledged as a fundamental right. Yet while the Court has extended the scope of First Amendment guarantees to statements and actions during peacetime, it has limited dissent in times of military crisis. According to the doctrine enunciated in Schenck, the courts must decide if the situation is such that the expression would create a "clear and present danger" of a crime. For example, speech designed to obstruct recruiting during a time of war is not protected (Debs, Abrams). However, during peacetime, states cannot limit their legislators' capacity to express opposition to the Selective Service Act or U. S. foreign policy (Bond). Provocative, offensive, or threatening speech is only provisionally protected. When the speaker creates disorder, the expression is not protected (Feiner). When the audience itself erupts, though, the police cannot ban the speech (Terminiello). "Fighting words," aimed at creating a breach of peace, are clearly not allowed (Chaplinsky). The free speech claims are outweighed by the public interest in preventing disorder. Merely offensive words, however, cannot be automatically banned; such action risks suppression of ideas (Cohen, Bachellor). Threatening words must be judged in the context of their utterance. Mere political hyperbole uttered under pressure of a specific event is allowable (Watts). In essence, words may legitimately be restricted when a compelling state interest overrides constitutional claims of free expression.

The Court has never been completely free of political pressures to restrict the constitutional guarantees of "undesirable" groups of individuals. This tendency is most apparent in cases involving the Communist Party. At one time, merely being a member of a party which advocated criminal syndicalism was a serious offense (Whitney). The Court eventually required demonstration of sufficient and compelling evidence of a defendent's active and knowing membership in the Communist Party (DeJonge, Scales, Noto). During the 1920s, merely teaching or advising others of the abstract doctrine of communism was punishable (Gitlow). In Yates, the Court distinguished between advocacy of abstract doctrine and advocacy of action. Today, states cannot proscribe advocacy, unless such advocacy is directed at producing imminent lawless action (Brandenburg) or constitutes a "clear and present" danger of violent overthrow of the government (Dennis).

The Court has protected symbolic expression when a substantial state interest is not impaired (Spence). States cannot abridge the espousal of peaceful change (Street). Students' rights of free expression also cannot be abridged, either by schools or courts (Tinker, Burnside). Yet, when subsidiary conduct entails the destruction of national symbols or the impairment of a state function, the Court has consistently banned such means of dissent. Draft card burning or flag desecration, for example, are not protected (O'Brien, Radich, Street, Smith). A flag can, however, be flown in protest (Stromberg). Recently, the Court has drawn the line of allowable expression closer to the point of action (Cohen,

Spence, Goguen). The distinction between pure speech and subsidiary conduct has become increasingly blurred.

Assembly

Within the past two decades, the Court has increasingly restricted picketing as a means of protest and petition. The Court has held that an individual has a right to picket (Thornhill), but has maintained that picketing is not the equivalent of speech. On occasion, the State may even ban peaceful picketing (Hughes). As Justice Douglas noted, "picketing is free speech plus, the plus being physical activity that may implicate the public interest, convenience, or necessity" (Logan Valley). Unlike its approach to other forms of symbolic speech, the Court continues to separate picketing into the component parts of pure expression and subsidiary conduct.

The acknowledged right to demonstrate (Edwards) is only provisionally protected. Though peaceful, orderly demonstrations have generally been allowed (Gregory), demonstrations on private property are subject to regulation, owing to the circumstances of the case (Adderly). Moreover, demonstrators cannot picket noisily near schools which are in session (Grayned).

The right of assembly, though more protected than picketing, has nonetheless been subject to considerable regulation. Assembly must be exercised in the public interest so as to not interfere with the comfort, convenience, peace, and order (Hague). Parades or processions can be controlled as to time, place, and manner. Yet assembly cannot be denied because of a perceived shortage of police protection (Hague). Every effort must be made to secure the constitutional right of assembly to all citizens and groups so requesting.

The Court has consistently acknowledged the individual's right to join any social, political, or religious group of his or her choice. This right, however, is subject to reasonable regulation not aimed at prohibiting the associational rights of a particular group (NAACP). During times of crisis, the concern for national security overrides that of individuals or groups (Korematsu, Communist Party). An individual is usually expected to be legally responsible for disclosing any information about his organizational ties before a legislative committee or court (Konigsberg). The individual, nonetheless, is protected from any unreasonable inferences as to his organizational memberships. A state may not exclude a person from a profession solely because he is a member of a particular political organization (Baird). The guilt by association so inferred from membership in a particular organization clearly contradicts First Amendment guarantees (Robel, Baird, Communist Party).

Groups, themselves, enjoy significant First Amendment protection. Organizations have the right to protect membership lists on behalf of the private interests of their members (Bates, NAACP, Gibson). Groups also enjoy the right to recruit new members, raise needed funds, and inform the public of their activities and objectives (Staub, Cantwell, Thomas). Such solicitation cannot be separated from general speech-making (Thomas). Moreover, licensing or censorship of such activity constitutes a prior restraint of free speech (Staub, Cantwell). This form of expression, though, is not protected absolutely. A privately-owned shopping center, for example, may control handbilling that is unrelated to the center's operation (Lloyd, Hudgens). Clearly, solicitation on behalf of an organization may be regulated as to time, place, and manner.

Academic Freedom

The rights of free speech and inquiry are nowhere more important than in the educational system. Teachers traditionally have been accorded almost unbridled discretion in matters of curriculum. Laws banning the teaching of evolution or foreign languages have been declared unconstitutional (Epperson, Meyer). Overall, teachers have broad control over the educational materials that they choose to use (Keefe, Parducci). The U. S. Supreme Court, however, has not made a definitive ruling on the issue of book banning. The question had been left largely to teachers, parents, school boards, and other self-appointed censors. The teacher's right to express his or her views is limited to specific conditions (Meinhold).

The Court has held that teachers possess specific procedural and associational rights. Non-tenured faculty have less procedural rights than tenured faculty (Perry). All teachers, however, have certain common associational rights (Sweezy). Teacher-fitness tests based on guilt by association have thus been declared unconstitutional (Adler, Beilan). Knowing membership in an "undesirable" organiza- tion is not sufficient grounds for termination or non-renewal of employment. The school must demonstrate the teacher's intent to further the unlawful aims of the organization (Keyishian). Moreover, any teacher or professor subject to dismissal must be given a summary hearing (Slochower). Decisions based on loyalty oaths deny procedural and sub- stantive due process (Shelton, Carr, Cramp); such oaths are facially unconstitutional (Baggett). In addition, merely in- voking the Fifth Amendment cannot be cause for dismissal (Slochower).

Students similarly enjoy rights of expression (Tinker), association (Healy), and due process of law (Goss, Wood). Mandatory flag-salute exercises, for example, are unconsti- tutional (Barnette). Required Bible reading and school prayer are also prohibited (Murray, Schempp). Students have rights to publish written materials (Dickey), and to hear outside speakers talk on campus (Molpus, Stacy, Dickson). Univer- sities, in short, have only limited discretion in prohibiting student publications or student-organized lectures. Only when the requirements of school discipline so indicate can the school justify punishment of students for exercising First Amendment rights (Fujishima). For the most part, when the Court has ventured into the area of academia, First Amend- ment rights have been strengthened for faculty and students alike.

Obscenity

While the Court has generally strengthened the First Amendment freedoms concerning most forms of expression, it has unequivocally denied protection to obscenity. For many years the rigid Hicklin rule was applied. Any printed mate- rial that was thought to have a corruptive influence on minors, sexually deviant adults, or a specific subclass of society was prohibited. In 1957, the Court adopted the Roth test. A work was considered obscene if an average person applying contemporary community (i. e. , national) standards would find the dominant theme of the piece, taken as a whole, as appealing to the prurient interest. A work that had re- deeming social value could not be prohibited (Memoirs). In effect, all but the most disgusting and useless of works were granted First Amendment protection. Taking a more aggres- sive stance against obscenity, the Burger Court adopted the

Miller test. Individual communities now have the responsibility for determining whether a work is obscene or not. Disparities in local attitudes have been thereby exacerbated. At the same time, the defendant's burden of proof has been significantly increased. The work must possess serious literary, artistic, political, or scientific value.

The Court has consistently guarded against any appearance of government censorship. Prior restraints on expression are acceptable only in extreme circumstances (Freedman). Postmasters cannot censor obscene mail (Hannegan, Grove Press). Police have only limited discretion in executing a search warrant; moreover, the warrant itself must be sufficiently precise to protect non-obscene works (Marcus). In order for a film to be declared obscene there must be previous judicial determination of obscenity in an adversary hearing (Heller). Though censorship by a state board was upheld in 1915 (Mutual Film), the Court has, in recent cases, avoided judging the acceptability of such boards (Burstyn, Kingsley). In the final analysis, jurors are probably the most acceptable censors (Smith). They are best equipped to apply contemporary community standards.

The Court, however, has not saddled individual jurors with the entire responsibility for controlling obscene expression. It has provided guidelines concerning procedural and substantive rights of publishers, distributors, and consumers of obscene materials. It is clear that pandering is not allowable (Ginzburg). Distributors cannot send obscene materials to unsolicited or unwilling addressees (Rowan). In order to obtain a conviction, it is necessary to show that the purveyor had known that the material was obscene (Smith). The Court also ruled that mere possession of pornography in the privacy of one's home is not punishable (Stanley). Yet the zone of privacy does not extend beyond the home (Orito). The unique problems associated with displaying obscene movies at drive-in theatres (Rabe, Erznoznik), and with zoning local theatres (Young), have not, at this time, been thoroughly resolved.

Silence

The right to silence has been supported by the Court. Most notably, the procedural and substantive rights of silence adhering to criminal proceedings have been considerably strengthened in the past two decades. A criminal suspect

clearly has a right not to communicate (Miranda, Escobedo).
Similarly, witnesses cannot be forced to testify against themselves before a committee or court, nor can they be deprived
of due process of law (Watkins). However, if such constitutional rights are not abridged, and the questions asked by a
legislative committee are pertinent to an investigation, testimony can be compelled (Barenblatt).

In addition to strengthening the rights of witnesses and
criminal suspects, the Court also has expanded the rights of
public employees. A public employee need not swear to an
oath contrary to his religious beliefs (Torcaso). Also, loyalty
oaths that provide for summary dismissal are unconstitutional
(Connell), as are those that impute guilt by association (Cole).

Intrusion

In some cases involving the question of intrusion the
Court has determined that personal inconvenience and annoyance resulting from unsolicited distribution of literature is
outweighed by the public interest in maintaining a free flow
of information. Cities cannot ban the distribution of all
literature; ordinances must be sufficiently precise (Lovell).
Notice posted to deter solicitors adequately prevents any resulting inconvenience. The Court has held, however, that
door-to-door solicitation for a commercial purpose may be
banned (Breard).

In addition to intrusion into the home, government
intrusion into one's personal lifestyle has also been permitted.
Though a person has a right to travel regardless of his
political beliefs or associations (Aptheker, Kent), the Executive authority of the government can impose area restrictions
on travel for national security purposes (Zemel). The freedom to travel abroad does not apply similarly to foreigners
wishing to enter the United States (Kleindienst). Another
intrusion into personal lifestyle concerns sexual conduct.
The First Amendment protects against unnecessary intrusion
into the zone of privacy regarding such conduct for married
couples (Griswold) and single persons (Eisenstadt). Sodomy
between two consenting adults in the privacy of one's home,
though, is only provisionally protected. Couples voluntarily
relinquish all rights to privacy by allowing photographs of
their sex acts to be seen by others (Lovisi). Another instance of intrusion into one's lifestyle concerns personal
reputation. Posting or other publications of embarrassing

personal information tending to implicate one's reputation is permissible if the information involves official public acts (Paul).

Perhaps the freedom from intrusion is greatest for criminal suspects. The Court has held that wiretapping clearly invades individual privacy (Katz). Evidence obtained from electronic surveillance is not admissible in either state or federal courts (Lee). Further, a search is valid only when the warrant is issued on probable cause by a neutral magistrate, and is incident to the arrest (Ker). However, a permissible area of search exists beyond the person proper (Rabinowitz). First Amendment protection from searches and seizures, for example, is much less when conducted in an automobile than within the domain of the home (Martinez-Fuerte, Sifuentes).

Epilog

The protection of freedom of expression is not absolute. Certain types of expression, notably obscenity, are never protected. Dissent, picketing, silence, as well as other communication rights, are only upheld provisionally. They are subject to regulation by federal and state laws. Any statute or ordinance, however, must be validly drafted and enforced. The Court has determined that a law cannot be so broad as to prohibit expression, rather than regulate it (Robel, Lovell). Narrow, objective, and definitive standards must be provided as to the implementation of the law (Gooding, Shuttlesworth, Poulos). The operative terms must be sufficiently precise so as to avoid ambiguity (Burstyn, Interstate Circuit, Hynes). Due notice must be given of the law and its effects (Wright, Princess Anne).

A law, nonetheless, is presumed valid until otherwise demonstrated. Therefore, it is an offense to disobey an ordinance before determination of its constitutionality (Walker, Princess Anne). If an ordinance or statute is properly drafted and enforced, and reasonably perceives a compelling state interest in controlling the exercise of some communication right, the Court will uphold the law.

How the Court will deal with future cases is quite unpredictable. The changing interpretations of the essential First, Fourth, Fifth, Sixth, and Fourteenth Amendment freedoms roughly parallel the rapid changes in American society itself. However, no matter how the Court deals with specific issues regarding these Amendments, it will most likely continue to provide a needed source of stability and continuity in the face of challenges to free speech.

SELECTED BIBLIOGRAPHY

Abernathy, Glenn. The Right of Assembly and Association. Columbia: University of South Carolina Press, 1961.

"Academic Freedom in the Public Schools: The Right to Teach," New York University Law Review 48 (December, 1973), 1176-99.

Aldrich, Ann, and JoAnne V. Sommers. "Freedom of Expression in Secondary Schools," Cleveland State Law Review 19 (January, 1970), 165-76.

Alfange, Dean, Jr. "Free Speech and Symbolic Conduct: The Draft-Card Burning Case," Supreme Court Review (1968), 1-52.

Alpert, Robert. "Lloyd v. Tanner: Handbilling Within a Shopping Mall Not Directed at a Store Is Not Protected by the First Amendment Unless No Adequate Alternative Location Exists," New York University Review of Law and Social Change 3 (Winter, 1973), 70-82.

"Applying Freedman v. Maryland to Campus Speaker Bans," University of Pennsylvania Law Review 119 (January, 1971), 512-20.

Arkes, Hadley. "Civility and the Restriction of Speech: Rediscovering the Defamation of Groups," Supreme Court Review (1974), 281-335.

"Army Surveillance of Lawful Civilian Activity Does Not Constitute Objective Harm Within the Meaning of the Standing Doctrine--Laird v. Tatum," Indiana Law Review 6 (1972), 341-8.

Artigliere, Ralph. "Privacy v. Free Expression in Public Areas," University of Florida Law Review 28 (Winter, 1976), 588-96.

Aspelund, Carl L. "Free Speech Rights of School Children," Loyola Law Review 16 (1969-70), 165-76.

Barker, Lucius J., and Twiley W. Barker, Jr. Freedoms, Courts, Politics: Studies in Civil Liberties. Englewood Cliffs, New Jersey: Prentice-Hall, 1972.

Barrier, Mary L. "Restriction of the First Amendment in an Academic Environment," University of Kansas Law Review 22 (Summer, 1974), 597-605.

Bassiouni, M. Cherif, ed. The Law of Dissent and Riots. Springfield, Illinois: Charles C Thomas, 1971.

Beaney, William M. "The Constitutional Right to Privacy in the Supreme Court," Supreme Court Review (1962), 212-51.

Belair, Robert R. "Less Government Secrecy and More Personal Privacy? Experience with the Freedom of Information and Privacy Acts," The Civil Liberties Review 4 (May-June, 1977), 10-8.

Berkman, Richard L. "Students in Court: Free Speech and the Functions of Schooling in America," Harvard Educational Review 40 (November, 1970), 567-95.

Berns, Walter. The First Amendment and the Future of American Democracy. New York: Basic Books, 1976.

Blasi, Vince. "Prior Restraints on Demonstrations," Michigan Law Review 68 (August, 1970), 1481-574.

"Board of Education's Removal of Selected Books from Public High School Library Violates Student's First Amendment Right to Receive Information," Texas Law Review 55 (February, 1977), 511-23.

"Board of Regents v. Roth: Procedural Rights of Non-Tenured Teachers," Columbia Law Review 73 (April, 1973), 882-92.

Boccarosse, Ralph N. "Lloyd Corporation v. Tanner: Expression of First Amendment Rights in the Privately Owned Shopping Center--A Re-evaluation by the Burger Court," Catholic University Law Review 22 (Summer, 1973), 807-29.

Bolmeier, Edward C. Landmark Supreme Court Decisions on Public School Issues. Charlottesville: The Michie Company, 1973.

"Border Search Exception Held Inapplicable to International Letter Mail," Washington University Law Quarterly (Summer, 1976), 493-502.

Bosmajian, Haig A. "Restricting Speech at the Shopping Center, Banning Assembly at the Military Base, Prohibiting Obscenity in the Marketplace," Free Speech 41 (May, 1977), 4-6.

_____, ed. Dissent: Symbolic Behavior and Rhetorical Strategies. Boston: Allyn and Bacon, 1972.

_____. Obscenity and Freedom of Expression. New York: Burt Franklin, 1976.

_____. The Principles and Practice of Freedom of Speech. Boston: Houghton Mifflin, 1971.

Bosworth, Allan R. America's Concentration Camps. New York: Wm. Norton, 1967.

Bragg, Morgan Stevenson. "State Loyalty Oaths: A Constitutional Resurrection," University of Florida Law Review 24 (Spring, 1972), 555-63.

Braunstein, Michael. "First Amendment Chill Resulting from Army Surveillance Nonjusticiable," Tulane Law Review 47 (February 1973), 426-36.

Breckenridge, Adam Carlyle. The Right to Privacy. Lincoln: University of Nebraska Press, 1970.

Brigman, William E. "The Controversial Role of the Expert in Obscenity Litigation," Capital University Law Review 7 (1978), 519-51.

Brown, Ernest J. "Quis Custodiet Ipsos Custodes?--The School-prayer Cases," Supreme Court Review (1963), 1-33.

Burkholder, Christina M. "Recent Supreme Court Developments of the Vagueness Doctrine: Four Cases Involving the Vagueness Attack on Statutes During the 1972-73 Term," Connecticut Law Review 7 (Fall, 1974), 94-115.

Caplis, Kevin J. "Electronic Surveillance and the Fourth Amendment: Warrant Required for Wiretapping of Domestic Subversives," De Paul Law Review 22 (Winter, 1972), 430-50.

Chafee, Zechariah, Jr. Free Speech in the United States. Cambridge: Harvard University Press, 1954.

Chambers, M. M. "Speaker Bans and the Courts," Educational Forum 35 (May, 1971), 471-8.

Church, Thomas, Jr. "Conspiracy Doctrine and Speech Offenses: A Reexamination of Yates v. United States from the Perspective of United States v. Spock," Cornell Law Review 60 (April, 1975), 569-99.

Clor, Harry M. Obscenity and Public Morality: Censorship in a Liberal Society. Chicago: University of Chicago Press, 1969.

Coen, Ronald S. "Cohen v. California: A New Approach to an Old Problem?" California Western Law Review 9 (Fall, 1972), 171-83.

Cohen, Felix. "Flag Desecration Statutes in Light of United States v. O'Brien and the First Amendment," University of Pittsburgh Law Review 32 (Summer, 1971), 513-32.

"College Authorities Improperly Deny Recognition to a Local Chapter of the Students for a Democratic Society," Boston University Law Review 52 (Spring, 1972), 311-21.

"Community Standards, Class Actions, and Obscenity Under Miller v. California," Harvard Law Review 88 (July, 1975), 1838-74.

Cord, Robert L. Protest, Dissent and the Supreme Court. Cambridge, Massachusetts: Winthrop Publishers, 1971.

Cox, Lawrence A. "Brubacker v. Board of Education: Teacher Dismissals for Use of Objectionable Material in the Classroom," Connecticut Law Review 7 (Spring, 1975), 580-608.

Cutlip, James. "Symbolic Speech, High School Protest and the First Amendment," Journal of Family Law 9 (1969), 119-25.

Danzig, Richard. "How Questions Begot Answers in Felix Frankfurter's First Flag Salute Opinion," Supreme Court Review (1977), 257-74.

DeGrazia, Edward, ed. Censorship Landmarks. New York: R. R. Bowker, 1969.

Denno, Theodore F. "Mary Beth Tinker Takes the Constitution to School," Fordham Law Review 38 (October, 1969), 35-62.

DeVol, Kenneth S., ed. Mass Media and the Supreme Court: The Legacy of the Warren Years. 2nd ed. New York: Hastings House Publishers, 1976.

Dionisopoulos, P. Allan, and Craig R. Ducat. The Right to Privacy: Essays and Cases. St. Paul: West Publishing, 1976.

"Dismissal of Public School Teacher for Symbolic Expression of Political Opinion in the Classroom Held Unconstitutional," Fordham Law Journal 1 (Spring, 1973), 467-80.

"Distribution of Handbills in a Privately Owned Shopping Mall Is Not Protected by the First Amendment When the Handbilling Is Unrelated to the Operations of the Shopping Mall, When the Mall Is Not Dedicated to a General Public Use and When There Is a Reasonable Alternative Place to Distribute the Handbills--Lloyd Corp. v. Tanner," Georgia Law Review 7 (Fall, 1972), 177-88.

"Distribution of Handbills in Mall of Private Shopping Center Is Not Constitutionally Protected When Purpose of Handbilling Is Unrelated to Shopping Centers' Operations," Alabama Law Review 25 (Fall, 1972), 76-97.

Dixon, Robert G., et al. The Right to Privacy: A Symposium on the Implications of Griswold v. Connecticut. New York: DaCapo Press, 1971.

Doherty, Patrick. "Freedom of Speech in Disturbing the Peace Cases," Loyola Law Review 18 (1972), 403-10.

Donnelly, Paul Edward. "The Pervasive Effects of McCarthyism on Recent Loyalty Oath Cases," Saint Louis University Law Journal 16 (Spring, 1972), 437-58.

Dow, Dennis R. "Municipal Zoning Ordinance May Restrict Location of Adult Motion Picture Theatres," Washburn Law Journal 16 (Winter, 1977), 479-89.

Eagle, Steven J. "Shopping Center Control: The Developer Beseiged," Journal of Urban Law 51 (May, 1974), 585-647.

Earle, Valerie, ed. On Academic Freedom. Washington, D. C.: American Enterprise Institute, 1971.

Edelstein, Stephen J., and Kenneth Mott. "Collateral Problems in Obscenity Regulation: A Uniform Approach to Prior Restraints, Community Standards, and Judgment Preclusion," Seton Hall Law Review 7 (Spring, 1976), 543-87.

"Electronic Surveillance and the Supreme Court: A Move Back?" DePaul Law Review 21 (Spring, 1972), 806-21.

Emerson, Thomas I. The System of Freedom of Expression. New York: Random House, 1970.

_____. Toward a General Theory of the First Amendment. New York: Random House, 1966.

Erickson, Keith V., and Carrol R. Haggard. "Freedom of Expression and the Law Enforcement Officer," Communication Quarterly 25 (Fall, 1977), 21-7.

Erskine, Hazel. "The Polls: Freedom of Speech," Public Opinion Quarterly 34 (Fall, 1970), 483-96.

"The Exercise of First Amendment Rights in Privately Owned Shopping Centers," Washington University Law Quarterly (Spring, 1973), 427-35.

Fellman, David. "Constitutional Rights of Association," Supreme Court Review (1961), 74-134.

_____. The Constitutional Right of Association. Chicago: University of Chicago Press, 1963.

"First Amendment Analysis of Peaceful Picketing," Maine Law Review 28 (1976), 203-21.

Fischer, Louis, and David Schimmel. The Civil Rights of Teachers. New York: Harper and Row, 1973.

"Freedom of Speech--Dismissal of Public School Teacher for Symbolic Expression of Political Opinion in Classroom Held Unconstitutional," Fordham Urban Law Journal 1 (Spring, 1973), 467-80.

"Freedom to Communicate versus Right to Privacy: Regulation of Offensive Speech Limited by 'Captive Audience' Doctrine," Washington Law Review 48 (May, 1973), 667-85.

Friedman, Leon. "The Ginzburg Decision and the Law," The American Scholar 36 (Winter, 1966-67), 71-91.

_____, ed. Obscenity: The Complete Oral Arguments Before the Supreme Court in the Major Obscenity Cases. New York: Chelsea House, 1970.

Gard, Stephen W. "Obscenity and the Right to Be Let Alone: The Balancing of Constitutional Rights," Indiana Law Review 6 (1973), 490-508.

Gatti, Richard D. "Teachers and the First Amendment," Willamette Law Journal 7 (December, 1971), 435-49.

Gatton, Edwin R. "Free Speech Regulated in Shopping Centers," Wake Forest Law Review (October, 1972), 590-97.

Gibbons, John J. "Hague v. CIO: A Retrospective," New York University Law Review 52 (October, 1977), 731-44.

Gibson, Eddie. "A City's Board of Censors May Not Prevent Production of a Rock Musical Without Adequate Procedure Which Assures Prompt Judicial Determination with the Board of Censors Assuming the Burden of Persuasion," Texas Southern University Law Review 4 (1976), 101-27.

Gibson, Gerry S. "Freedom of Speech: Property Rights Triumphant in the Shopping Center," University of Florida Law Review 28 (Summer, 1976), 1032-43.

Gilmor, Donald M. , and James A. Barron. Mass Communication Law. 2nd ed. St. Paul: West Publishing, 1974.

Goldstein, Stephen R. "The Asserted Constitutional Right of Public School Teachers to Determine What They Teach," University of Pennsylvania Law Review 124 (January, 1976), 1293-357.

Gordon, Robert T., Jr. "Loyalty Oaths--Oath to Oppose Overthrow of Government Does Not Violate First and Fourteenth Amendments: No Administrative Hearing Required When Oath Constitutional," Mississippi Law Journal 43 (1972), 543-548.

Graham, Edward M. "Freedom of Speech of the Public School Teacher," Cleveland State Law Review 19 (May, 1970), 382-92.

Haiman, Franklyn S. Freedom of Speech. Skokie: National Textbook Company, 1976.

_____. Freedom of Speech: Issues and Cases. New York: Random House, 1965.

_____. "The Rhetoric of the Streets: Some Legal and Ethical Considerations," Quarterly Journal of Speech 53 (April, 1967), 99-114.

_____. "Speech v. Privacy: Is There a Right Not to Be Spoken To?" Northwestern University Law Review 67 (May-June, 1972).

Haney, Roger D. "Obscenity and Pornography: Legal Arguments and Empirical Evidence," Free Speech Yearbook 1976, 46-59.

Harris, Richard. Freedom Spent. Boston: Little-Brown, 1976.

Hazard, William R. Education and the Law: Cases and Materials on Public Schools. New York: The Free Press, 1971.

Himes, Scott M. "Zoning, Adult Movie Theatres and the First Amendment: An Approach to Young v. American Mini Theatres, Inc.," Hofstra Law Review 5 (Winter, 1977), 379-411.

Holmes, Charles. "Non Renewal of Untenured Teacher's Contract: Cook v. Hudson," North Carolina Central Law Journal 6 (Fall, 1974), 107-16.

Hook, Sidney. Academic Freedom and Academic Anarchy. New York: Cowles Book Company, 1970.

Horn, Robert A. Groups and the Constitution. New York: AMS Press, 1971.

Hudon, Edward G. Freedom of Speech and Press in America. Washington, D. C. : Public Affairs Press, 1963.

Hughes, Michael D. "California v. LaRue--The Supreme Court's New Overbreadth Doctrine," Utah Law Review (Summer, 1973), 320-7.

Imwinkelried, Edward J. , and Donald N. Zillman. "The Legacy of Greer v. Spock: The Public Forum Doctrine and the Principle of the Military's Political Neutrality," Georgetown Law Journal 65 (February, 1977), 773-806.

Israel, Jerold H. "Elfbrandt v. Russell: The Demise of the Oath?" Supreme Court Review (1966), 193-252.

James, Raymond C. "The Right to Travel Abroad," Fordham Law Review 42 (May, 1974), 838-51.

Jayson, Lester S. , ed. The Constitution of the United States of America: Analysis and Interpretation. Washington, D. C. : U. S. Government Printing Office, 1973.

Joughin, Louis, ed. Academic Freedom and Tenure: A Handbook of the American Association of University Professors. Madison: University of Wisconsin Press, 1969.

Kalven, Harry, Jr. "The Concept of the Public Forum: Cox v. Louisiana," Supreme Court Review (1965), 1-32.

_____. The Negro and the First Amendment. Chicago: University of Chicago Press, 1965.

Kane, Peter E. "Erosion of the First Amendment: Freedom of Speech and the Nixon Court," Free Speech 38 (May, 1976), 7-9.

Karst, Kenneth L. "Public Enterprise and the Public Forum: A Comment on Southeastern Promotions, Ltd. v. Conrad," Ohio State Law Journal 37 (1976), 247-63.

Katz, Al. "Privacy and Pornography: Stanley v. Georgia," Supreme Court Review (1969), 203-18.

Kirp, David L. , and Mark G. Yudof. Educational Policy and the Law: Cases and Materials. Berkeley: McCutchan Publishing, 1974.

Kitch, Edmund W. "Katz v. United States: The Limits of the Fourth Amendment," Supreme Court Review (1968), 133-52.

Kitchens, Dean Joel. "The Constitutional Limits of the Speech or Debate Clause," UCLA Law Review 25 (April, 1978), 796-820.

Kochly, Robert J. "The Shopping Center: Quasi-Public Forum for Suburbia," University of San Francisco Law Review 6 (October, 1971), 103-16.

Konvitz, Milton R. , ed. Bill of Rights Reader: Leading Constitutional Cases. 5th ed. Ithaca: Cornell University Press, 1973.

_____. Expanding Liberties: Freedom's Gains in Postwar America. New York: Viking Press, 1966.

_____. Fundamental Liberties of a Free People: Religion, Speech, Press, Assembly. Ithaca: Cornell University Press, 1957.

Krislov, Samuel. "From Ginzburg to Ginsberg: The Un-hurried Children's Hour in Obscenity Litigation," Supreme Court Review (1968), 153-97.

Kruse, M. Russell. "From Logan Valley Plaza to Hyde Park and Back: Shopping Centers and Free Speech," Southwestern Law Journal 16 (August, 1972), 569-88.

Kurland, Philip B. , ed. Free Speech and Association: The Supreme Court and the First Amendment. Chicago: University of Chicago Press, 1975.

"Laird v. Tatum: The Supreme Court and a First Amendment Challenge to Military Surveillance of Lawful Civilian Political Activity," Hofstra Law Review 1 (Spring, 1973), 244-75.

Lambeth, Evelyn J. "Hudgens v. NLRB: A Final Definition of the Public Forum?" Wake Forest Law Review 13 (Spring, 1977), 139-59.

Law, Robert E. "Lloyd v. Tanner: Death of the Public Forum?" University of San Francisco Law Review 7 (April, 1973), 582-95.

LeDuc, Don R. "'Free Speech' Decisions and the Legal Process: The Judicial Opinion in Context," Quarterly Journal of Speech 62 (October, 1976), 279-87.

Lewis, Felice Flanery. Literature, Obscenity, and Law. Carbondale: Southern Illinois University Press, 1976.

Lewis, Robert. "Free Speech and Property Rights Reequated: The Supreme Court Ascends from Logan Valley," Labor Law Journal 24 (April, 1973), 195-200.

"Lloyd Corp. v. Tanner: A Shopping Center Open for Business but Not for Dissent," Maine Law Review 25 (1973), 131-46.

"Lloyd Corp. v. Tanner: The Demise of Logan Valley and the Disguise of Marsh," Georgetown Law Journal 61 (May, 1973), 1187-1219.

"Loyalty Oaths--The United States Supreme Court Relaxes Its Stringent Safeguards--Cole v. Richardson," University of Richmond Law Review 7 (Fall, 1972), 162-170.

McCoy, Joseph L., and Roger T. Clark. "Do College Students Have a Constitutionally Protected Right to Hear Outside Speakers?" Mississippi Law Journal 41 (Winter, 1969), 135-41.

McDonald, Kevin D. "First Amendment--Content Neutrality," Case Western Reserve Law Review 28 (Winter, 1978), 456-492.

McGaffey, Ruth. "Local Option on the First Amendment?" Free Speech Yearbook 1974, 11-17.

McKay, Robert B. "Self-Incrimination and the New Privacy," Supreme Court Review (1967), 193-232.

Magrath, C. Peter. "The Obscenity Cases: Grapes of Roth," Supreme Court Review (1966), 7-77.

Mallies, Harry C. "Freedom of Expression in the Public Schools and the Law," Journal of Secondary Education 46 (March, 1971), 109-16.

Marble, Kenneth R. "Lloyd Corporation, Ltd. v. Tanner: Property Rights in a Privately Owned Shopping Center v. the Rights of Free Speech," Willamette Law Journal 9 (March, 1973), 181-91.

Martin, Philip L. "The Improper Discharge of a Federal Employee by a Constitutionally Permissible Process: The OEO Case," Administrative Law Review 28 (Winter, 1976), 27-39.

Mathews, David J. "Civilians' Claim that Army's Data-Gathering System Works a Chilling Effect on Their First Amendment Rights Held Not to Be a Justiciable Controversy Absent Showing of Objective Present Harm or Threat of Future Harm," Villanova Law Review 18 (February, 1973), 479-91.

Meiklejohn, Alexander. "The First Amendment Is an Absolute," Supreme Court Review (1961), 245-66.

Meiklejohn, Donald. "Privacy in the Burger Court: The Influence of Mr. Justice Black," Vermont Law Review 2 (1977), 35-68.

Memmer, Anthony W. "Free Speech: Prior Restraint in the Military Upheld," JAG Journal 26 (Fall, 1971), 117-25.

Michaud, Leonard J. "Zoning: Content Classification for Adult Movie Theatres," Loyola Law Review 22 (Fall, 1976), 1079-86.

Miller, Beverly G. "Miller v. California: A Cold Shower for the First Amendment," St. John's Law Review 48 (March, 1974), 568-610.

Miller, Simon A. "Teacher's Freedom of Expression Outside the Classroom: An Analysis of the Application of Pickering and Tinker," Georgia Law Review 8 (Summer, 1974), 900-18.

Mims, Stephen S. "Eisenstadt v. Baird: Massachusetts Statute Prohibiting Distribution of Contraceptives to Unmarried Persons Held Unconstitutional," Southwestern Law Journal 6 (October, 1972), 775-80.

Morris, Arval A. The Constitution and American Education. St. Paul: West Publishing Company, 1974.

Murphy, Paul L. The Meaning of Freedom of Speech: First Amendment Freedoms from Wilson to FDR. Westport, Connecticut: Greenwood Publishing, 1972.

Nahmod, Sheldon. "Black Armbands and Underground News-papers: Freedom of Speech in the Public Schools," Chicago Bar Record 51 (December, 1969), 144-53.

"Narrowing the Overbreadth Doctrine?" University of Colorado Law Review 45 (Spring, 1974), 361-77.

Naylor, David T. Dissent and Protest. Rochelle Park, New Jersey: Hayden, 1974.

Nelson, Harold L. , and Dwight L. Teeter. Law of Mass Communications. Mineola, New York: Foundation Press, 1969.

Nozette, Mark D. "Loyalty Oaths--Vagueness Standard Relaxed for 'Affirmative' Oaths," Cornell Law Review 58 (January, 1973), 383-98.

O'Meara, Joseph. "Abortion: The Court Decides a Non-Case," Supreme Court Review (1974), 337-60.

O'Neil, Robert M. Free Speech: Responsible Communication Under Law. 2nd ed. Indianapolis: Bobbs-Merrill, 1972.

Owen, W. C. "Plazas, Parking Lots, and Picketing: Logan Valley Plaza Is Put to the Test," Labor Law Journal 23 (December, 1972), 742-57.

Parker, Frank M. "Shopping Centers and the 'Quasi-Public' Forum," North Carolina Law Review 51 (November, 1972), 123-34.

Pearlstein, Mark. "The 'Fighting Words Doctrine' as Applied to Abusive Language Toward Policemen," DePaul Law Review 22 (Spring, 1973), 725-36.

Peebles, Thomas H. "State Regulation of 'Fighting Words'--Gooding v. Wilson," Journal of Urban Law (February, 1973), 498-504.

Pennington, Francis E. "First Amendment Suits Against Governmental Surveillance: Getting Beyond the Justiciability Threshold," St. Louis University Law Journal 20 (1976), 692-721.

Perlman, Gilbert T. "The Public Forum from Marsh to Lloyd," American University Law Review 24 (Fall, 1974), 159-203.

Phillips, James M., Jr. "Southeastern Promotions, Ltd. v. Conrad: A Contemporary Concept of the Public Forum," North Carolina Law Review 54 (February, 1976), 439-49.

Pincoffs, Edmund L., ed. The Concept of Academic Freedom. Austin: University of Texas Press, 1975.

Podgor, Ellen S. "Symbolic Speech," Indiana Law Review 9 (June, 1976), 1009-32.

"Police Dossiers--'Chilling Effect' First Amendment--Standing--Ripeness for Adjudication: Anderson v. Sills," Rutgers Law Review 25 (Winter, 1971), 300-40.

Policy Documents and Reports. Washington, D. C.: The American Association of University Professors, 1977.

Polsby, Daniel D. "Buckley v. Valeo: The Special Nature of Political Speech," Supreme Court Review (1976), 1-43.

"Privacy in the First Amendment," Yale Law Journal 82 (June, 1973), 1462-80.

Ragan, Fred D. "Justice Oliver Wendell Holmes, Jr., Zechariah Chafee, Jr., and the Clear and Present Danger Test for Free Speech: The First Year, 1919," Journal of American History 58 (June, 1971), 24-45.

Ragsdale, J. Donald. "Last Tango in Paris et al. v. The Supreme Court: The Current State of Obscenity Law," Quarterly Journal of Speech 61 (October, 1975), 279-89.

Rice, Charles E. Freedom of Association. New York: New York University Press, 1962.

Rodgers, Raymond S. "Congress Shall Make No Law ... A Computer-Assisted Content Analysis of the Decisions of Justice William O. Douglas on the Issues of Obscenity and Pornography," Free Speech Yearbook 1977, 91-101.

Rogge, O. John. The First and the Fifth: With Some Excursions into Others. New York: DeCapo Press, 1971.

Rosenthal, Elden. "Symbolic Speech: A Constitutional Orphan," Free Speech Yearbook 1971, 69-79.

Sager, Alan M. "The Impact of Supreme Court Loyalty Oath Decisions," American University Law Review 22 (Fall, 1972), 39-78.

Saunders, Eric F. "Electronic Eavesdropping and the Right to Privacy," Boston University Law Review 52 (1972), 831-47.

Schauer, Frederick F. "Hudgens v. NLRB and the Problems of State Action in the First Amendment Adjudication," Minnesota Law Review 61 (February, 1977), 433-60.

_____. The Law of Obscenity. Washington, D. C. : Bureau of National Affairs, 1976.

_____. "Reflections on 'Contemporary Community Standards': The Perception of an Irrelevant Concept in the Law of Obscenity," North Carolina Law Review 56 (January, 1978), 1-28.

Schechter, Alan H. Contemporary Constitutional Issues. New York: McGraw-Hill, 1972.

Schroeder, Stephen K. "Symbolic Speech--Policeman's Refusal to Wear Flag Emblem Not Protected by First Amendment Since Municipality Has Right to Prescribe Uniform Design," Creighton Law Review 6 (1972), 264-76.

Shaffer, Karen A. "Tatum v. Laird: Military Encroachment on First Amendment Rights," American University Law Review 21 (September, 1971), 262-80.

Shapiro, Martin. Freedom of Speech: The Supreme Court and Judicial Review. Englewood Cliffs, New Jersey: Prentice-Hall, 1966.

Sharp, Donald B. , ed. Commentaries on Obscenity. Metuchen, New Jersey: The Scarecrow Press, 1970.

Shattuck, John H. Rights of Privacy. Skokie: National Textbook, 1977.

Shea, Thomas F. "Don't Bother to Smile When You Call Me That--Fighting Words and the First Amendment," Kentucky Law Journal 63 (1974-75), 1-22.

286 / FREE SPEECH

86.

er Not Open to First Amendment Activities Unrelated to Use," Minnesota Law Review 57 (January, 1973), 603-20.

Shulman, Carol Herrnstadt. "Employment of Nontenured Faculty: Implications of Roth and Sindermann," Denver Law Journal 51 (1974), 215-33.

Sinowitz, B. E. "Court Rulings and Teacher's Right to Speak Out," Today's Education 62 (September-October, 1973), 50-60.

Smith, Paul D. "Gooding v. Wilson: Where from Here?" Southwestern Law Journal 26 (October, 1972), 780-86.

"Spence v. Washington: Smith v. Goguen: Symbolic Speech and Flag Desecration," Columbia Human Rights Law Reserve 6 (Fall/Winter, 1974-75), 535-50.

Starr, Isidore. The Idea of Liberty: First Amendment Freedoms. St. Paul: West Publishing, 1978.

Stine, Alan C. "Base Access and the First Amendment: The Right of Civilians on Military Installations," Air Force Law Review 18 (Fall, 1976), 18-32.

Stone, Geoffrey R. "Fora Americana: Speech in Public Places," Supreme Court Review (1974), 233-80.

Strong, Frank R. "Fifty Years of 'Clear and Present Danger': From Schenck to Brandenburg--and Beyond," Supreme Court Review (1969), 41-80.

Stuart, Shelly R. "Young v. American Mini Theatres, Inc.: A Limit on First Amendment Protection," New England Law Review 12 (Fall, 1976), 391-418.

Suffet, Stephen L. "The Resistance and the Court: The Punitive Draft Cases," Free Speech Yearbook 1971, 50-63.

Summers, Marvin, ed. Free Speech and Political Protest. Boston: D. C. Heath and Company, 1967.

Sunderland, Lane V. Obscenity: The Court, the Congress and the President's Commission. Washington, D. C. : American Enterprise Institute for Public Policy Research, 1974.

Tefft, Sheldon. "Neither Above the Law Nor Below It: A Note on Walker v. Birmingham," Supreme Court Review (1967), 181-92.

Thayer, Ted J. "Freedom of Speech and Symbolic Conduct: The Crime of Flag Desecration," Arizona Law Review 12 (Spring, 1970), 71-88.

"Threatening the President: Protected Dissenter or Potential Assassin," Georgetown Law Review 57 (February, 1969), 553-72.

Trager, Robert. "The Legal Status of Underground Newspapers in Public Secondary Schools," University of Kansas Law Review 20 (Winter, 1972), 239-51.

Tucker, Angula Gay. "Arnett v. Kennedy: Restriction on Public Employee's Freedom to Criticize," Free Speech Yearbook 1976, 31-6.

Vento, John S. "Chilling Effect on First Amendment Rights-- Army Surveillance of Civilian Political Activity," Duquesne Law Review 11 (Spring, 1973), 419-28.

Wall, Joseph E. "Fighting Words or Free Speech?" North Carolina Law Review 50 (February, 1972), 382-90.

Ware, Russell M. "The Black Armbands Case--Freedom of Speech in the Public Schools," Marquette Law Review 52 (Winter, 1969), 608-13.

Watkins, Barry. "Captivity of an Audience Viewing Screen of Drive-in Theatre Outside of Premises," Arkansas Law Review 30 (Spring, 1976), 82-8.

Widmer, Eleanor, ed. Literary Censorship in the '70s. Belmont: Wadsworth, 1970.

Wilkinson, J. Harvie, III. "Goss v. Lopez: The Supreme Court As School Superintendent," Supreme Court Review (1975), 25-75.

Worton, Stanley N. Freedom of Assembly and Petition. Rochelle Park, New Jersey: Hayden, 1975.

_____. Freedom of Speech and Press. Rochelle Park, New Jersey: Hayden, 1975.

Wright, Charles. "The Constitution on the Campus," Vanderbilt Law Review 22 (October, 1969), 1027-88.

Young, Marilyn Archbold. "Flag Desecration: A Constitutionally Protected Activity?" University of San Francisco Law Review 7 (October, 1972), 149-62.

GENERAL INDEX

absolutism 10

bad tendency 7, 19
balancing 9, 66, 67
Black, Hugo 10, 64, 95,
  165, 215, 219, 247
Blackmun, Harry 170
Brandeis, Louis 6, 239
Brennan, William 32, 167,
  195
Burger Court 12, 204, 266
Burger, Warren 138, 170,
  245

Clark, Tom 167
Clarke, John 18
clear and present danger
  6, 8, 16, 125, 126, 127,
  128, 262, 263

Douglas, William 1, 8, 10,
  11, 35, 43, 90, 95, 97,
  130, 151, 155, 165, 209,
  215, 220, 242, 245

Espionage Act 15, 17, 18

fighting words 30-33, 46,
  94, 263
Fortas, Abe 46, 52, 131
Frankfurter, Felix 2, 10,
  11, 65

free speech plus 264

Goldberg, Arthur 82,
  247

Hand, Learned 9
Harlan, John 39, 61,
  165
Holmes, Oliver Wendell
  6, 16, 17
Hughes, Charles 181

Jackson, Robert 112

McCarren Act 65
Marshall, Thurgood 99
Minton, Sherman 117

National Labor Relations
  Act 72, 89

pandering 195-197, 267
Powell, Lewis 32, 90,
  170
preferred position 11,
  125, 226, 229
prior restraint 69, 71,
  74, 75, 76, 77, 100,
  101, 103, 127, 128,
  134, 135, 136, 181-
  183, 188, 192, 220,
  230, 265, 267

INDEX OF CASES